Library of
Davidson College

Medical Writing
and Communicating

Medical Writing and Communicating

John J. Gartland, M.D.

Medical Editor, Thomas Jefferson University
James Edwards Professor, Emeritus, of Orthopaedic Surgery
Jefferson Medical College of Thomas Jefferson University
Philadelphia

University Publishing Group
Frederick, Maryland

University Publishing Group Inc.
Frederick, Maryland 21701

Copyright 1993 by University Publishing Group. All rights reserved
Printed in the United States of America

ISBN 1-55572-018-8

*For creating the environment, and providing
the opportunity, this book is gratefully dedicated to
Paul C. Brucker, M.D., President
Thomas Jefferson University, and
Joseph S. Gonnella, M.D., Dean
Jefferson Medical College of
Thomas Jefferson University*

Contents

Preface ix

1. Physicians as Communicators 1
2. Physician Writing Skills 23
3. Medical Writing Style 37
4. Organizing and Starting to Write 53
5. Medical Writing Formats 71
6. Revising and Rewriting 93
7. Presenting Conferences and Talks 103
8. Graphics for Written and Spoken Material 121
9. Grant Writing 137
10. Communicating with Patients 155
11. Computers in Medical Communicating
    Marvin E. Gozum, M.D. 189
12. Improving Medical Writing and
    Communication Skills 203

Appendix
    Thomas Jefferson University Hospital Approved
    Abbreviations List 231

Preface

Awareness that a need exists for a book such as this was generated by an unsuccessful search for a textbook suitable for use in an elective course in medical writing and communicating I taught to second-year students at Jefferson Medical College. To the best of my knowledge, no book focusing on the communication and interpersonal skills physicians need in practice, written by a physician with clinical practice experience, and addressed to medical students, physicians, and allied health professionals is now in print. It is important for medical students, physicians, and allied health professionals to recognize that their professional effectiveness can be enhanced by possessing improved communication and interpersonal skills, and this book was written to assist in fostering that recognition. At the moment, not much curricular time is devoted to developing these skills during the busy period of medical student education. This book was also written to become a textbook for communication skills courses as medical schools develop such courses in the near future.

The medical profession regards communication and interpersonal skills as necessary for physicians to possess, and the ability to interact well with patients has long been an acknowledged goal of medical education. Despite this professed importance, obtaining proficiency in these skills has been given little prominence in the traditional medical school curriculum when contrasted with the emphasis placed on biotechnology. As a consequence, medical schools produce some graduates who display a lack of balance between emphasis on curing and emphasis on caring. Admittedly, medical knowledge and clinical skills are the cornerstones of good patient care, but what needs to be emphasized to medical students and physicians is that the catalyst for transforming *good* patient care into *effective* patient care are the communication and interpersonal skills of physicians.

The need for physicians to communicate better among themselves, and with patients and others, takes on added urgency in light of the social and political changes threatening to affect the medical practice environment and the delivery of medical care. Improvement in the communication and interpersonal skills displayed by physicians in their interactions with patients and others is necessary if there is to be improvement in the level of satisfaction people have with physicians and the delivery of medical care in this country. Those in the medical profession can ill afford to lose the support of their patients and the public as debates about the future of the health-care delivery system in this country begin to unfold. An essential step in moving toward a consistently positive correlation between patient care outcomes and the possession of good communication and interpersonal skills by physicians is to effect a better balance between biotechnology, prevention of disease, and the teaching and fostering of these skills in the curricula of medical schools. The recommendation is made in this book that medical schools accept more of the responsibility for fostering and enhancing the communication and interpersonal skills of their graduates.

The ability to write clearly and logically is recognized as an important and desirable skill for physicians to possess but, unfortunately, it seems to be a professional skill more honored in the breach than in the attainment. A vital element of effective medical communication is clarity in the written material physicians produce. Repeated criticisms of physicians' writing skills, however, speak to a lack of clarity in much of what physicians write. Confused and convoluted writing by physicians can be a danger to patients and others because such writing lends itself to misinterpretation and misunderstanding of its intended meaning. Developing acceptable writing skills, then, should be a major goal for physicians because the nature of the medical profession is such that physicians can not escape the need to write, be it a patient's medical record, a letter to a referring physician, a progress note on a hospital chart, or an article for submission to a medical journal. The content matter of what physicians write must be clear and incapable of being misinterpreted or misunderstood because, quite often, what physicians write concerns itself with issues of critical importance, such as the health and welfare of a particular patient or a group of patients.

I am grateful for the friendly collaboration of Marvin Gozum, MD, who shares with readers his technical knowledge of computer systems and programs in Chapter 11.

Rare is the book that can be written without the help and advice of others, and this book is not that unprecedented. At Jefferson, I extend my appreciation and thanks to Jussi J. Saukkonen, M.D.; O.D. Kowlessar, M.D.; Ronald P. Jensh, Ph.D.; Joseph R. Sherwin, Ph.D.; Malcolm Clendenin, and Louise M. Lang, R.N.

Among orthopaedic colleagues around the country who shared with me their expertise and wisdom, I extend my appreciation and thanks to Reginald R. Cooper, M.D.; Henry R. Cowell, M.D., Ph.D.; and Roby C. Thompson, Jr., M.D.

Finally, my special thanks to Theresa A. Wilson, Center for Research in Medical Education and Health Care at Jefferson, for cheerful and very able secretarial assistance.

John J. Gartland, M.D.

1

Physicians as Communicators

After choosing medicine as a career, physicians face additional choices about career options and opportunities for service. A popular and visible opportunity for service lies in treating the injured and healing the sick, but other options exist. Combined with a clinical career, or as an independent option, physicians may elect to teach in order to share their knowledge and experience with students, residents, and other physicians. Some physicians may seek a career in research so as to contribute to the scientific knowledge base supporting clinical decision making. Still others may combine a clinical and teaching career with disseminating pertinent medical information to peers, colleagues, patients and others by the printed or spoken word. Regardless of choice, these differing career paths and opportunities for service are bound together by the common thread of effective written and spoken communication. To receive, to record, and to transmit information accurately, succinctly, and with clarity is a skill that is basic to the practice of every branch of medicine and a skill that all physicians should strive to possess, no matter what medical career option is chosen. Good physician communicators recognize that communication is the key to clinical success and know that knowledge combined with effective communication skills is a powerful tool for physicians to possess.

THE COMMUNICATION PROCESS

Communication is both an interaction and a process based on a background of human behavior and social science research, and defined by a body of knowledge.[1,2] Communication as a word is derived from a Greek root meaning to bring together. Although the activity encompassed by communication includes the transmitting and imparting of information, the action involved with bringing people together for the sharing of information is a dynamic process that goes far beyond the passive activity implied by simply transmitting or imparting information. Information that is shared in an effective communication process initiates changes in the behavior, thinking, life style, or attitude of the person receiving the information. The communication process achieves its full potential when appropriate relationships exist, or are developed, among communicator, message, and recipient of the message. Communication is an interaction or relationship between humans, involving the production of a written or spoken message by someone and the receipt of the message by someone else. It is this ongoing process of sending and receiving messages that results in the creation of a positive or negative communication relationship among humans. It is often the manner or style in which a spoken message is communicated from physician to patient that is important to the development of their relationship, determining whether or not the ensuing relationship has positive or negative connotations for the participants. There is reason to believe that all use of language has a persuasive dimension; in fact, one can not communicate at all without some attempt to persuade in one way or another. All communication behavior, therefore, has as its purpose the eliciting of a specific response from a particular person or group of persons. In order to become effective communicators, physicians must first understand the purposes of communicating by either the written or spoken word. Effective communication with patients and others, for example, involves more skills than the giving of a message delivered, not infrequently, in a stern tone of authority and in a time frame just short of being rude.

Communication is a process that is in a constant state of change. Its content is influenced by the environment and situation in which the communication takes place, as well as by the relationship existing between the communicating participants. In a sense, the communication process, either written or spoken, can be considered a continuum in that the content or impact of the message can influence both parties in the interaction for an indefinite period. Communication can be affected, positively or negatively, by the purpose and nature of the message, the style or form in which it is delivered, the audience to whom the communication is addressed, the behavioral attitudes of the communicator and audience, and by social, educational, and cultural differences between the communicator and the message recipient, be it a single patient, a readership, or a large professional audience.[3] The perception of the quality of medical care delivered to patients by physicians, for example, depends largely on the assessment by patients of the quality of the human communication developed between them and their physicians. Regardless of their professional qualifications, physicians who are perceived by patients as poor communicators are not highly regarded as care givers by these patients. Effective communication, then, not only includes the outcome desired by the message that is communicated, but also a perception of satisfaction with the encounter experienced by both parties involved in the communication process.

THE IMPORTANCE OF COMMUNICATING EFFECTIVELY

Human communication is believed to be the physician's single most important tool for providing medical care to patients.[2] This belief underscores the importance of why physicians should strive to develop effective medical writing and communicating skills for use in their professional careers. This ability to communicate effectively with readers, patients, and others in need of health related information is both a skill and an art. Available evidence, however, supports the suspicion that many physcans are deficient in both the skill and art of effective communication. Like the skills needed to practice clinical medicine, facility in communication skills requires a familiarity with its techniques but, like the art of medicine, also has a more intuitive and intangible aspect. It is generally agreed that the professional competence of physicians involves not only medical knowledge and technical skills, but also clinical judgment, interpersonal skills, professional attitudes, and ethical behavior. Among the interpersonal skills considered desirable in physicians is the ability to communicate effectively with patients and others.[4] Unfortunately, little assessment of or even training in medical writing or communication skills is provided at present in the curricula of most medical schools and residency programs. Instead, these skills are left to be learned in hit or miss fashion through personal initiative or by imitation of role models, usually busy clinicians or residents who focus their time in a hospital setting.[5]

Written and spoken communications by physicians must be clear in meaning, precise in words and terminology used, and honest, accurate, and scientifically valid in information that is conveyed. These requirements are not subject to individual modification as might be acceptable in other types of communication for the very good reason that more is at stake in medical communicating. The content matter of medical communications concerns itself with critical issues, such as the health and welfare of a patient or groups of patients. Regardless of specialty, all physicians require a common foundation of knowledge, values, professional attitudes, and basic clinical skills, including the ability to communicate with patients and others.[6] Obtaining information from patients, communicating information to patients, and sharing medical information with peers and colleagues is inherent to the practice of medicine. Good communication promotes a relationship between physician and patient that facilitates care of the illness, enhances patient self-reliance, and helps to ensure that all relevant issues are brought to bear on the diagnostic and therapeutic process.[7] This is accomplished to its fullest extent by those physicians who develop rapport and trust with patients, instill confidence in patients that recommended procedures and treatments are in their best interests, and who exhibit positive attitudes toward people. Effective medical communicating allows the exchange of thoughts, ideas, data, conclusions, and other forms of information to bring about beneficial changes between communicators and audiences.[8] The ability to discuss medical problems with patients and other physicians with equal effectiveness is a mark of a good physician communicator. The ability to communicate well with patients, listeners, or readers, however, is a skill that requires a conscious effort to possess and hard work to master. This task takes a dedicated effort by physicians because the ability to communicate well is an acquired skill for most physicians and mastering this skill takes learning and practice.

The need for physicians to communicate better among themselves and with patients and others has taken on added importance in light of the social and political changes affecting the medical practice environment and the delivery of medical care.[9] There is growing concern in government, among the general public, and within the medical profession that the technical competence of physicians needs to be complemented with a well developed set of interpersonal skills.[10] A study of the Medicare program by the Institute of Medicine lists several deficiencies noted in the practice behavior of physicians, including poor relationships with patients.[11] This new emphasis highlights the recognition that medical care has become a type of mutual participation activity in which health care decisions are believed to be a responsibility properly shared between physicians and patients. This view makes it even more essential that physicians function as patient advocates and practice medicine more as teachers of patients and less as authority figures. To be able to teach patients, physicians must be able to communicate with them effectively in order to elicit their understanding and cooperation in the management of medical problems. Unfortunately, some physicians in practice believe themselves too busy or too important to spend much time communicating with patients. It is unlikely that data exist to support these vain pretensions. Those physicians who continue to cling to an outmoded non-communicating "doctor knows best" style of medical practice are discovering an increasingly larger number of dissatisfied patients and malpractice suits.[12]

The time has long since passed since physicians were the sole providers of medical information to patients and the general public. Health and wellness are topics of great interest to the public at large and the mass media provide health information and health education material in large quantities. Patients used to believe that questioning their physicians about medical decisions implied a lack of confidence in them, but that attitude no longer prevails. Patients no longer hesitate to ask about treatment options, expectations of results, treatment risks, and a lot more.[13] As patients become more sophisticated and knowledgeable about their medical problems, physicians will need to share more information with them. As far as patients are concerned, the basic and, possibly, the most important type of communication with physicians, and the cornerstone upon which good medical care is built, is the interpersonal interaction and communication that occurs during clinical encounters between physicians and patients. Unfortunately, other factors can act to blunt the effectiveness of a clinical encounter from a patient's viewpoint. As medical care becomes more technical, complex, and impersonal, health professionals other than physicians become increasingly involved in the patient communication process, thus providing more opportunity for the process to break down. When one considers office receptionists, secretaries, technicians, nurses, physician assistants, medical students, residents, and clinical fellows, patients may have to deal with numerous people before getting to see their selected or assigned physician. These assistants may cause the clinical encounter to operate more smoothly from the physician's point of view but, not infrequently, may provide a communication nightmare for patients.

It is not possible to give excellent care to patients in a quick, easy, or offhand fashion, or by delegating the responsibility to someone else. Patients want and need to discuss their problems and concerns with their physician of choice and they have every right to expect that will occur. Communication nightmares for patients can be avoided by teaching all involved health professionals, including physicians, the reasons for accepting their roles as patient advocates and patient teachers, and by structuring the clinical encounter and its environment in such a way that the primary goal of the effort is not physician convenience, but rather improved outcome of patient care from the patient's viewpoint. The general attitude and atmosphere of a medical practice office or other outpatient site must be set by the physician in charge who should be aware that communication problems with patients can arise, but who is professional enough to plan ahead in an attempt to prevent such problems from occurring. The goal should be to create an atmosphere in which patients feel welcome, cared for, and respected as human beings. This viewpoint should apply not only to patient visits, but should also apply to telephone calls and messages received from patients. If their roles are clearly defined and understood, and if the agreed upon purpose of the clinical encounter is to increase patient satisfaction with the interaction and compliance with treatment efforts, health professionals other than physicians can be important assets in successful patient management and patient communication efforts.

From the standpoint of clinicians, a major and desirable goal of good physician-patient communication is to improve the outcome of patient care from the patient's viewpoint. The outcomes of diagnosis and treatment depend, largely, on unimpaired communication between physician and patient. Failure to establish empathic relationships with patients can be a serious bar to communication and patient response. The quality of medical care rendered depends, greatly, on the interactions between physicians and patients, and the suspicion exists that these interactions, all too often, are disappointing to both parties.[14]

From the standpoint of physician writers and speakers, the goals of effective medical writing and communicating will vary with the purpose of the communication effort.[15] One desirable goal of medical communicating by writing or speaking is to disseminate useful information to readers or listeners, convincing them of the strength of the presented material and the validity of the conclusions derived from that material.

THE EFFECTIVE PHYSICIAN COMMUNICATOR

Physicians depend on their abilities to communicate with peers, colleagues, patients, and patients' families in order to carry out their professional responsibilities appropriately. Physicians need to possess basic writing skills so their written records and patient referral letters are clear, concise, and accurate, say what the physician writer intended them to say, and will so appear on later retrieval and review for whatever purpose. Good communications with patients and patients' families are characterized by warmth, sensitivity, cordiality, and courtesy on the physician's part. How well or how poorly these communication efforts turn out will depend upon how well or how poorly these abilities have been developed in physicians, and can serve to distinguish effective from ineffective physician communicators. Effective communication skills do not just happen, nor do they necessarily develop naturally. Communication skills are learned behaviors that have to be examined and practiced before being mastered. Physicians, in particular, need to develop an increased awareness of the ways in which their own communication skills, or lack of them, affect the meanings created in written materials, the clinical encounters with patients, and the resulting behaviors taken by others. Physicians are not, necessarily, believed to be poor communicators at the start of their medical education period, but, by the time they have completed their medical education, it is believed most have lost much of their communicating and interpersonal sensitivity.

There may be insensitive communications between physicians and patients for a variety of reasons, and the fault may lie with either party. Patients can be querulous, demanding, hostile, suspicious, exceedingly sensitive, and highly dependent. A large measure of patient dissatisfaction and resentment arising out of clinical encounters with physicians, however, originates because physicians respond to these patient attitudes in careless, thoughtless, or insensitive fashion. Regardless of cause or origin, insensitivity on the part of physicians is a major deterrent to the development of effective communication with patients. Those physicians who treat patients with respect and have recognized the need for mastering the techniques of good communication skills are more likely to gather full and accurate information from patients, dispense clear and persuasive information to them and their families, and elicit cooperation in the details of patient management from patients and others.

Effective physician writers are able to compose their material so it is clear to readers and cannot be misinterpreted or misunderstood. Effective physician communicators are able to share ideas and information with patients and others in a clear and concise manner, yet are adaptable enough to adjust their communication strategies and behaviors to the specific individual and specific situation in which they find themselves. They understand the difference between talking *with* people and talking *at* people, and are able to accept information from patients and others in order to encourage true dialogue among people. These physicians are sufficiently aware of the communication process to be able to react perceptively to the wide range of verbal and nonverbal messages patients and colleagues transmit in medical care situations and then to respond accordingly. Physicians who can communicate compassion, sensitivity, caring and empathy to patients are successful in establishing good interpersonal relationships with them.

WHAT OTHERS THINK OF PHYSICIANS AS COMMUNICATORS

Despite the personal nature of their professional calling and a better than average educational background, physicians are frequently charged with serious deficiencies in their communication and interpersonal skills.[16] Physician writers have been accused of filling their written material and published articles with confused thought and amibiguity, ungrammatical and pretentious constructions, subspecialty jargon, and a tendency to pontification, among other shortcomings. All too often, physicians seem to lack a facility to write clearly, speak effectively in professional settings, or use language that can be easily understood by patients, readers, or listeners. There is nagging and persisting evidence that medical care, in spite of its professional and technical advances, may not be meeting the perceived needs of patients, and the reason is believed to be lack of effective physician-patient communication.[17]

Most patients seem to like their personal physicians, but have a poor and often deteriorating image of physicians as professionals. It appears that a large segment of the public does not regard physicians as effective communicators, at least as far as their own health care needs are concerned. The American Medical Association maintains a file on the public image of physicians as measured by beliefs about physicians held by the public (Survey of Physician and Public Opinion on Health Care Issues). According to the 1988 Survey, a frequently recorded dissatisfaction about physicians expressed by patients is that physicians, as a group, are not communicating with them well enough or thoroughly enough. Many patients regard physicians as arrogant and do not believe physicians do a very effective job in either communicating information to them about their medical condition or expressing concern about their welfare as patients.[18] Unfortunately, according to the 1991 Survey, this physician image gap has widened.[19] If such views and opinions are widespread among the general public, it is not surprising that the outcomes of medical care, as viewed by patients, should be adversely affected. However, there is evidence that physicians will voluntarily change their practice behavior when pertinent information about practice patterns and patient outcomes is available to them.[20] While considerable attention has been paid to process and outcome in many problems relating to medical care, the fact that process includes the physician-patient relationship has been infrequently studied.[21] While practice patterns and patient outcomes are of singular importance within the medical care system, they are not the sole factors involved in providing effective and satisfying medical care. Good communication with patients must be recognized as a principal cornerstone of effective and satisfying medical care. Interpersonal and communication skills of physicians play a crucial role in the medical care delivery process and, it must be hoped, that as a more solid and scientific base of knowledge is developed about these skills, this new information will play a similar role in changing physician practice behavior.[22]

Poor communication with patients risks being associated with misinterpretation and misunderstanding of medical information, which could result in inappropriate or ineffective patient care and an increase in malpractice suits.[23,24] A heightened professional awareness of the need for good communication and good relationships between physicians and patients has resulted from the growing number and cost of malpractice actions. In general, patients' level of satisfaction with a medical experience is an important determinant of cooperation with the physicians' recommended treatment programs. It appears that patient cooperation with treatment programs depends more on how the physician's communication skills are perceived than on anything else.[25] Patient satisfaction with a medical experience appears to be related more to the physician's skill as a communicator than to the perceived quality of the medical care received, the patient waiting time, or even the cost of the medical care.[15,26] Unfortunately, many patients believe they are given inadequate information about their progress while in the hospital or during a treatment phase of the illness.[27] A frequent patient complaint is that when physicians do offer explanations to them, these explanations are difficult to understand because the physician uses cryptic and obscure terms and medical jargon. It has become increasingly evident that how well or how poorly physicians communicate with patients has a direct relevance to the accuracy of their diagnoses and the compliance, satisfaction, and response to treatment of their patients.[28]

Although the ability to communicate, to explain complex medical points in simple terms, and to seek out a common language with patients, listeners, or readers is a sound basis for success in medical practice and an achievement all physicians should strive to attain, indications are that many physicians fall far short of this goal.[29] When questioned in surveys, most patients report satisfaction with the quality of medical care they received, but study after study indicates that most patients are generally not satisfied with the physician-patient communication accompanying the medical care. In one study carried out in a hospital outpatient clinic, the majority of patients interviewed complained that their physician did not listen to them, did not permit them to make decisions about their own treatment, did not make treatment or medication information clear to them, did not tell them why they were given certain treatments, and did not make them feel at ease.[30] It does not necessarily follow that more communication with physicians is going to create more satisfied patients. What really matters is not how *much* is said to patients, but *what* is said and *how* it is said.

A frequent criticism of physicians expressed by patients and others is that the rigorous scientific training required for their medical education depersonalizes some of them so that effective medical technicians are produced who, upon entering clinical practice, have fewer communication and interpersonal skills than they had upon entering medical school.[31,32] Medical care, in these instances, can become system-efficient, but not patient-centered and effective communication with patients and others suffers accordingly. It is believed that as medical students become more and more focused on medical problems associated with the human body, many students become less focused on the person in the human body with the medical problem. In addition, personal relationships with patients can be attenuated and distorted by physicians depending too heavily on data reported by sources extraneous to both themselves and their patients. Consequently, many of the interpersonal problems arising out of the physician-patient encounter are believed caused by physicians' perceived lack of balance between emphasis on curing and emphasis on caring.[33] Medical care tends to be further depersonalized by the recent but regrettable custom of referring to physicians as "providers of care" and patients as "consumers or customers of care," and by the unfortunate custom of referring to patients used for teaching purposes as "patient material." Being a competent physician implies behaving and communicating in a professional, ethical, and sensitive manner, and use of such terms tends to denigrate this characterization. True compassion for the medical problems of patients is a product of sensitive and aware communication. The absence of satisfying communication between physicians and patients thwarts physicians' medical skills and diminishes their sensitivity for patients. The need for understanding the problems of communicating with patients and others and coping with them effectively is increasing as the delivery of medical care is more and more fragmented by specialized professionals and technicians so that patients are increasingly forced to relate to a galaxy of different physicians and health care workers.

The communication and interpersonal skills displayed by physicians can have a positive, or negative, influence on clinical interviews with patients; patients' satisfaction with the tone and conduct of clinical encounters with physicians; recall by patients of offered medical advice; patient compliance with recommended treatment programs; and the impact of potentially distressing medical and surgical procedures.[28] Although patients regularly cite dissatisfaction with physicians' communication styles when asked in surveys, they rarely complain directly to the involved physicians who, therefore, may not be aware of their own cited deficiencies. The biggest barriers to good verbal communication between physicians and patients appear to be the use of medical jargon by physicians, an intimidating awe of physicians by some patients, and physicians projecting, verbally or nonverbally, to patients a perceived lack of time for the patient and a need to hurry the clinical encounter. Although fluent in the jargon of their own specialty, physicians often can not communicate well with persons outside the field of medicine, or even with physicians in other medical disciplines. In addition, physicians' writing skills, or lack of them, affects their ability to transmit information in an effective and useful manner by the written word. Improved and more useful communications between physicians, patients, and others is an absolute essential if there is to be any improvement in the level of satisfaction people have with physicians and the medical care delivery system in this country.[34]

MEDICAL JARGON

Most physicians are articulate but many, nevertheless, find it difficult to communicate with patients effectively. Some find difficulty choosing the appropriate level of communication needed to carry out effective interchanges with patients because they have never learned that a less specialized level of language can not only be just as precise, correct, and appropriate, but can also actually facilitate communication with patients and others. However, the attempts made by physicians to communicate with patients and others too often confuse rather than enlighten, and complicate rather than simplify the exchange. The reason usually is the inappropriate choice of colorful buzzwords, creative acronyms and abbreviations, eponyms, and euphemisms that combine to make up the jargon of medicine, a language nearly unintelligible to the uninitiated.[35] Jargon can be defined as a somewhat esoteric language spoken by a particular group, class, or occupation. The jargon of medicine has been called "medspeak" by some observers who do not mean the term to be complimentary.[36]

"Medspeak" is a type of language shortcut, based on the arcane terminology of the medical profession, that is used among physicians and other health professionals to express medical complexities in the most efficient manner.[37] This type of medical jargon is permissable in discussions among health professionals, particularly when patient confidentiality is an issue. However, "medspeak" is inappropriate for communicating with patients or the public, and is inappropriate for use in professional writing, including patient medical records. The use of jargon and creative abbreviations is particularly inappropriate in patient medical records where words or phrases might be misinterpreted or misunderstood on later retrieval of the medical record. Skilled physician communicators do not use medical jargon, narrowly understood medical terms, or excessive abbreviations because they know their use severely limits understanding and dissemination of the information being communicated. The use of medical jargon in conversations with patients is out of place because such use obscures clear meaning and only serves to highlight the physician user's lack of sensitivity and awareness to the breakdown in communication. The argument against the use of medical jargon by physicians in conversations with patients is strengthened by knowing that patients fail to understand the meaning of many common medical terms used by physicians, particularly medical jargon. Of added interest is the information that physicians themselves generally overestimate what their patients have understood in conversations with them.[38] Koos quotes one of his patients who, in an earlier time, sums up the matter of physician-patient communication clarity quite succinctly: "Nobody should blame the doctor if he doesn't fix them up right away-or maybe never. But maybe things would be better if the doctor understood us, and if we always knew what the hell he was driving at-and not in big words, either."[39]

PHYSICIAN WRITING SKILLS

A large part of a physician's professional responsibility is to write pertinent information in patients' hospital or office medical records and to write letters to referring physicians about the care of mutual patients. A short experience in reviewing such communication efforts is usually long enough to cause even the most tolerant of reviewers to wonder why so many physicians express themselves so obscurely, so verbosely and, therefore, so ineffectually. Lois DeBakey, a professor of scientific communications, has pointed out the fondness some physicians appear to have for pompous, confusing, vague, monotonous, and ambiguous language.[40] It is believed, for example, that most medical students learn to write patient medical records by taking medical records written by their predecessors and teachers and adapting them to the patients immediately at hand. If this is universally true, it is easy to understand how poor medical writing skills would have a tendency to perpetuate themselves. Physicians need to possess basic writing skills so that their written records and referral letters are clear, concise, accurate, and say what the physician writer intended them to say, and will so appear on later retrieval and review for whatever purpose. In addition, some physicians write medical articles and case reports for publication and present talks to professional and lay audiences in formal and informal settings. Audience needs and interests vary for each of these different forms of medical communicating, and good physician communicators are aware of and responsive to these different audience needs and interests.

Most physicians do not find writing to be a very exciting activity and many, unfortunately, find no place at all for medical writing in their professional careers. A tendency exists among physicians to regard writing as hard work and to associate all kinds of professional writing with the rules and regulations of grammar and syntax, remembered not kindly from earlier schooling. Writing is hard work, but only in the sense that most worthwhile activities involve some hard work. The truth of the matter is that writing, more than any other form of medical communicating, is a creative act which can provide a unique and important kind of self-education to the writer, as well as bring rewards like professional visibility and peer respect. The ability to write well is recognized as an important and desirable professional skill for physicians to possess. Good writing, because it is methodical and disciplined work, requires planning, organization, and the ability to translate mental images into prose. Good writing also requires communicating to an appropriate audience, using an appropriate format, followed by reading, editing, and revising what has been written.[41] Once the requisite skills are mastered, most physicians who write find it a liberating and enjoyable experience.

Those physicians for whom writing is an important part of their professional careers appreciate that writing is not only a unique means for knowing and learning, but also a powerful tool for composing meaning and for making sense. Good medical writing is crisp, clear, and elegant, and begins with a commitment to language and a desire to use language effectively as an accompaniment to a professional career. Writing is a special discovery process in which learning comes by doing because writing well depends considerably on language mastery.[42] Learning good writing skills, whether for the preparation of letters to referring physicians, patients' histories, articles for publication, or research protocols, comes only from doing and by attaining mastery over language, which is the servant of clear thought. Successful writing requires practice in writing, thinking hard about what has been written, and a compulsive need to find the correct or most appropriate word to express ideas clearly.[43] Ultimately, good writing is based on a commitment to good writing, and an appreciation for carefully selected words and sentence structures, the materials from which good writing is constructed. For most physicians, writing is not a natural skill like talking; it must be learned and practiced like any other skill.

Knowledge gaps in medicine are filled when basic and clinical scientists disseminate new information through publication of research results. Such widespread sharing of information by the printed word allows easy transference and translation of new findings into the delivery of better patient care. A principal reason for learning good medical writing techniques is to assist in the preparation of manuscripts that will have a high probability of being accepted for publication, and of being fully understood when published and read. The process starts with a good idea and a good study design, followed by the production of a written document that tells readers what the investigator did, why it was done, and what was learned by doing it. Although good writing should never lead to the publication of bad science, bad writing can, and often does, prevent or delay publication of good science. Beginning physician writers are well advised to become careful and critical readers of respected peer reviewed journals, such as the *New England Journal of Medicine* and the *Journal of the American Medical Association*. Frequent and critical reading of such journals assists beginning physician writers to become familiar with both the structure and form of published medical articles, and the writing styles, both good and bad, of published physician writers.

Writing for publication in medical journals requires a stylized type of writing with the written material divided into distinctive and clearly separate component parts (see Chapter 5). These component parts and the order of their presentation to readers make up the form of medical writing, as distinct from the content of medical writing which is constructed from the ideas, data, and conclusions reported by the author. Physicians who have learned to become critical readers of published medical articles tend to become better writers because they are more likely to understand readers' needs for a clear statement of the author's purpose in writing the article, and for a limited amount of highly specialized data in its presentation. In other words, they are better able to understand, as they write their own articles, just how readers will read. Such physicians are better able to appreciate what signposts to meaning in the form of grammatical structures, background information, and intermediate steps in reasoning their readers will need to have a full understanding of the written message. Physicians who have been frustrated as readers by medical writing that is poorly organized or overly technical in its presentation, or medical writing in which the point of the article is never clearly stated by the author, are better able to understand readers' needs for a clear statement of purpose from the author in the introductory section of the article, and a limited amount of highly specialized data in the body of the article.

Good medical writing is a combination of good data, good vocabulary, good sentence structure, good organization of the material being presented, and is written with an appropriate sense of readership.[44] In addition, good medical writing requires the author to have an ability to organize ideas into logical sequences of information flow, an understanding of sentences and how they work, and a sense of how well the expressed ideas have been distributed through the different parts of the written material. An ability to string appropriately selected words together in sentences that are pleasing to hear and read imparts an effective style to the writing. Good medical writing is constructed with plain, clear language, and is written with the readers' needs in mind. This means avoiding medical jargon, unfamiliar eponyms and abbreviations, unnecessary words, and excessive use of technical terms. Good medical writers are considerate of their readers, think carefully about their vocabularies, and do not misuse technical and specialized words in vain attempts to impress readers. Such attempts only confuse readers and defeat the purpose for which the writing was originally intended. Physicians have limited time for reading and little patience with poorly written articles. Some of the common writing errors that irritate medical readers are taking too much for granted by assuming the readership knows more than it does about a specific subject, including too much irrelevant material in the article, the use of medical jargon, and writing in a disjointed and wandering fashion. Information that physician writers present to readers must be properly organized and should be capable of being read as a logical flow of ideas. Whenever possible, paragraphs should lead off with topic sentences that help orient readers to the information contained in the paragraph. The message conveyed by the article should be expressed simply and in the fewest words consistent with clear meaning. The most effective medical writing is lucid, direct, and accurate. If appropriate word choice is a problem, use of a thesaurus can be helpful by supplying a list of words from which a choice can be made.

COMMUNICATION AND INTERPERSONAL SKILLS OF PHYSICIANS

The medical profession has long regarded communication and interpersonal skills as necessary for physicians to possess, and the ability to interact well with patients has been an accepted goal of medical education.[45] Despite the professed importance of these skills, attaining proficiency in these skills has been given little prominence in traditional medical education curricula and, until recently, relationships between patient care outcomes and possession of these skills has been studied infrequently. There is a great deal of information about what should and should not happen in a clinical encounter in regard to communication and interpersonal interactions between physicians and patients, but few studies have attempted to define a relationship between patient care outcomes and possession or lack of these skills.[46] Available evidence suggests that poor physician communication and interpersonal skills are neither a new phenomenon nor a specific byproduct of medical practice but, rather, a deficiency persisting in many physicians since medical school.[47] This suggested deficiency assumes added significance in view of descriptive studies in which ratings given by patients for physician courtesy and information giving correlate strongly with patient satisfaction with the clinical encounter.[25]

Charney reviewed in 1972 what was then known about the body of knowledge concerned with physician-patient communication and observed: "The subject of patient-physician communication has often been discussed in literature and philosophy. Within medicine itself, the topic tends to be reserved for commencement speeches and other occasions characterized by speakers, long in the tooth, whose expertise lies elsewhere, and audiences, short in attention span, who recognize truisms when they hear them. In short, it is relegated to the "art of medicine" wastebasket; important to be sure, but lacking the precision and prestige of the bulk of scientific medicine."[22] In 1983, Wasserman and Inui noted: "Few would dispute the importance of clinician-patient interaction in health care. These interactions are not merely a ubiquitous feature of our health care system; they also provide the primary means for the diagnosis and treatment of disease, the management of illness, and the prevention of many health problems. Ultimately, clinician-patient interactions form the basis of the 'clinician-patient relationship.' Yet, surprisingly, little is known about these interactions, their antecedents, and their effects."[48]

Most of the useful information presently available about the content and value of communication and interpersonal skills of physicians and the relationship of these skills to outcomes of physician-patient interactions comes from work in the social sciences, particularly behavioral science, and the clinical disciplines of psychiatry, internal medicine, pediatrics, and family medicine.[49] Engel brought the need for physician improvement in the acquisition and use of these skills to the attention of clinicians with the suggestion that what was needed was a biopsychosocial model of medical care.[32] This proposed model suggests that all factors influencing a person within his or her environment need be considered to most productively identify and evaluate a patient's concern, provide for ongoing preventive services, and treat illness successfully. In a 1984 review of the clinical implications of social scientific research in physician-patient communication, Waitzkin notes there has been a recent but growing interest in empirical studies of communication and observes: "Typically, this research confirms the disconcerting misunderstandings, confusions, and barriers that often arise in doctor-patient communication. The process of communication takes on added importance because it can affect the outcomes of medical care, such as satisfaction, compliance, and physiologic responses to treatment. Educational efforts that aim to improve practitioners' communication skills can lead to encouraging results."[29] It must be pointed out, however, that the lessons of social science about physician and patient behaviors are observations about human nature. While many physicians might argue that human nature is very difficult to change, it can also be argued in rebuttal that the need for change must be recognized and acknowledged before change itself can become possible.

Although medical educators believe communication and interpersonal skills should be taught to medical students, convincing assurance that this desired belief is being fulfilled does not exist.[6] Particularly unsettling is the expressed belief that communication skills of medical students deteriorate throughout medical school.[50] A body of literature attesting to deficiencies in these subjects within traditional medical education has led to an increased awareness among some medical educators of the value and usefulness of teaching communication and interpersonal skills to medical students.[51,28] As a result of this new awareness, the curricula of some medical schools have been expanded to include instruction in interviewing techniques, interpersonal relationships, and communication skills, but the majority of medical schools still provide little curricular time for the teaching of these skills.[52,28]

Medical students and residents need help with communication skills, particularly obtaining a good history from a patient, conveying information about diagnosis and treatment to patients and patients' families, reassuring patients, achieving patient compliance and satisfaction with the clinical encounter, and monitoring how patients and their families adapt to illness and treatment.[53] Residents have been found to lack the ability to explain an illness to a patient, to determine the patient's level of understanding and emotional response to an illness, and to acquire an adequate social history from patients.[54] Despite the relevance of communication and interpersonal skills to the success of clinical practice, and evidence that at least one-half of physicians' time with patients during clinical encounters is spent talking, medical schools have been slow to introduce formal education in these skills for medical students. When teaching of these skills has been introduced, little time for them is allocated in the curricula and the teaching of these skills has usually been taken on as an extra commitment by the departments of psychiatry and family medicine.[55]

The basic clinical skills that must be taught to medical students include history taking, physical examination, and the ability to synthesize all relevant data into a differential diagnosis. Eventually, clinical proficiency extends to all compartments of patient care, including the acquisition of effective communication and interpersonal skills. Although not required in most medical schools at the present time, it has been shown that education of medical students in communication and interpersonal skills is both feasible and effective.[23,56,57] A critical question, however, that has not yet been addressed, but needs answering, is whether or not these skills, once taught in medical school, are retained throughout the period of medical education and into clinical practice.[6] Some evidence does suggest that these skills, as taught currently in some schools, are not retained throughout the period of medical education.[58]

Medical students and residents, for the most part, are unprepared when they have to deal with the spectrum of human emotions that patients and their families experience during the course of a serious illness. Until recently, an absence of any formal education, discussion, or even recognition of emotionally influential issues during the educational period tended to desensitize developing communication and interpersonal skills in medical students and residents.[59] Traditionally, students and residents are expected to learn how to cope with these emotions and interactions by trial and error. Most medical schools, until recently, left the learning of interpersonal skills to the students' own initiative and intuition, despite the information that more than one-half of a physician's working time in patient care, particularly in fields such as family practice, pediatrics, and internal medicine, is spent on problems involving, primarily, psychosocial factors which require interpersonal skills rather than technical knowledge.[14] As a consequence, communication and interpersonal skills have been found to be underdeveloped in medical students, and no improvement has been noted as the students progress through medical school.[47] It is probably unrealistic to expect that communication and interpersonal skills, if not acquired by physicians during medical school, can be learned during the period of graduate medical education. It is difficult to teach these needed skills during the clinical years because, in most settings, the emphasis tends to be more on the technical aspects of care. Overwhelming responsibility for patients and the necessity of acquiring technical competence during the period of graduate medical education may, to some extent, act as a deterrent to the acquisition of effective communication and interpersonal skills for many physicians during this period of career development.[60]

To the extent that the practice of medicine has become more scientific and more dependent upon technology, the physician-patient relationship has been weakened. As the physician-patient relationship declines, so does physician availability and familiarity with the total patient. A frequently voiced patient opinion about the way medicine is now practiced is that touch has been replaced by technology. In light of these and other changes occuring in the practice environment, it seems evident that physicians need to develop an improved professional image for themselves, and a more cordial relationship with their patients. Professional pride in practice patterns and behaviors is an additional reason why physicians and patients need to communicate with each other effectively. It has been shown in more than one study that how physicians communicate with patients affects the accuracy of their diagnoses, their patients' compliance and satisfaction with the medical experience, and their patients' responses to investigations and treatments.[22] The fact that patient satisfaction with their relationships with physicians correlates strongly with ratings for physician courtesy and information giving underscores the recommendation that the professional image of physicians would be greatly enhanced by administering to themselves a strong dose of common courtesy and common sense, along with the skills of information giving and listening.[31]

Two dimensions of communication important to effective physician-patient interaction are content and expressive function of the material being communicated. Content refers to the type of information that is being shared, and can pose a communication problem for physicians. The intense emotionality in dealing with patient suffering, fear, death, problem patients, and the uncertainties involved in medical decision making have always been part of a physician's life, but may be poorly handled from a communication standpoint by some physicians. Delivering bad news to patients is a type of communication some physicians find difficult to carry out, and communication between physicians and patients' families becomes particularly difficult if things are not going well with the patient, or in the event of a patient's death. Being able to talk about death as a reality after it occurs is an important outlet both for the physician and family members provided the communication interaction takes place in an atmosphere of dignity, respect, and sensitivity.

The expressive function of communication refers to the relationship the communication creates between physician and patient. The kind of relationship that develops, be it warm and empathic, or cold and impersonal, determines the type of interaction that follows. A relationship that allows for expressive communication that is warm and empathic is more likely to be effective, and is more likely to lead to open sharing of information between the participants. Physicians have an obligation to address the anguish that accompanies a patient's suffering, but how this obligation is fulfilled often becomes a problem in physician-patient communication. Sickness and pain strip away the usual social intercourse that makes human interactions unique and pleasant. Many times patients expect greater sympathy for their suffering and more skill in relieving their pain than physicians are able to provide. Objective measurement of pain is uncertain, and this uncertainty about pain level and intensity often leads to communication problems between physicians and difficult patients because physicians frequently allow their fallible intuitions to become the determining factor. Unless and until proof exists that the extent of suffering by the patient is actually much less than expressed by the patient, physicians should show patience and compassion, offer reassurance, and continue to give such patients the benefit of the doubt. Such an approach to a problem patient allows continuation of good communication while the medical problem is being addressed and clarified.

Two additional dimensions of effective physician-patient communication which have been repeatedly emphasized in the literature relate to needs expressed by patients. One is the need for the physician to understand the patient's concern about his or her illness, including its cause, severity and prognosis, the results of tests, and the availability of treatment. The other need is for the physician to give the patient the desired information about the illness and its treatment in clear and understandable language, and be willing to answer questions the patient may have. A critical component of effective physician-patient interaction is the attentiveness displayed by physicians toward the information and nonverbal clues given by patients.[61] Equally important to a good communication exchange are the nonverbal clues expressed by the physician who, more often than not, is unaware of expressing them, and usually unaware of their effect on patients. Patients watch their physicians' faces closely, and are quite sensitive to the tone of voice employed by physicians when talking to them.[14] The physician's facial expression should reflect equanimity, and the speaking voice should be calm, friendly, and clearly audible to the patient. Empathy is the clinician's essential tool in understanding patients and their problems, and in selecting and reviewing appropriate treatment with them. It also must be remembered that adherence to the physicians' Code of Ethics makes it mandatory that physicians include in their communication with patients the disclosure of financial interests in ancillary services, if any, as well as providing information about alternative referral services, where available. Adhering to ethical guidelines in communicating with patients and others eliminates the appearance of conflict of interest, and retains the primary focus of the communication interaction on the quality and continuity of patient care.

The clinical encounter is a complex interaction between a physician and patient, each of whom has overlapping, but not entirely congruent, values and goals. How effective the outcome of the clinical encounter will be from a patient care standpoint depends, largely, on the communication and interpersonal skills possessed by the physician. How a patient assesses the warmth displayed, the information given verbally and nonverbally about the medical problem, the laying on of hands, and other reassuring techniques employed by the physician during the encounter, generally reflects the professional attitudes of the physician as these attitudes relate to what is referred to as the art of medicine and bedside manner, which are component parts of professional behavior. The key features of a good bedside manner have been described as a cheerful optimism with kindness, and engendering faith and hope, while minimizing pain and fear.[62] Although vital components of effective medical care, many physicians regard references to the art of medicine and bedside manner with suspicion and even disdain. Physician attitudes toward this vital component of medical care reflect, mostly, their belief that the scientific basis for these interpersonal interactions lacks the precision and prestige of the bulk of scientific medicine.[22] Consequently, each physician tends to have his or her own unique definition of what constitutes "skill" in relating to patients.[45] Professional bias notwithstanding, physician communication with patients will not improve substantially until compassion, warmth, kindness, respect for and interest in patients as people, and physician concern for the welfare of patients begin to play a more prominent role in the physician-patient interaction. Improvement in medical communicating and, consequently, improvement in the delivery of effective and satisfying medical care will take concerted action by physicians and patients, as well as contributions by social and behavioral scientists. Physicians and patients must value and respect each other for the needs and obligations each brings to the clinical encounter. Physicians need to collaborate with social and behavioral scientists to develop creative investigations that explore the biopsychosocial model of care, and encourage the type of clinical practice that is satisfying to all participants.[63]

Patients list kindness, understanding, interest in them as people, sympathy, and encouragement as the most important attributes they wish their physicians to possess. Therefore, patients evaluate a physician's attitude of caring by assessing the humaneness, warmth, cordiality, and courtesy extended to them by the physician. Patients evaluate a physician's competence and the quality of care rendered to them by assessing the thoroughness the physician displays during a clinical encounter, the use of preventive measures, and the physician's willingness and ability to share information with them about their medical problem.[64] It seems that patients are most satisfied with the communication interaction when the physician discovers and deals with the patient's concerns and expectations; when the physician's manner communicates warmth, interest, and concern about the patient; and when the physician explains things to the patient in terms that can be understood. Consequently, patients want a physician whose attitude toward them creates trust and confidence, whose manner suggests thoroughness and concern and allays their tensions, anxieties, and fears, and who shows compassion by extending as much help to a fellow human being as is possible. The fact that a frequent criticism of physicians offered by patients is their lack of warmth, and a caring attitude toward them as patients suggests that patients find their ideal physician infrequently, and supports the conclusion that a real need exists for physicians to improve their communication and interpersonal skills.

References

1. Berlo DK. *The Process of Communication; An Introduction to Theory and Practice*. New York, NY: Holt, Rinehart and Winston; 1960.
2. Kreps GL, Thornton BC. *Health Communication*. New York, NY: Longman; 1984.
3. Pendleton D, Hasler J. (eds.). *Doctor-Patient Communication*. London,

England: Academic Press; 1983.
4. Physicians for the Twenty First Century. Subgroup report on clinical skills. *J Med Educ.* 1984; 59(2):139-147.
5. Burchard KW, Rowland-Morin P. A new method of assessing the interpersonal skills of surgeons. *Acad. Med.* 1990; 65: 274-276.
6. Physicians for the Twenty-First Century. Report of the Project Panel on the General Professional Education of the Physician and College Preparation for Medicine. *J Med Educ.* 1984; 59(2): 1-3.
7. Matthews JJ. The communication process in clinical settings. *Soc Sci Med.* 1983; 17(18): 1371-1378.
8. Thompson TL. *Communications for Health Professionals: A Relational Perspective.* New York, NY: Harper & Row; 1986.
9. Radovsky SS. U.S. medical practice before Medicare and now-differences and consequences. *N Engl J Med.* 1990; 322: 263-267.
10. Kahn GS, Cohen B, Jason H. The teaching of interpersonal skills in U.S. medical schools. *J Med Educ.* 1979; 54: 29-35.
11. Lohr KN, Schroeder SA. A strategy for quality assurance in Medicare. *N Engl J Med.* 1990; 322(10): 707-712.
12. Sloan FA, Mergenhagen PW, Burfield WB, Bovbjerg RR, Hassan M. Medical malpractice experience of physicians. Predictable or haphazard? *JAMA.* 1989; 262(23): 3291-3297.
13. Mathis D. Paternalism and patient education: personal responsibility for wellness. *Am Med Writers Assoc J.* 1989; 3(3): 22-25.
14. Korsch BM, Negrete VF. Doctor-patient communication. *Scient Amer.* 1972; 227: 67-74.
15. Francis V, Korsch BM, Morris MJ. Gaps in doctor-patient communication: patients' response to medical advice. *N Engl J Med.* 1969; 280(10): 535-540.
16. Barnlund DC. The mystification of meaning: doctor-patient encounters. *J Med Educ.* 1976; 57: 716-725.
17. Catlin RJO. Does the doctor understand what I am asking? *Am J Pub Health.* 1981; 71: 123-124.
18. Gartland JJ. A reappraisal of some professional attitudes in orthopaedic surgery. *J Bone Joint Surg.* 1989; 71-A: 319-320.
19. Physician Image Gap Widens. *Amer Acad Orthop Surg Bull.* 1991; 39(3): 12.
20. Agency for Health Care Policy and Research. AHCPR Program Note. *Medical Treatment Effectiveness Research.* March 1990.
21. Starfield B, Wray C, Hess K, Gross R, Birk PS, D'Lugoff BC. The influence of patient-practitioner agreement on outcome of care. *Am J Public Health.* 1981; 71: 127-131.
22. Charney E. Patient-doctor communication. Implications for the clinician. *Pediatr Clin North Am.* 1972; 19(2): 263-279.
23. Hickson GB, Clayton EW, Githens PB, Sloan FA. Factors that prompted families to file medical malpractice claims following perinatal injuries. *JAMA.* 1992; 267(10): 1359-1363.

24. Vaccarino JM. Malpractice: The problem in perspective. *JAMA*. 1977; 238: 861-863.
25. Lane SD. Compliance, satisfaction, and physician- patient communication. *Communication Yearbook*. 1983; 7: 772-799.
26. Korsch BM, Gozzi EK, Francis V. Gaps in doctor- patient communication. Doctor-patient interaction and patient satisfaction. *Pediatrics*. 1968; 42(5): 855-871.
27. McGhee A. *The Patient's Attitude to Nursing Care*. London, England: Livingstone; 1961.
28. Sanson-Fisher R, Maguire P. Should skills in communicating with patients be taught in medical schools? *Lancet*. 1980; 2: 523-526.
29. Waitzkin H. Doctor-patient communication. Clinical implications of social scientific research. *JAMA*. 1984. 252: 2441-2446.
30. Shuy RW. The medical interview: Problems in communication. *Primary Care*. 3(3): 365-368; 1976.
31. Comstock LM, Hooper EM, Goodwin JM, Goodwin JS. Physician behaviors that correlate with patient satisfaction. *J Med Educ*. 1982; 57: 105-112.
32. Engel GL. Enduring attributes of medicine relevant for the education of the physician. *Ann Intern Med*. 1973; 78: 587-593.
33. Engel GL. Are medical schools neglecting clinical skills? *JAMA*. 1976; 236(7): 861-863.
34. Weaver B. Physicians need to improve their relationship, image with their patients. *Am Med Writers Assoc J*. 1990; 5(1): 2-6.
35. Woods D. Good english is good medicine. *Can Med Assoc J*. 1981; 125: 624-629.
36. Shaughnessy AF. Toward less picturesque speech. *AMA News*. February 13, 1987: 4.
37. Smith DA. Editorial. *Medical Jargon*. Penna. Med. 1988; 91(2): 6.
38. Boyle C. Difference between patients' and doctors' interpretation of some common medical terms. *Br Med J*. 1970; 21(1): 286-289.
39. Koos EL. *The Health of Regionville*. New York, NY: Columbia University Press; 1954.
40. DeBakey L. The persuasive proposal. *J Tech Writing and Commun*. 1976; 6: 5-25.
41. Boice R, Jones E. Why academics don't write. *J Higher Educ*. 1984; 55(5): 567-582.
42. Alper PH. Writing is the perfect hobby. *AMA News*. August 2, 1985: 27.
43. Schwager E. *Medical English Usage and Abusage*. Phoenix, Ariz: Oryx; 1991.
44. Birkby SJ. A sense of audience: Know your readers' background and interest before devising writing strategies. *Amer Med Writers Assoc J*. 1987; 2(4): 17-18.
45. Hess JW. A comparison of methods for evaluating medical student skill in relating to patients. *J Med Educ*. 1969; 44: 934-938.
46. Rossiter CM Jr. Defining therapeutic communication. *J Comm*. 1975;

25(3): 127-130.
47. Poole AD, Sanson-Fisher RW. Understanding the patient: a neglected aspect of medical education. *Soc Sci Med.* 1979; 13A: 37-43.
48. Wasserman RC, Inui TS. Systematic analysis of clinician-patient interactions. A critique of recent approaches with suggestions for future research. *Med Care.* 1983; 21(3): 279-293.
49. Maguire P. Doctor-patient skills. In: Argyle JM, ed. *Social Skills and Health.* London, England: Methusen; 1981.
50. Ceropski JM, Kline SL. Social perception processes and person centered communication in the medical setting: research findings and implications for medical education. Presented to the Annual Meeting of the Speech Communication Association; 1982; Louisville, Ky.
51. Pacoe LV, Naar R, Guyetti IPR, Wells R. Training medical students in interpersonal relationship skills. *J Med Educ.* 1976; 51: 743-750.
52. Preven DW, Kachur EK, Kupfer RB, Waters JA. Interviewing skills of first-year medical students. *J Med Educ.* 1986; 61: 842-844.
53. Maddison DC. What's wrong with medical education? *Med Educ.* 1978; 12: 97-102.
54. Duffy DL, Hamerman D, Cohen MA. Communication skills of house officers. A study in a medical clinic. *Ann Intern Med.* 1980; 93: 354-357.
55. Monahan DJ, Grover PL, Kavey REW, Greenward JL, Jacobsen EC, Weinberger HL. Evaluation of a communication skills course for second year medical students. *J Med Educ.* 1988; 63: 372-378.
56. Sanson-Fisher R, Fairbairn S, Maguire P. Teaching skills in communication to medical students-a critical review of the methodology. *Med Educ.* 1981; 15: 33-37.
57. Werner A, Schneider JM. Teaching medical students interactional skills. A research-based course in the doctor-patient relationship. *N Engl J Med.* 1974; 290(22): 1233-1237.
58. Kauss DR, Robbins HS, Abrassi I, Bakaitis RF, Anderson LA. The long-term effectiveness of inter-personal skills training in medical schools. *J Med Educ.* 1980; 55: 595-601.
59. Wertheimer MD, Bertman SL, Wheeler HB, Siegel I. Ethics and communication in the surgeon-patient relationship. *J Med Educ.* 1985; 60: 804-806.
60. Werner ER, Adler R, Robinson R, Korsch BM. Attitudes and interpersonal skills during pediatric internship. *Pediatrics.* 1979; 63: 491-499.
61. Friedman HS. Nonverbal communication between patients and medical practitioners. *J Soc Issues.* 1979; 35(1): 82-99.
62. Spencer FC. The vital role in medicine of commitment to the patient. *Bull Am Coll Surg.* 1990; 75(11): 6-19.
63. Fisher S, Todd AD, eds. *The Social Organization of Doctor-Patient Communication.* Washington, DC: Center for Applied Linguistics; 1983.
64. Ware JE Jr, Snyder MK. Dimensions of patient attitudes regarding doctors and medical care services. *Med Care.* 1975; 13(8): 669-682.

2

Physician Writing Skills

Writing is believed by many communication experts to be the most challenging, creative, and rewarding of the communication skills used by physicians because of its potential for disseminating information of benefit to patients. Developing acceptable writing skills, then, should be a major goal for physicians because the nature of the medical profession is such that physicians can not escape the need to write, be it a patient's medical record, a letter to a referring physician, or an article for submission to a medical journal. Although some writing experts believe that writing can not be taught, it is believed that writing can be learned as a skill.[1] Writing is a personal and sensitive skill which can be enhanced to a remarkable degree by reading good writing and by writing practice. For most physicians, the ability to write well is not a natural talent; it takes a dedicated effort to become a good physician writer. Those physicians who are good writers became so because they wanted to become good writers and, in the course of learning the required technical skills, also learned to write in a clear, informative, and pleasing style. They learned to avoid jargon and imprecise writing and, along the way, came to realize that creativity in writing is not limited just to poetry and fiction. Writers know that nothing is so stimulating as the discovery that their writing has reached and engaged the interest of readers. Having a medical article accepted for publication, for example, is a tangible expression of the fact that, in the judgment of some detached professionals, the writer has something of value to say to colleagues and other professionals.[2] Physician writers have the added satisfaction of knowing the information contained in their written material can be instrumental in helping patients and bettering the human condition, provided they have the ability to convey their message to readers in clear and understandable prose.

Because of its relevance to the clarity and comprehension of what physicians write, it is essential that physicians understand the requirements of the language they use in their professional writing. Language is the essential, and perhaps the only, medium by which information and ideas are transferred from one mind to another. The first requirement of language is that it should be understood. The second is that the information or ideas that are given by one mind and received by another should not be distorted in the process by factors such as faulty grammar, imprecise terms, poor word selection, disorganized structure, or difficult style.[3] The precise and accurate transfer of information by whatever means is a goal all physicians should strive constantly to achieve. Information and ideas can be transmitted easily and accurately by physician writers only if the details of writing structure and style are given their proper degree of importance. The use of grammatical standards and conventions are essential for clear communication and must be appreciated and understood by physician writers. Proper use of these standards and conventions can result in the giving of information in a writing style that is lucid, simple, and pleasing to read.

Writing requires the physician to possess certain technical skills such as a facility for the language and a sense of grammar, syntax, and writing structure which allow the writer to turn vague thoughts into concrete paragraphs, sentences, and words on a page. Writing is a fairly complex process because each word selected should represent a thoughtful decision on the part of the writer. In addition to structural decisions, the emphasis given the writing will vary depending on the writing task the writer wishes to accomplish.[4] A part of the emphasis that good writers never neglect is a sense of audience because good writing is keyed to the readership which makes up the audience for physician writers. For the written material to be both read and understood, the author must know the intended audience. Writing without any sense of audience is as bad as writing without any sense of purpose. Because physicians may write for both lay and professional audiences, knowing something about the background of the readership is an important consideration. Articles written by physicians for medical readers, for instance, are compartmentalized and targeted specifically to an expected audience. Writing by physicians for lay or non-professional readers requires quite a different approach to the writing task. In this instance, a sense of audience is necessary to know how many technical words, for example, would be appropriate without compromising clarity and understanding. Because writing is an important form of communicating, clarity in writing has to be considered a vital element of effective medical communicating. A reader who has to work too hard to obtain useful information from a piece of writing will soon lose interest in that writing.[5]

Given an appreciation of reader needs for clearly expressed information, good physician writers fulfill these needs by making correct language choices and appropriate structural decisions when composing the written material. Good writers know not to use more words than are necessary to express intended meaning clearly, know not to use superfluous adjectives and adverbs, and know not to use complicated phrases in places where single words would serve just as well. Familiar, rather than unusual, words are preferred if they express the writer's intended meaning equally well because familiar words are more understandable to readers. Physician writers, because of an inherent responsibility to their readers to convey clear and accurate information, can best fulfill this responsibility by using precise rather than vague, and concrete rather than abstract words to assist clarity of expression and meaning. In medical writing, as in medical practice, being "almost right" can be dangerous. Absolute accuracy in what is put into writing is essential. Above all, those physicians who wish to develop good writing skills must learn to avoid ambiguity, wordiness, imprecision, vagueness, disorganization, writing clutter which ensures that no noun or verb goes unmodified, and pomposity in their writing. Good writing reflects the writer's capacity to think logically, and physicians who possess good writing skills combine clarity of thought with common language so that readers understand clearly what has been written.

TYPES OF WRITING

Non-fiction writing, of which medical writing is an example, can be subdivided into four areas or types of writing according to what task the writer wishes to accomplish. These four writing types are called *description, narration, exposition,* and *persuasion or argument*. This classification serves as a convenient device to point out that differing writing tasks exist and the writing emphasis must vary according to the task the writer wishes to accomplish. Although such a writing classification has its conveniences for some purposes, it must be realized that in most written material these four writing types frequently overlap.

Description

This type of writing paints a picture and its purpose is to create in the reader, to the extent that is possible, sensory impressions such as seeing, hearing, smelling, tasting, and touching. The writer may also try to describe a feeling. An author writing a description wants the reader to imagine a thing or an experience accurately enough so as to be able to participate vicariously in seeing or experiencing it.

- As an example of this type of writing, imagine how an internist would write a social and demographic description of the typical patient mix encountered in a general medical clinic for use in a syllabus to be given to second year medical students for an introduction to a clinical medicine course.

Narration

This type of writing tells a story and its purpose is to clearly communicate to the reader some series of events. One can narrate a series of events that happened to oneself, to other people, or to other things.

- As an example of this type of writing, imagine how a newspaper columnist would, in later columns, tell readers of personal experiences while hospitalized for coronary artery bypass surgery.

Exposition

This type of writing informs the reader and its purpose is to explain something to the reader. It assumes that the writer understands the subject to be explained and the reader does not, but is nevertheless capable of understanding, and wants to be given the explanation. Most medical writing is expository in nature.

- As an example of this type of writing, imagine how an orthopaedist would write material directed to a family medicine readership for the purpose of explaining the benefits of school screening programs for the early detection of scoliosis.

Persuasion (Argument)

This type of writing persuades the reader by arguing the validity of a set of data or points of logic to support a thesis, and its purpose is to get the other person to think differently. Persuasion proceeds from an assumption very different from the assumption exposition is based upon. Whereas exposition assumes the writer merely wants to transmit to an uninformed reader information that is essentially non-controversial, persuasion assumes that the information may very well be controversial and that the reader may be informed on the subject. Even if the reader is not informed on the subject, the debatable nature of the subject will require that the writer explain both the topic and his or her point of view on it in such a way that the reader thinks differently after reading the material.

- As an example of this type of writing, imagine how a health economist would write material attempting to convince a radiology readership that routine mammography for all adult female age groups is not cost effective.

MEDICAL WRITING

Writing for publication in medical journals is a purposeful exercise in organization and clarity of expression that tends to follow stylized formats. The purpose of medical writing is to convey accurate information to readers who can act upon the information to relieve human suffering and improve the human condition. Not only does medical writing differ significantly from literary writing in orientation and purpose, but even differs among the types of stylized formats used for different medical writing tasks. The stylized format used for a Case

Report, for example, differs in significant details from the stylized format used for a grant application to the National Institutes of Health. The purpose of medical writing is to communicate information to readers and its intrinsic value lies in the message it conveys, the research it summarizes, the questions it raises, and the thinking behind the decisions it announces. In literary writing the personality and writing style of the writer frequently assumes the dominant position, but in medical writing the message conveyed by the writing must always be dominant. Medical writing must satisfy the reader's needs for information, not the physician writer's needs for self expression.

Two frequent mistakes made by inexperienced physician writers are: (1) they do not target their article to an appropriate journal. Medical journals have special and differing requirements and authors must write to these requirements, and (2) they do not write for the reader who is the author's audience. Poor writers are easily identified by either writing for themselves with no concept of reader needs or by using the writing exercise to show off personal knowledge. Good medical writing, then, becomes a matter of helping readers find information quickly, understand it better, and recall it more accurately. Even with these constraints, medical writing need not be boring to read, but can be correct as to purpose, structure, and style and still be pleasing to read.

EFFECTIVE MEDICAL WRITING

Good physician writers understand that effective writing skills afford them a unique opportunity for learning and teaching, and for persuading others. They possess a sense of audience which directs them to write from a reader's point of view and enables them to keep their responsibility to the readers' need for information foremost in mind. In the long view, better physician-patient communication and enhanced patient compliance depends, in part, on the realization by physicians that the production of competent and clear prose is part of the solution.[6,7] In a more traditional view, medical writing represents an opportunity for physicians to add to the knowledge base supporting their profession and the clinical decision making required for its practice.

Ideally, medical articles by physicians should provide information that meets the four criteria of new, true, important, and comprehensible.[8] The transfer of scientific information by the printed word is a process that should be associated with inherent or implied responsibilities at three levels. Physician writers have a responsibility to report accurate data and draw reasonable and logical conclusions derived from the reported data. Second, editors and manuscript reviewers have a responsibility to apply the peer review process in a dispassionate, analytic, and objective manner.[9] To close the loop, physician readers have an implied responsibility to use the newly acquired information to effect better patient care. A responsibility that effective physician writers bear constantly in mind is the understanding that the accuracy and validity of the presented facts and conclusions must be beyond question because they know other physicians will act on the content and conclusions of the published article in the delivery of patient care.

One unfortunate by-product of the "publish or perish" attitude in some academic medical centers is the misguided attempts by a few physicians to deliberately pass off the same information or data to different journals without notifying editors that the information or data has been published elsewhere. In some instances this misrepresentation has resulted in essentially the same information being published in more than one journal. Editors of peer reviewed medical journals consider this misrepresentation a form of intellectual dishonesty. The *New England Journal of Medicine*, in response to such misrepresentation, cites the Ingelfinger Rule as a guide to its editorial decisions in such matters.[10] This rule states that prior publication of research results will disqualify them from publication in the *New England Journal of Medicine*. Grounds for editorial disqualification include prior publication in the scientific or lay press or what is described as extensive medical "news conferences." Specifically exempted from the Ingelfinger Rule, however, are publication of abstracts or presentation of the data at scientific meetings. This exemption is uniformly endorsed by all editors of medical journals.

The most valuable contributions to medical literature, but also the most rare, are significant new concepts or innovations derived from original material or new ideas. Regardless of originality and ultimate value to the medical knowledge base, truth and scientific validity must be an intrinsic part of every effort to record medical information in print. Trust is the essence of scientific endeavor, and readers of published medical articles have the right to expect that data were collected and results observed and presented exactly as the author states it happened.[11] No matter whether the project is basic science or clinical research, each step in the acquisition and interpretation of information must meet the test of accuracy. It does not take much imagination to realize the havoc that could result from the publication of inaccurate or incorrect medical information. Errors can creep in at any stage of a study and the effects of these errors would be magnified if not detected before publication. The study design itself can be faulty, observations can be incorrect, the analysis of results inappropriate, or the conclusions not justified by the evidence or data. Errors like these usually occur because of a lack of thoroughness in performing the study or evaluating the results, or by failing to meet criteria already established by prior work. Medical journal editors and manuscript reviewers have the task of trying to assess the validity of papers submitted in hope of publication. Medical manuscripts are frequently rejected for publication by editors or reviewers because either the evidence or the data presented by the author are insufficient to justify the conclusions drawn by the author.

Readers of medical articles are looking for answers to questions or solutions to problems, but they also must be convinced that the answer or the solution presented by the writer is correct, or at least reasonable. It is the responsibility of the physician writer to convince the reader, through the use of critically selected and evaluated evidence arranged in logical sequence, that the conclusions deduced from the reported study are correct and fully supported by the presented evidence. The physician skilled in writing techniques is in the best position to achieve this convincing effect because such techniques help clarify the writer's thinking. A good physician writer knows what he or she is trying to say to a reader when beginning to write, but it may not become totally clear in the paper until the final draft. New details, thoughts, and associations constantly come to mind during the writing and what the writer wants to say to the reader may not be clearly said to the writer's satisfaction until multiple drafts have been written and the scientific argument fully developed in the text. The scientific argument is a coherent series of reasons, statements, or facts used to support or establish a point of view. Whether a reader is convinced or not depends not only on how well the physician writer presents the argument, but also on the logic and clarity of the thinking as expressed in the writer's organization of the evidence, the sequence of its presentation, and the clarity of its explanation as expressed by the writer's choice of words and sentence structure. To help present this argument to a reader with logic, clarity, and precision, medical writing follows a stylized format which can be used for reporting the results of either basic medical science research or clinical research and which is described in detail in Chapter 5.

EVALUATION OF PHYSICIAN WRITING SKILLS

The ability to write clearly and logically is recognized as an important and desirable skill for physicians to possess but, unfortunately, seems to be a professional skill more honored in the breach than in the attainment. Some believe that professional writing by physicians, if not a lost art, seems at times to be a losing one.[12] Physician writers have been charged with filling their written material and published articles with confused thought and ambiguity, ungrammatical and pretentious constructions, subspecialty jargon, and a tendency to pontification, among other shortcomings.[13] Many physicians write poorly in a technical sense and others have little to no sense of audience and tend to ignore readers because of their preoccupation with the subject matter of the communication. Such physician writers approach writing quite differently from the way their audience reads the material. The writing problem of such physician writers is a tendency to confuse their technical tasks as medical information sharers with their rhetorical tasks as writers. The poor quality of medical writing, and the negative consequences of ineffectual writing by physicians, have long been a concern of medical educators and physician communicators.[14,15] Almost half a century ago, Gregg pointed out how seriously communication of information was being compromised by physicians poorly educated in the arts of communication.[16] Thirty years later Blake, in an historical view of the literary style in

American medical writing, noted that the opinion of the day was that the literary style in medical writing has been getting steadily worse.[17] A later opinion maintained that medical writing is so verbose, pedantic, and equivocal that it is a genuine bar to communication.[18] A look at present day medical journals shows that, with few exceptions, good science and good writing rarely go together and that easily understood writing is often too much for readers to expect.[19] Each year, editors at the *Southern Medical Journal* hand out the Dizzy Awards for "bewildering, unintentionally comical, or just plain terrible medical writing."[20] The contest gets its name from baseball pitcher and sports announcer Dizzy Dean, whose mangled language became legendary in the 1950s and 1960s. Three recent examples:

- The test was regarded as positive when any of the three solutions exactly reproduced the globus symptoms of which they complained.

- Besides causing lung damage, our data suggests . . .

- Hours after admission, the referring hospital called to report. . . .

If the ability to write clearly and logically is an important and desirable skill for physicians to possess, why are they characterized as poor writers and why are the articles physicians write criticized so frequently?[21]

Critics of the writing skills demonstrated by physicians generally include reasons they believe underlie poor medical writing skills. Reasons that have been identified by these critics as contributing to this undesirable situation are many and include poor basic writing skills superimposed on a poor grounding in grammar, syntax, and composition; poor physician reading habits, so a broadly based vocabulary is rarely developed; and disorganized thinking processes, so that disjointed papers are produced. For physicians to understand why others believe they write badly, they need to know something of the basic fundamentals of good writing so they can look at a sentence and understand how it works, how the ideas should be distributed through the different parts of the written material, and then be able to decide how to write it better. Other reasons believed to underlie poor physician writing skills are cultural factors, use of medical jargon, an indifference to good writing on the part of many physicians, a tendency for physicians to write to impress rather than inform, a fondness for technical terms to the exclusion of simpler words which would help reader understanding, and a propensity among physicians to write articles with multiple authors.[21,19,13] Ingelfinger notes that of 97 original articles published in the *New England Journal of Medicine* in the last half of 1975 (Volume 293) not one was written by a single author, and only 13 were written by two. The average number of authors per article was 4.55.[22] As young physicians begin to develop what they think are writing skills, they often imitate the writing styles of those physicians already in print and the poor writing cycle tends to take on a life of its own.[19]

Another, but not as widely appreciated, reason to explain poor physician writing skills is the absence of instruction in medical writing skills in the curricula of most medical schools. The Association of American Medical Colleges states, in describing prerequisites for a career in medicine, that refined communication skills, the use and understanding of written and spoken language, are essential for the study of medicine and for communicating with patients, and that effective communication is the foundation of a physician's successful relationship with the public and with other professionals.[23] Despite this AAMC prescription for professional success, the reality is that physicians are regarded as poor communicators and medical writers. One reason for the disparity between what is prescribed and what is achieved is the minimal amount of attention presently paid to the development of effective physician communication skills in most medical schools. It is apparently assumed by medical educators that entering medical students bring writing skills with them in a state of sufficient development to obviate need for further attention, but evidence exists to cast doubt on this assumption.[24,17,18] Even more unfortunate is the realization that convincing arguments supporting the belief that writing well is an important communication skill for physicians to possess are rarely pointed out to medical students during the medical education process.[15] Most medical educators fail to appreciate that writing is a poorly developed skill in the majority of medical students and physicians and most medical schools fail to provide a curriculum that includes instruction in medical writing and communication skills at the present time. It seems apparent that such instruction needs to be included in the medical curricula if the situation, as it is presently believed to exist, is to be remedied.

A survey of U.S. medical school deans carried out in 1982 found that only 15 of the 101 medical schools responding offered courses in writing skills, but in 7 of these 15 schools the offered instruction consisted of only brief seminars or workshops.[24] Lack of time, lack of interest on the part of those needing instruction, or lack of qualified faculty members have been offered as reasons by medical schools for not offering courses in medical writing skills to students. Another survey of U.S. medical schools was carried out in 1987 to determine which types of medical writing are considered most important for physicians and medical students to learn and whether such types of writing are taught as part of the formal curricula.[15] According to the responding medical schools, the five most important writing tasks for which physicians should have some writing skills were: write-up of the patient history and physical examination, progress note, discharge summary, peer-reviewed published paper, and grant proposal. Although these represent important, complex, and different writing tasks, they are not taught extensively in medical schools at the present time or thoroughly explained in the available literature on medical writing. According to the findings in this survey, a majority of responding medical schools do not teach, in a formal fashion, the major writing tasks needed by students and physicians or offer any other kind of systematic writing instruction. The results of this survey support the need to develop courses in medical schools that address the systematic teaching of effective medical writing skills.

IMPROVEMENT IN PHYSICIAN WRITING SKILLS

Most writing experts argue that the best way for physicians to learn how to write well in the literary sense is to read, analyze, and appreciate great writers and their writing.[25,26] In addition, most experts claim that the best time for students to develop a personal interest in literary writing skills is during their formal education period. For a variety of reasons, including stringent demands imposed on their available time by premedical and medical education requirements, this opportunity is neither appreciated nor sought by most students who ultimately become physicians. Admittedly, some physicians do bring good writing skills to the practice of medicine, such skills being natural or developed by a choice reflecting an educational background in English literature and composition, but the vast majority of physicians bring no such natural talent or educational background to the practice of medicine. It has been has been pointed out, however, that, although this traditional educational background of English literature and composition may provide physicians with some knowledge of fundamental writing skills, it does not provide them with the appropriate orientation needed for medical writing.[27] This view maintains that because literary and scientific writers have different purposes, each requires a different orientation toward their writing purpose and this orientation differs significantly between the two forms of writing.

Literary writing and writing in the humanities is oriented toward writing style and personal expression and emphasizes expression over communication. Literary writing orients writers to approach writing as an intrinsically valuable form of self expression in an individual context. On the other hand, technical writing, of which medical writing is a part, is oriented toward communicating information that can be shared with readers. In medical writing, therefore, the content of the material, not the writer, becomes the principal focus. Effective medical writing skills orient the physician to approach writing as instrumentally valuable in a professional context, not in a personal context. A writer's need to communicate and a reader's need to know are not always the same as these different orientations emphasize. The reader's need to know is a basic premise of effective medical writing which must never be neglected by physician writers. This basic premise requires the physician writer to develop a sense of writing from a reader's point of view so as to anticipate or respond to the reader's need for information. A good physician writer drafts the written manuscript for a specific audience by consciously placing himself or herself in the position of the readers and writes to please them. The needs of this specific audience require that good medical writing be simple, concrete, clear, and concise.

Technical and literary writing styles differ only in their orientation to writing purpose.[2] Both types share the same fundamental technical skills such as a sense of grammar and syntax, appropriate word choices, a sense of audience, and the ability to organize written material appropriately. If the aspiring physician writer has no specific background in the fundamentals of writing structure, helpful texts are available.[28-33] Studying the material presented in such texts will give physicians some familiarity with the fundamentals under which writing is formulated, but writing skills will not be mastered until each physician actually writes and rewrites. Physicians can usually learn something about writing by editing badly written drafts, written by themselves and others.[34] Learning the fundamentals of good writing and studying examples of good writing allows aspiring physician writers to develop the ability to discriminate good writing from bad and to identify specific factors that make bad writing bad. Once this ability has developed, the aspiring physician writer will be able to recognize writing that is clumsy and unclear or words that should be replaced with more appropriate choices and will know what to do to improve the writing. However, because medical writing is a form of technical writing, more is required of physician writers than a sound basis of English grammar and composition. Physician writers must think hard about the requirements for scientific proof, the logical development of scientific argument, and the precision of scientific expression. Physician writers have an obligation to readers to ensure that the study is worth reporting, that the claims made by the author are justified by the facts advanced, and that the writer has sufficient technical skills and knowledge of lay and technical language to present the material in a way that will be readily understood by readers.

The starting point for any written medical communication is having worthwhile information to share with readers. The next point to settle is to identify the audience with whom the information is to be shared. Problems usually occur when a physician writer, used to writing for peers who share the same general background, must communicate with a group with a different background. If a physician writes for a lay audience, particular attention must be paid to the depth of the vocabulary and extent of prior information potential readers may possess. Physician writers must take care not to overwhelm readers with a vocabulary choice that is overly technical and professional. Conversely, a too simplistic style and a patronizing tone can be equally offensive to some lay readers. Complex medical information must be explained in clear and everyday language and this transition may be easier said than done for some physician writers. A way this transition can be accomplished is for the physician to exchange places, mentally, with the lay reader and keep at the writing task until comprehension and complete clarity follows. This transition can be assisted by referring to a checklist of readers' needs which include:

1. Have I stated my purpose clearly in the opening paragraph?
2. Have I let the readers know what to expect from the text?
3. Have I provided a context for my ideas?
4. Have I highlighted the main ideas?

5. Have I told readers everything they need to know?
6. Have I included anything they do not need to know?
7. Is the level of language consistent with the readers' background and familiarity with the subject?
8. Does the style of presentation serve my underlying purpose of persuading, informing, or moving the reader to action?[35]

Once a physician writer can make this transition successfully, he or she has developed a writer's sense of audience, a capability Brazelton calls "finding a comfortable voice."[36]

Physicians are busy people and many argue that professional time constraints keep them from writing. Unquestionably, writing takes time because it is an almost endless process of sifting, sorting, and organizing. Physicians who want to become successful medical writers must understand that time must be reserved for writing in any schedule, no matter how busy or cluttered that schedule appears to be. In a busy professional life, time for writing means the physician must take charge of the time available and simply reserve time for writing. Writing will not happen unless physicians take the time to learn to construct relationships between language and thought and reserve time for writing as a conscious and deliberate act. In like manner, physicians can develop a broad general vocabulary only by becoming better readers of the general literature. Reading is perhaps the most valuable formative influence on a writer. Those physicians who read only the biomedical literature will write as they read. In order to find pleasure in the form and precision of words it is necessary to read widely. An appetite for reading good literature is an excellent route to better writing. Some guidelines to assist physicians develop more effective writing skills include:

1. Increase your facility with words and proper language flow through reading.
2. Increase your familiarity with the form and structure of good medical writing by reviewing articles published in peer reviewed journals.
3. Remember two commandments of good medical writing:
   - Use clear uncomplicated language that flows in a continuous and sensible fashion.
   - Be alert to awkward constructions which should stand out as you read, and reread, your written material.
4. Avoid medical jargon, pretentiousness in the tone of the writing, and a style that suggests you are writing down to readers.
5. Above all, know the material about which you are writing.
   - Be certain that all conclusions can be supported by evidence presented in the body of the paper.
   - Avoid global statements and speculation.
   - Vacuous space-filling language is easy to spot and will not be accepted by good editors.

Physician writing skills would be improved if they were included in the physician communication skills taught to students during medical school. When medical school curricula are reorganized and strengthened with additional emphasis placed on subjects such as the humanities, wellness and fitness, nutrition, and geriatrics, time must also be found for formal instruction in medical writing and communicating. It can be anticipated that the ultimate outcome of such instruction will be better physician-patient communication and higher standards for medical writing.

References

1. Chernin E. First, do no harm. In: Warren KS, ed. *Coping with the Biomedical Literature*. New York, NY: Praeger Publishers; 1981:40-65.
2. Walby BJ. Training the scientific author. *J Res Comm Studies*. 1981; 3: 111-120.
3. Pickering G. Language: The lost tool of learning in medicine and science. *Lancet*. 1961; 2: 115-119.
4. Weaver FS. Teaching, writing, and developing. *J Higher Educ*. 1982; 53: 586-592.
5. Birkby SJ. A sense of audience: know your readers' background and interest before devising writing strategies. *Amer Med Writers Assoc J*. 1987; 2(4): 17-18.
6. Becker MH, Maiman L. Strategies for enhancing patient compliance. *J Com Health*. 1980; 6: 113-135.
7. Ley P. Towards better doctor-patient communication. In: *Communication Between Doctors and Patients*. AE Bennett, ed. London, England: Oxford University Press; 1976; 75-98.
8. DeBakey L. *The Scientific Journal. Editorial Policies and Practices. Guidelines for Editors, Reviewers, and Authors*. St. Louis, Mo., The CV Mosby Company; 1976.
9. Cole S, Rubin K, and Cole JR. Peer review and the support of science. *Scient Amer*. 1977; 237: 34-41.
10. Relman AS. The Ingelfinger Rule. *N Engl J Med*. 1981; 305: 824-826.
11. Engler RL, Covell JW, Friedman PJ, Kitcher PS, Peters RM. Misrepresentation and responsibility in medical research. *N Engl J Med*. 1987; 317(22): 1383-1389.
12. Garland J. Annual Oration. The New England Journal of Medicine and the Massachusetts Medical Society. *N Engl J Med*. 1952; 246: 801-806.
13. Woodford FP. Sounder thinking through clearer writing. *Science*. 1967; 156: 743-745.
14. Medical literature and medical writing (editorial). *JAMA*. 1900; 35: 626.
15. Yanoff KL, Burg FD. Types of medical writing and teaching of writing in U.S. medical schools. *J Med Educ*. 1988; 63: 30-37.
16. Gregg A. Language and the practice of medicine. *Diplomate*. 1943; 15: 115-122.

17. Blake JB. Literary style in American medical writing. *JAMA*. 1971; 216(1): 77-80.
18. Roland CG, Cox BG. A mandatory course in scientific writing for undergraduate medical students, *J Med Educ.* 1976; 51: 89-93.
19. Radovsky SS. Medical writing: another look. *N Engl J Med.* 1979; 301 (3): 131-134.
20. Doctors' diction causes black eyes. *The Editorial Eye.* 1991; 14(4): 3.
21. Crichton M. Medical obfuscation: structure and function. *N Engl J Med.* 1975; 293: 1257-1259.
22. Ingelfinger FJ. "Obfuscation" in medical writing. *N Engl J Med.* 1976; 294: 546-547.
23. Farley L, ed. *Medical School Admission Requirements, 1982-1983.* Washington, DC: Association of American Medical Colleges; 1981:8.
24. Bjork RE, Oye RK. Writing courses in American medical schools. *J Med Educ.* 1983; 58: 112-116.
25. King LS. *Why Not Say it Clearly. A Guide to Scientific Writing.* Boston, Mass: Little, Brown and Company; 1978.
26. Lock S. *Thorne's Better Medical Writing.* 2nd ed. New York, NY: Wiley; 1977.
27. Lang TA. Technical writing is not one of the humanities. A fundamentally different approach. *Amer Med Writers Assoc J*. 1987; 2(5): 3-8.
28. Day RA. *How to Write and Publish a Scientific Paper.* 3rd ed. Phoenix, Ariz: Oryx; 1988.
29. Ebbitt WR., Ebbitt DR. *Writer's Guide and Index to English* 7th ed. Glenview, Ill: Scott and Foresman Co; 1982.
30. Huth EJ. *How to Write and Publish Papers in the Medical Sciences.* Philadelphia, Pa: ISI Press; 1982.
31. Strunk W. Jr, White EB. *The Elements of Style.* New York, NY: The Macmillan Co; 1959.
32. Williams JM. *Style. Ten Lessons in Clarity and Grace.* 2nd ed. Glenview, Ill: Scott, Foresman and Co; 1985.
33. Zinsser WK. *On Writing Well. An Informal Guide to Writing Nonfiction.* 2nd ed. New York, NY: Harper & Row; 1980.
34. Weiss EH. *100 Writing Remedies: Practical Exercises for Technical Writing.* Phoenix, Ariz: Oryx;1990.
35. Snyder D. Honor the readers' bill of rights. *The Editorial Eye.* 1990; 13(2): 1-3.
36. Brazelton TB. Finding a comfortable voice aids in patient interaction for physician-educator. *Amer Med Writers Assoc J*. 1989; 4(4): 9-10.

3

Medical Writing Style

Because physicians can not escape the need to write during their professional careers, it becomes an additional responsibility for them to learn how to express themselves clearly in the English language. The one cogent purpose of all medical writing is to communicate information to readers. Physicians who understand the requirements of the language, who are able to express themselves in logically derived written sequences, and who appreciate the roles grammar, syntax, usage, and tone play in medical writing, possess the ability to transfer clear and understandable information to readers. The information a physician writer wishes to convey to a reader must be transferred in a crisp and clear writing style that leaves no room for reader misunderstanding or misinterpretation of the written material. The structure of the written material should match its purpose. Convoluted, complex, or poorly constructed writing by physicians may be associated with serious patient misadventures in a busy clinical practice. Physician writers should know how the language works and why certain constructions are allowed while others are not. It is also necessary for physicians to appreciate that the written word is more formal than the spoken word and that words selected to be used in written materials should be chosen with care in light of that formality. Style in medical writing refers to correct usage of the English language and English syntax, and not to the flair and panache of the writing as expressed by the author.

Grammar relates to the rules that govern the proper use of language. These rules attempt to define the structural requirements of proper language usage so that communication between persons can be made more clear. Grammar is not concerned with word choice but, rather, with the relationships among words, which is the structure of the language. Syntax, on the other hand, relates to the way the elements of language are put together. That the subject of a sentence comes before the predicate, for example, is a feature of English syntax. Questions about usage arise because, like other languages, English makes available a range of choices appropriate to different language situations. Knowing what the alternatives are and recognizing how and why they differ puts the writer in a better position to suit the language to the subject, to the readership, and to the occasion.[1]

In writing a medical article or research protocol, a physician writer's primary concern should be the content of the written material, the message or information that is to be conveyed to readers. If the content is judged to be worthwhile and valuable, editorial assistance can help with the mechanics of writing. For physician writers, the decision to publish or not rests more often on the content of the paper than on its mode of expression. If an editor of a medical journal believes a manuscript is worth the attention of the journal's readership, minor defects in style or structure are not likely to block publication. However, if an editor believes a manuscript carries a less important message, defects in grammar and syntax may tilt the editorial decision toward rejection. The manner in which the information or message is expressed, therefore, is worth the attention and study of physician writers.

Style in writing is a characteristic way of making writing choices, and those with style possess a feeling for words and for alternate ways of saying something. For medical writing, these choices involve word selection, grammatical choices, and sentence structure as used in building properly constructed sentences and well organized paragraphs. *Style* is a word used to describe patterns of writing, and when used in reference to writers carries with it the inference that they possess a critical sense and an ability to make discriminating judgments in the writing effort.[2] An effective writing style for physicians combines a good vocabulary, a feel for correct sentence structure, and an ability to link well selected words together in sequences that are pleasing to read.

The importance of writing style comes into play at that time in manuscript preparation or manuscript revision when the physician writer must make certain that what needs to be said in the written material is said with accuracy, clarity, brevity, and grace. In the writing sense, grace means that the assembled words move smoothly along a clear line of thought. Physician writers need to have their ideas understood exactly because their writing often deals with critical issues, such as the health of patients. To achieve this purpose, physicians must attempt to state each idea as accurately and concisely as possible by building sentences methodically. Reader comprehension requires that sentences be developed efficiently and in logically derived sequences. This should be followed by careful editing by the writer, which entails keeping the sentence building processes of word choice, predicating, and modifying as simple as possible. Physician writers should make certain their sentences contain no unnecessary words and their paragraphs no unnecessary sentences.

Good medical writing style is characterized by objectivity, brevity, and crispness, and is achieved by way of plainness, simplicity, and orderliness in the writing effort. A physician writer's own style will depend, largely, on his or her ability to build ideas with properly constructed sentences. The written words should flow together without awkwardness, and unnecessary complexity in its tendency to become unnecessarily complex in its sentence structure. Such a sentence structure tends to convey information that is ambiguous in meaning and capable of being misunderstood or misinterpreted. The core of sentences should be simple, intact, and contain the most important information. Words should be chosen thoughtfully so that readers are provided with the clearest possible representation of the physician writer's thoughts, but the expression of those thoughts does not have to be couched in language that makes for dull reading.

Style problems that should be avoided but are commonly encountered in medical writing include wordiness, poor word choice, and excessive use of the passive voice. The seven deadly sins of writing, the antithesis of good writing, have been identified as ambiguity, wordiness, imprecise word choice, vagueness, disorganization, pomposity, and word clutter.[3] There also appears to be an unfortunate tendency for physicians to write, speak, and, indeed, think in terms of neologisms, or newly made up and self-coined words, and technical jargon. Use of unnecessary and undesirable technical jargon has become a bad habit of many physician writers. Style manuals are useful to assist physician writers eliminate style errors, grammatical mistakes, and structural inconsistencies in their writings that detract from the quality of published articles and distract readers.[4,5]

WRITING STRUCTURE

The purpose of structure in writing is to allow the transfer of information and meaning from the mind of the writer to the mind of the reader in a clear and precise manner. Structure affects meaning and, therefore, should match meaning. Said another way, what is easier to grasp is easier to consider, and easier to remember. Physician writers who fail to impose a structure on their writings will fail to gain the attention of readers. Awareness of the importance of structure is derived from writing experience, and development of such sensitivity is of particular importance in medical writing which requires clarity of thought and expression to insure reader understanding. Physician writers who possess an appreciation for writing style and the requirements of structure know, for example, to put closely related thoughts in the same sentences, but to put less related thoughts in separate sentences. They know to write with nouns and verbs, not with adjectives and adverbs. In particular, they know that the more of their meaning they can put into verbs, the stronger their statements will be. Structural problems frequently encountered in material written by physicians are errors in grammar, faulty punctuation, and poor sentence structure.

Sentences

A sentence in the English language has two key parts: a *subject* and a *predicate*. The subject, in the form of a noun or a pronoun, identifies what the sentence is about, and the predicate is that part of the sentence containing the verb and all its modifiers. A sentence that contains the normal word order of *subject-verb-object/complement* is known as a *core sentence*. The *object* may be a noun, pronoun, noun clause, infinitive, infinitive phrase, gerund, or gerund phrase. A *complement* may be a noun or equivalent as listed above, or a modifier of various kinds. The meaning of the complement is related to the subject by a *linking verb*, but it does not receive action from the verb nor describe the verb

Example:
He was the chairman.

Verbs convey action in two ways, by *active* or *passive* voice, and both voices can be used in medical writing. If the subject a sentence *performs* the action, the verb is in the active voice because active voice emphasizes the doer of the action

Example:
The students took the examination.

If the subject *receives* the action, the verb is in the passive voice because passive voice de-emphasizes the doer of the action

Example:
The examination was taken by the students.

This is why passive voice is used frequently in published medical articles where the emphasis must be on the *message* of the article, and not on the *writer* of the article. The subject of a sentence determines whether the verb should be singular or plural. A collective noun, such as faculty or army for example, takes a singular verb and singular pronoun. A compound subject, however, takes a plural verb.

Subject-verb agreement means that a singular subject takes a singular verb and a plural subject takes a plural verb. As discussed later, factors exist in writing, however, which can obscure the relationship between a subject and its verb. For example, inverted sentences and collective nouns tend to mask their subjects, and prepositional phrases coming between a subject and a verb can confuse this relationship for writers.

As a general rule, physicians should avoid constructing long and involved sentences because these types of sentences are difficult for readers to follow. Readers have difficulty following the flow of thought in long and complicated sentences and do better with sentences of about eighteen to twenty words in length. Unless a longer sentence is required for meaning or to clarify a point, it is better to break a long sentence apart, replacing it with two or more shorter ones. Short and compact sentences written in the normal word order convey the most emphasis to readers.

A balanced sentence is one that is well constructed, and one in which the beginning of the sentence is the strongest part, the end is the next strongest, and the middle is the weakest part. A strong sentence has the subject do something.

MEDICAL WRITING STYLE 41

The more of their meaning physician writers put into verbs, the stronger will be the resulting sentence.

Examples:
Weak construction: Misinformation might be given to the patients and caregivers regarding when no further improvement in strength could be expected based on the M.M.T.
Strong construction: Reliance on the M.M.T. might provide misinformation to patients and caregivers concerning when muscle strength plateaus.

Inversion away from the normal word order in constructing a sentence may be appreciated in poetry, but in medical writing it can be confusing to readers, and is likely to draw editorial attention. Sentences that are poorly constructed and contain extraneous words or clauses are called *loose sentences* and are certain to draw editorial attention.

As often as possible, physician writers should follow the writing rule which stipulates, *"one sentence, one idea."* Putting too many details in one sentence makes it awkward and confusing for readers to follow. Consider this sentence from a physician's dictated operative report: "The patient was taken to the operating room and prepped and draped in the usual manner under satisfactory general endotracheal anesthesia in the supine position with the knee flexed over a bolster." In one thirty-two-word sentence this physician lists five pieces of information, but leaves the reader confused and puzzled. Readers of this poorly structured sentence might well wonder if the patient was prepped and draped under the anesthesia equipment, or even if the anesthetist was in the supine position. When dictating operative reports it is not necessary, under ordinary circumstances, to state that the patient was taken to the operating room. It would appear obvious that the operation could not have taken place if the patient was not present in the operating room. A clearer picture of what occurred in this operating room would emerge if this one long sentence was restructured into two shorter and more compact sentences, as follows: "After the administration of satisfactory general endotracheal anesthesia, the patient was placed in the supine position. The leg was prepped and draped in the usual manner and the knee was flexed over a bolster."

A sentence can be structurally correct, yet not be concise, so that it conveys its information to readers in an improper or confusing fashion. Consider the confusing message conveyed in the following sentence from the written medical history of a young boy admitted to a hospital for a surgical procedure: "This 12 year old white male presents now with severe valgus deformity of his right knee secondary to a motor vehicle accident which resulted in a malunion of his distal femur with premature epiphyseal closure." The physician who wrote this history constructed a thirty-five-word sentence containing a list of misfortunes for this boy, but failed to mention the one fact that is key to understanding the entire sequence of events leading to this admission. The omitted fact was that the boy had sustained a supracondylar fracture of his right femur as a result of the motor vehicle accident. It was the fracture that led to the patient's subsequent misfortunes, not the motor vehicle accident. Careless, imprecise writing conveys careless, imprecise information.

Considerate writers avoid the use of the *periodic sentence,* which is a sentence that does not make its meaning clear until the end. Things in a sentence are related, and readers must hold each structural component in mind until its necessary relationships are found. Physician writers are cautioned not to construct sentences that require too much to be suspended while readers seek out its necessary relationships. The best sentences are those constructed to follow the *subject-verb-object/complement* formula.

Examples:
A periodic sentence: Based on paralytic poliomyelitis, paralysis from SCI may follow a pattern similar to patients with post-polio syndrome who develop secondary complications of pain and progressive weakness.
A subject-verb-object/complement sentence: Paralysis associated with SCI may follow a pattern similar to that seen in patients with post-polio syndrome who develop secondary complications of pain and progressive weakness.

If readers are forced to seek relationships that writers fail to make clear in sentences, the invariable result is reader confusion and a garbled message.

Physician writers should present informational items, and structural clues, at the points where the reader will need them so the written sentences give a sense of rhythm when being read. Punctuation marks are used to assist reader comprehension. They are used to separate sentences and indicate the relationship of words and word groups within sentences, joining them, separating them, or setting them off. Properly used punctuation makes the meaning of complicated sentences precise and clear.

Five suggestions to assist physician writers in constructing better sentences are:

1. Make something important the subject of the sentence.
2. Make the subject do something. The more of his or her meaning the physician writer puts into verbs, the stronger will be the written sentence.
3. Make the object (or complement) match.
4. Do not put unnecessary words in between the strong elements in a sentence, or between the main words.
5. Do not overwrite, overstate, or use an excess number of qualifier words.

Paragraphs

A *paragraph* is the writing structure in which relevant facts are given to readers and ideas are developed for readers. Paragraphs should be composed of groups of related statements presented as units to readers by writers. Each individual sentence, therefore, is a unit of the fact or step contributing to the construction of the idea, but the paragraph is the unit of the completed idea. Sentences which supply bits of information to the development of the idea should be smoothly connected together to form the paragraph which is the writing form in which writers express ideas to readers. Whenever possible, each paragraph should lead off with a topic sentence that serves to alert readers to the facts and ideas that follow. A paragraph functions as a structural unit because of the connections that exist between the statements it contains. A paragraph appears as a unit to the eye of a reader because it is physically set off from what precedes and what follows, either by indentation or by spacing above and below.

Each paragraph, or cluster of related statements, is meant to form a stage or bridge in the flow of the writer's thoughts. While statements in a paragraph should have a connection with one another, each new paragraph is expected to take a somewhat different tack. However, each paragraph must do something for the total writing effort, such as make a point, convey an idea, or create an impression. A paragraph can meet these requirements only if all the sentences contained in it contribute to its core of meaning, and if that meaning is an integral part of the stream of ideas running through the writing effort. Connecting words, phrases, or clauses are frequently used by writers to provide a rhythmic and coherent transition between paragraphs. Good physician writers know how to organize their material and present their sentences and paragraphs to readers in such logically derived sequences that their written material and published papers are easily read and clearly understood.

Transition Words

Transition words, such as, for example, "while," "and," "but," "although," and "therefore," are essential for clear writing. Their use contributes to the flow and coherence, ease of understanding, and logical presentation of the written material. Transitions indicate and clarify the relationship among ideas by linking all relevant ideas explicitly, thus preventing reader misunderstanding. Transition words, phrases, sentences, or paragraphs help the reader understand the writer's perspective and clarify the relationship between the ideas that are being presented. When transitions are omitted or used incorrectly, readers can misinterpret the writer's intentions.

Examples:
Without transition: The doctor's instruction to the nurse was vague. The patient was not brought to the operating room on time.
With transition: The doctor's instruction to the nurse was vague, hence the patient was not brought to the operating room on time.

Common Grammatical Mistakes

Grammatical mistakes frequently encountered in physician writing include subject-verb disagreements, unclear or missing antecedents for pronouns, nonparallel constructions, misplaced modifiers, misuse of subordinate clauses, and punctuation errors with semicolons and colons. Style manuals, dictionaries, colleagues who are experienced and skillful writers and, in some institutions, medical editors can assist physician writers with the details of proper sentence structure.[4,7,8,9]

Subject-Verb Disagreement

Subject-verb agreement means that a singular subject takes a singular verb and a plural subject takes a plural verb. However, factors exist that can obscure this relationship and that can act to make the correct choice a difficult decision. If an incorrect choice is made, the resulting sentence will contain a subject-verb disagreement. Among the factors that can act to obscure appropriate subject-verb agreement are:

"Neither-Nor" or "Either-Or"
When these forms are used, the verb should agree with the subject nearest to it.

Example:
Neither the surgeon nor the assistants are ready to begin the operation.

The subject nearest the verb is "assistants," hence the verb must be plural. If the words "surgeon" and "assistants" were in reverse order, the verb would be singular.

"None" and "Number"
"None" can take either a singular or plural verb depending on the meaning of its use. When "none" means "not one," it takes a singular verb.

Example:
None of the residents is presenting a case today.

When "none" means "not any," it takes a plural verb.

Example:
None of the case presenters today are residents.

"The number of" takes a singular verb.

Example:
The number of physicians in the doctors lounge is six.

"A number of" takes a plural verb.

Example:
A number of physicians are in the doctors' lounge.

Collective Nouns
These are nouns whose singular form names a group of persons, objects, or acts. When the group as a whole takes the action, the collective noun takes a singular verb and singular pronoun.

Example:
The faculty is expected to attend the lecture.

However, when the individual units of the group take the action, the noun takes a plural verb and a plural pronoun.

Example:
Members of the faculty are expected to attend the lecture.

Other Nouns
Nouns that are plural in form but singular in meaning usually take singular verbs.

Example:
Pediatrics is a required clerkship during the third year of medical school.

Some nouns can take either singular or plural verbs. A few nouns that end in "-ics," such as "pediatrics" or "statistics," are considered singular when referring to an organized body of knowledge, and plural when referring to qualities, activities, or individual facts.

Examples:
Statistics is considered to be a difficult course.
Statistics are useful to support the conclusions derived from the results of a research project.

Compound Subject
A compound subject takes a plural verb, but a compound subject joined by "or" takes a verb that agrees with the subject closest to the verb.

Examples:
Students or the teacher is expected to lock the door after class.
The teacher or the students are expected to lock the door after class.

Unclear Antecedents

An *antecedent* is a substantive word, phrase, or clause referred to by a pronoun. Each pronoun used should have a clear and immediate antecedent, and must agree with its antecedent in number, gender, and person. The noun, phrase, or clause that a pronoun is meant to replace in a sentence should be readily apparent to a reader. An antecedent can be in a preceding sentence, but not normally in a preceding paragraph. An unclear antecedent is said to be present if a sentence contains a pronoun without a clearly obvious antecedent, so that the meaning conveyed by the sentence is unclear to readers.

Example:
Didactic presentations focus on technical aspects of surgery. They are designed to be brief with ample time for questions and answers.

In this example, taken verbatim from a university-sponsored CME course brochure, it is not clear if the antecedent for the pronoun "they" is "didactic presentations" or "technical aspects of surgery." The meaning the writer of this course brochure wants to convey would be more apparent to readers if the two sentences were rewritten as one sentence: "Didactic presentations, focusing on technical aspects of surgery, are designed to be brief with ample time for questions and answers."

Parallelism

Parallelism means that parts of a sentence that are parallel in meaning should be made parallel in structure. The benefit of parallelism in sentence construction is that it improves reader understanding of what is written. Parallelism is achieved by balancing a word with another word, a phrase with another phrase, an infinitive with another infinitive, and so on. If a writer constructs a list of items, all items in the list should be made parallel, and should not contain parts of speech that are not parallel. For example, a noun is not parallel with an infinitive, nor is a noun parallel with a clause. Not only must all the elements in a list begin with the same part of speech, the beginning capitalization and ending punctuation must also be consistent. Lack of parallelism in writing upsets the rhythm of the written words, and jars the consciousness of readers.

Examples:
Improper: The duties of the resident were patient care, the teaching of medical students, and to write hospital discharge summaries.
Proper: The duties of the resident were *to care* for patients, *to teach* medical students, and *to write* hospital discharge summaries.

Modifiers

A *modifier* is a word, phrase, or clause that adds descriptive detail to another word, phrase, or clause (The cloudless, blue sky was wonderful to see). Modifiers can be adjectives, adverbs, appositives, or clauses. Clauses used as modifiers can be either *restrictive* (essential to the meaning of the sentence) or *nonrestrictive* (not essential to the meaning of the sentence). A restrictive modifier limits or restricts the meaning of the term or word it modifies so that the meaning is clear and unambiguous. Restrictive modifiers are frequently introduced by the subordinate connective "that," and are not set off by commas.

Example:
The operating room that is assigned to Dr. Brown is well equipped.

Nonrestrictive modifiers are explanatory in meaning. They add information to a sentence, but are not crucial to the meaning of the sentence. Nonrestrictive modifiers are frequently introduced by the subordinate connective "which," and are set off by commas.

Example:
Dr. Smith was assigned Operating Room 6, which happens to be the best equipped of all the operating rooms.

A memory device that can be used to distinguish between "that" and "which" is: *that defines; which describes.*

Good writers know that proper word order is important and match the modifier with the word being modified. Single adjectives are usually placed just *before* the words they modify. Adjective phrases and clauses are placed immediately *after* the words they modify, except when a phrase and a clause modify the same word; then the phrase precedes the clause. Adverb modifiers should be placed so that the meaning is expressed exactly. A modifier word, phrase, or clause that is incorrectly placed next to a word it can not sensibly describe is said to be a *misplaced* or *dangling modifier*.

Examples:
Improper: The patient left the operating room in good condition.
Proper: The patient was in good condition on leaving the operating room.

A phrase or clause that is written as a dangling modifier needs to be differentiated from a *non sequitur*, which occurs when one thing in a sentence bears no relationship in meaning with the other thing or things in the sentence.

Examples:
Dangling phrase: A lifelong sports enthusiast, John became the team's first coach.
Correct: John, a lifelong sports enthusiast, became the team's first coach.

Non sequitur: Born in St.Louis, John learned to coach while playing sports in college.

Clause

A clause is a group of words that has a verb and its subject, and possibly other elements related to them, and is used as part of a sentence. Clauses can be structured in two forms. A clause that expresses a complete thought, and can stand alone as a sentence, is called a *main* or *independent clause.* Also known as a *restrictive clause,* this type of clause is not set off by commas in the sentence.

Example:
It was the most difficult examination the students ever remembered being given in the course.

A clause that requires a main clause to complete its meaning is called a *subordinate* or *dependent* clause. This type of clause, although containing a verb and its subject and possibly other elements related to them, can not stand alone as a sentence, and is not crucial to the meaning of a sentence. Such clauses function as a unit, as a noun or as a modifier within the sentence. Every subordinate clause is introduced by a *subordinating connective* or, if not, one can be mentally supplied by a reader to relate the clause to the rest of the sentence, or to an element of the sentence. Also known as a *nonrestrictive clause,* this type of clause is always set off by commas in the sentence.

Example:
This type of clause, although containing a verb and its subject, and possibly other elements related to them, can not stand alone as a sentence, and is not crucial to the meaning of the sentence.

In this example, "although" is the subordinating connective. Other subordinating connectives are "because," " if," "since," " where," and "when."

Semicolon, Colon

The most frequent use for a semicolon is to separate two main or independent clauses that are not linked by a *coordinating conjunctive,* and whose relatedness the writer wishes to emphasize. Coordinating conjunctives ("and," "but," "or," "nor," "for,") join parts of equal grammatical weight and, in certain circumstances, can be used instead of a semicolon.

Example:
Some sentences have too much punctuation; others have too little.
Some sentences have too much punctuation and others have too little.

Semicolons can be used to separate elements in a series when there is interior punctuation, or when the elements in the series are long. If the items in a series are relatively short, commas are generally used instead of semicolons. Because in most places where a semicolon might be used, a period or a comma could also be used, the use of a semicolon is often as much a matter of style as of correct punctuation.

The *colon* is used as a mark of anticipation, indicating to the reader that what follows the colon will supplement what preceded it.

Example:
Three rules that pertain to vehicle highway safety are:

1. Do not exceed the posted speed limit.
2. Do not pass on the right.
3. Do not ride close to the vehicle in front of you.

Note that the three items in the above list are written in a parallel fashion.

Word Choice

Ranking in importance with the content matter of the written material is the need for readers to be able to understand what is written by physician writers. Whether or not this goal is achieved depends largely on the words physician writers choose to use in their written material. Proper word choice, in turn, depends on the physician writer's range of vocabulary and knowledge of word meaning.[10] Lack of clarity in medical writing is frequently a matter of degree that arises from a careless choice of words. Good medical writers resolve word usage questions in the direction of greater precision. Frequent references to a dictionary and thesaurus will help expand the range of a physician writer's vocabulary and knowledge of word meaning. A good vocabulary and a broad understanding of word meanings allows the choice of words that are accurate for the occasion, and which fit well into the context in which they are used. Much of the craft of writing comes in choosing words that, in context, will mean to the reader exactly what the writer intended them to mean. Good physician writers try hard to find the appropriate word for the particular situation. No word is, in itself, good or bad, or right or wrong. Whether a particular word is accurate in the context in which it is used, or is put to good use or not in the writing effort, can only be judged in the context of the writing situation.

An example of inaccuracy in word choice is the frequently seen incorrect interchange of the words "patient" and "case." These two words are not properly interchangeable because they have different meanings. "Case" is defined as the instance or episode of disease while "patient" is the person with the disease and the person needing care.

Examples:
Incorrect: Dr. Smith just admitted a case of pneumonia.
Correct: Dr. Smith just admitted a patient with pneumonia.
Correct: Last year, 14,729 new cases of the disease were reported to the U.S. Centers for Disease Control.

Another example of word inaccuacy is the use of the word "presently" to mean now when, in fact, the word means "soon."

Examples:
Incorrect: He is presently the department chairman.
Correct: He will be department chairman presently.

Physicians tend to use the terms "operative treatment" and "conservative treatment" when describing or contrasting treatment methods requiring surgical intervention with treatment methods not requiring surgical intervention. The term "conservative treatment" is inaccurate in this context in so far as it is used to delineate two different and opposing approaches to treatment. The opposing meaning for the word "conservative" is liberal or radical which is certainly not what those who use the word, even incorrectly, have in mind. The correct word choices when describing or contrasting these opposing approaches to treatment are "operative" and "non-operative" treatment.

The use of medical jargon also reflects poor word choice for physician writers. *Jargon* has been described as a language that combines the pretentiousness of big words and the deadliness of cliché with an unreal quality all its own. Jargon is an esoteric language constructed so that its users can communicate with only those few who understand its mysterious sounds. Consistent use of jargon by physician speakers and writers ensures that these users will fail to communicate with most people. Occasionally a big or "jargon" word more exactly expresses what the physician writer or speaker wants to say. If that is the case, the occasional use of the particular word is acceptable as long as it is the correct one for the meaning of the sentence. The best advice for physician writers is to learn to choose words that are clear, direct, and forceful, and to appreciate that medical jargon should almost never be used in responsible medical writing or speaking.

Some physician writers, possibly in the mistaken notion they are impressing readers, use big words, or unusual words, or jargon, or even attempt to introduce unnecessary new words. Journal editors usually consider such writers pedantic, and such writers risk losing the interest and attention of readers. If nothing else, such a writing style usually draws editorial attention. Consider this sentence taken from a published surgical article: "The surgeon must be well trained in the approach, anatomy, and potential complications of such an exposure before attempting such a noble undertaking." It takes a high degree of pomposity to classify a surgical exposure as a "noble undertaking." The physician who wrote this sentence should have been instructed by the journal editor to end the sentence by inserting the pronoun "it" after the gerund "attempting." To clothe a simple or familiar idea in strange language is to try to magnify its importance. Such attempts reflect badly on physician writers and will usually draw an editorial response.

Attention must be paid to the meaning of the words selected if reader understanding is to follow. Physician writers should choose words whose meaning they understand and, as far as possible, words whose meaning readers understand. A word encountered frequently in medical writing, but almost never in normal conversation, is "elucidate" which means to explain or to make something clear. Why select "elucidate" when the simpler and more widely understood word "explain" makes more sense for the purpose for which the medical writing was intended? Another word favored by some physician writers is "utilize," when the better choice would be the more generally understood word "use."

Writers who are careful of word usage avoid writing nouns as verbs, such as "to impact" or "to interface," and avoid foolish redundancies in writing such as "end result," "future plans," or "basic fundamentals." Thoughtful word choice helps physician writers avoid smothering verbs or adverbs in a group of extra words such as writing "to a great extent" instead of simply writing "largely," or writing "have a need for" instead of simply writing "need." In addition, most published medical articles are written in an impersonal style and the use of the first person singular or plural is not encouraged. However, use of the first person pronoun in either singular or plural form is appropriate when the writer is describing a judgment such as "I believe, etc., I concluded, etc." or "We believe, etc., or we concluded, etc."[11]

TONE

Less important than style, perhaps, but still worthy of attention is writing tone. Science traditionally affects an objective stance in its investigations, and in its presentations of results. Perusal of published articles in prestigious medical journals should convince physician writers that the accepted writing *tone* is one of objectivity. This convention requires physician writers to choose words that are deliberately neutral in terms of their emotional content. This is not to say there is no room for emotion in medical writing, but does say that in most medical publications emotion is subordinate to the more fundamental tasks of data presentation and interpretation. Casual, clever, witty, pompous, or pedagogic tones in submitted articles are not generally appreciated by editors of most respected medical journals.

References

1. Day RA. *Scientific English: A Guide for Scientists and Other Professionals*. Phoenix, Ariz:Oryx;1992.
2. Strunk W Jr., White EB. *The Elements of Style*. 3rd.ed. New York, NY:

Macmillan Company; 1976.
3.   Boston BO. In: Stoughton M. *Substance and Style: Instruction and Practice in Copyediting*. Alexandria, Va.: Editorial Experts, Inc; 1989:340-342.
4.   American Medical Association. *Manual of Style*. 8th ed. Baltimore, Md: Williams & Wilkins; 1989.
5.   Huth EJ. *Medical Style & Format*. Philadelphia Pa: ISI Press;1987.
6.   Ebbitt WR, Ebbitt DR. *Writer's Guide and Index to English*.7th.ed. Glenview, Ill: Scott, Foresman and Company;1982.
7.   Mattson M, Leshings S, Levi E. *Help Yourself: A Guide to Writing and Rewriting*.3rd.ed. Columbus, Ohio: Charles E. Merrill;1983.
8.   Quirk R, Greenbaum S. *A Concise Grammar of Contemporary English*. New York: Harcourt, Brace Jovanovich;1973.
9.   *The Chicago Manual of Style for Authors, Editors, and Copyeditors*. 13th.ed. Chicago,Ill; The University of Chicago Press; 1982.
10. Eibel P. Cacolalia. *Orthop. Rev.* 1986; 15(4): 114-119.
11. Roland CG. Why not "I" and "We?" *JAMA*.1968; 203(4): 121-122.

4

Organizing the Effort and Starting to Write

Physicians who might be encouraged to develop good medical writing skills are frequently deterred by the mistaken notion that writing is hard work and a difficult skill to master.[1] This misconception often has its origin in exaggerated emphasis on the need to master editorial conventions such as spelling, punctuation, and usage, rather than a focus on the real purpose of medical writing which is the information conveyed by the written material. In truth, what is required for successful medical writing is a good idea backed up with a good study design, good data to support the conclusions, and an ability to organize and present the information in such a way that it is both understandable and interesting to readers.[2] Writing is the intellectual act of expressing meaning through language, and, in the sense in which the term is used in this chapter, can be conceptualized as consisting of four component parts:[3,4]

1. Invention: the planning of the text with regard to audience, purpose, and topic;
2. Drafting: the actual writing of the text;
3. Revising: the refining of the text, often with substantial changes; and
4. Editing: polishing the text for clarity, style, and format.

Physician authors know that writing is a liberating and enjoyable experience and discover that nothing is so stimulating as the realization that their writing has reached and engaged the interest of readers. Medical writing is hard work, then, only in the sense that most worthwhile things are hard work to accomplish.

The process of writing, however, starts with the effort to organize the ideas underlying the project before actually starting to write the paper. The first step in the process should be to develop more fully the idea which stimulated the thought of writing the medical paper in the first place so the writer can have a clear focus in mind before beginning to write. The initial planning process should involve making written notes of ideas, data, references, secondary sources of information, and other pieces of information that might be useful in writing the paper. Notes are best kept together in a notebook where they can be maintained in an organized fashion, can be enlarged or deleted as necessary, and are readily available when needed. Next comes a thorough search of the pertinent literature, followed by the careful construction of a writing outline of the proposed paper, because outlines are the best way to move from notes to a finished manuscript.[5] In addition, outlining techniques assist the writer to develop a facility with logical sequencing and the development of ideas and topics. The writer must also be certain that the type of final written product is clearly established in his or her mind before starting to write because each type of writing, be it a traditional medical article, a scientific research paper, a review article or a case report, has a different format. Because each format has a different purpose and uses a slightly different structure and context, each requires a somewhat different writing style (Chapter 5).

Before beginning to plan the writing of a paper in detail, physician writers must make a clear choice as to the paper's intended audience. Writing style and data presentation will vary depending upon whether the paper is to be directed to a medical specialist, a general medical, or a lay audience. Inexperienced physician writers often seem to have difficulty understanding the first axiom of good medical writing which says to write for the reader who is your audience and not to write for yourself. Some physician writers seem to neither know nor care about their readers, except perhaps for the few readers working in their own narrow specialties. This apparent disregard for readers creates obstacles to comprehension for the very readers for whom the message of the paper was supposedly directed. A good writer drafts the paper for a specific audience by consciously placing himself or herself in the position of the readers and writes to engage their attention and interest. It is also strongly recommended that physician writers familiarize themselves with article lengths and writing styles found in issues of the journal to which they plan to submit their manuscripts. How the paper is written will be affected to a certain degree by the choice of journal because the selected journal defines the audience to whom the physician writer's message is directed.

The physician writer also needs to ask himself or herself some probing questions about the planned paper and should reflect a bit on how to handle editorial rejection if the finished paper is not accepted for publication. The physician writer should think seriously about the answers to these five questions before starting to work on the writing project:

1. What is my purpose in writing and what do I have to say?
2. Is the paper I plan to write worth writing?
3. What is the correct format for the message I wish to convey to readers?

4. Who is the appropriate audience for the message?
5. What is the right journal for the paper?

Answering these questions before starting the writing task could have a direct bearing on whether or not the completed paper will be ultimately accepted for publication.

Professional journals differ greatly in subject matter published, style, degree of specialization, frequency of publication, circulation and readership, editorial policy, and prestige. Some medical journals are highly specialized, while others are more general in scope of published material. In addition, some journals have an international reputation, while others are local and more parochial in outlook. It is essential that physician writers target their articles to appropriate journals. Writers learn patience through the delays inherent in editorial review, acceptance with or without suggested revisions, publication and, possibly, reader reaction to a published article. Physician writers also must understand that the editorial rejection rate for articles submitted to peer reviewed journals can run as high as eighty percent. Some of the principal causes of editorial rejection include manuscripts that are not considered original enough by reviewers, manuscripts that contain gross inaccuracies or claims not justified by the accompanying data, or manuscripts that are too long or presented so inadequately that no amount of revising or copy editing would set them right.[6] Even if the article represents the author's own analysis and findings, it may duplicate material recently published in the same or another journal. On the other hand, if the data or evidence opens up an entirely new approach to a previously well covered subject, the paper stands a good chance of being accepted for publication. Physician writers need to understand, however, that the material in the article must be appropriate for the audience served by the selected journal. Experienced physician writers have learned to live with these editorial odds and have developed strategies to deal with editorial criticism and rejection. The essential qualities a physician writer must develop in this regard include:

1. Readiness to accept editorial rejection and to react like a professional colleague, not a victim of injustice.
2. Readiness to submit a manuscript to another, possibly less prominent, journal.
3. Preparedness to reply to editorial criticisms rationally, particularly when the writer believes it to be unfair.
4. Willingness to revise and shorten the manuscript, and
5. Persistence in the face of failure and readiness to learn from failure.

In summary, organizing the effort and starting to write can be said to involve three essential steps:

1. Thinking
    - Develop the major idea for the study or project, writing notes as ideas and suggestions for additional topics come to mind and are developed more completely.
    - Think carefully about what needs saying and focus on the point or points that need to be presented, writing notes as the focusing progresses.
    - Search the pertinent literature thoroughly for background information and to make certain the proposed study has not been published before.
2. Planning
    - Plan or organize the development of the article using an outlining technique.
    - Gradually develop the form of the ideas and points to be presented in the article.
    - Refine the developed ideas and points to focus on essential data and to exclude material that is irrelevant, redundant, or speculative.
3. Writing According to Plan

The physician writer is required to possess a reasonable command of basic English and sentence structure. However, the writing itself emerges almost as a mechanical act and follows the writing formats described in Chapter 5.

ORGANIZING THE EFFORT

The key elements required for organizing the writing effort successfully and efficiently are the literature search and the use of an outlining technique. Effective writing begins with a clear sense of purpose and an organized scheme of some sort to group together bits of information or data collected in the writer's notebook. No one method of organization is believed to be better than another, so each physician writer must find the method with which he or she is most comfortable and develop a facility with it. This perception of relationships helps focus the literature search and is the key to organizing the writing effort. Clear organization of the material into appropriate subdivisions of the whole results in organized thinking and writing and is the principal reason why most experienced physician writers use some outlining technique as a writing blueprint at the start of the writing process.

SEARCHING THE LITERATURE

Practitioners, researchers, teachers, and students can keep reasonably up to date on what is being published on topics within their own special interests by scanning the contents of journals to which they subscribe or review in a library.[7] A wider range of current journals can be scanned by using one or more of the several editions of *Current Contents* found in the hospital or medical library. An

ORGANIZING AND STARTING TO WRITE

effective personal filing system is needed if good articles that are encountered during these scanning sessions are to be kept handy for future reference.[8] However, scanning current journals and maintaining a personal reprint or index card file derived from this scanning are not efficient and effective means for finding papers published in journals not regularly scanned and papers published in the past or in other languages. Most physician writers must rely on searching the literature of the medical sciences by making use of one or more of the major indexing and abstracting services available in most medical libraries or by initiating the search themselves from their own homes and offices if they have the proper computer equipment and appropriate software.[9]

Searching computerized data bases makes it possible for the physician to rapidly identify and use large volumes of information. However, the traditional method of going to the medical library and consulting printed sources is still recommended as the appropriate first step before going to the computerized data bases. Effective research requires reading source documents which is best done in a library. Reading printed documents leads to other references including the serendipitous discovery of additional or unexpected information which can only be discovered by reading source documents. Other sources of information such as presentations, technical reports, and symposia are usually not included in computerized data bases, but can be read in printed form in a library. The information gained by reviewing printed sources allows the physician writer the opportunity to focus the scope of the computerized data base search more efficiently and specifically. Although on-line searching can not replace other kinds of bibliographic research, it is an invaluable tool for locating specific information rapidly.[10]

Before starting a computerized literature search, the writer must first define and focus the subject or topic of his or her search because on-line searching can be too costly to use for broad based searching. The writer must decide what topics or subjects the search should cover, what time period it will include, what sources to consult, and what other possible constraints might be imposed on the search. By making use of appropriate indices, the writer should prepare a list of all the subject terms that may be relevant to his or her search.[11,12] The indices may have to be searched using synonymous terms found in the thesaurus for each index. If the assistance of a medical librarian is to be enlisted, the writer should be prepared to define the parameters of the search for the assisting librarian. These parameters include:

1. Topics to be covered;
2. Years to be included;
3. Language of periodicals to be searched; and
4. Sources to be examined.

Several sources are available to the physician writer for retrieving information from the medical literature. The source most accessible is *Index Medicus*, a printed subject and author index to over 3,000 journals and other periodicals in the medical sciences. Another source, the *Excerpta Medica* system, can be searched for article references in one or more of the many abstract journals and literature indices issued by *Excerpta Medica*. Manual systems, although valuable sources of information, are not capable of organizing and retrieving the growing body of published medical literature as well or as efficiently as on-line computerized data bases. As soon as the physician writer has defined and focused the subject or topic of his or her literature search, it is time to search the on-line system sources. Bibliographic searching is one of the most widely used applications of computers in medicine.

The National Library of Medicine offers two main groups of bibliographic services: (1) print indices, including *Index Medicus* and other indices of narrower scope, and (2) the MEDLARS on-line data bases (MEDLINE and related data bases). MEDLINE is believed to represent the state of the art in medical bibliographic data bases and is capable of accessing millions of medical literature references. The MEDLINE data base can be accessed through the National Library of Medicine or by using one of several commercially available software packages. One does not retrieve entire articles from MEDLINE, but the available abstracts usually give the searcher sufficient information to decide whether or not particular articles are worth reviewing in their entirety. Articles finally selected by the writer can then be located in the library in print form and photocopied for easy reference and filed with the writer's notes. Data base services are available which allow a user to print out an entire article if it is in that particular data base. For example, *BRS Colleague* has a Comprehensive Core Medical Library (CCML) data base containing the full text of more than 70 major medical journals and over twenty medical textbooks. With its LINK command, a publication cited in MEDLINE can be instantly retrieved from the CCML.

Some physician writers are sufficiently computer literate to conduct their own literature searches from their homes or offices.[9] The minimum equipment needed to provide access to the medical literature is a personal computer, a modem and telephone line, a printer, and a software program such as Grateful Med or Paper Chase.[13,14] Physicians wishing to do their own literature searching in MEDLINE from home or office will also need copies of Medical Subject Headings (MeSH) Annotated Alphabetic List,[11] and Medical Subject Headings Tree Structures[12] in order to get the appropriate indexing words and their hierarchical structure to properly access the MEDLINE data base. These two reference sources, obtainable from the National Technical Information Service, are updated yearly by the National Library of Medicine. Physician writers who lack the equipment, the skill, or the interest to do the searching themselves can consult medical librarians who are now experts in information systems and information retrieval and are willing to be of assistance to physician writers. Consultation with a medical librarian before beginning a literature search will show an inexperienced writer the most efficient way to find the medical articles needed for background research. When the writer locates printed articles he or she expects to use later when writing the paper, photocopies should be made and saved in a file. This precaution allows the writer to easily verify the content of each article and the bibliographic details of the reference that will be recorded in the bibliography or reference section of the paper. The writer should have copies in hand of every article he or she plans to cite in the bibliography. It is not recommended that references from abstracts or secondary sources be cited in the bibliography.

OUTLINING

Outlining, which lies at the heart of the traditional approach to all writing, is simply a tool used by writers to develop ideas in a neat and logical fashion. An outline is a temporary, preliminary, or working blueprint prepared by writers at the start of the writing process as a means of organizing and stimulating thoughts on the writer's subject matter. Outlining functions as a tool used by writers to gain control of multiple ideas and slot these ideas into their proper niches in the overall writing scheme. A working outline can make use of a formal technique or can be an informal approach that is fluid, subject to constant revision, and constructed without particular attention to form because it is destined to be discarded when it has served its purpose. Outlining rests on the assumption that research and thinking should precede writing and is the brainstorming part of the process that should occur before the start of the actual writing. It is a technique designed to assist writers to gather their thoughts about the topic into some kind of logical sequence or structure. Outlining addresses organization and organization reflects logic. Good organization of a paper allows readers and reviewers to concentrate on content and not to be distracted by poor structure.

Although outlining can serve several purposes in the writing process, its primary purpose is to function as a blueprint method for planning the writing of medical articles and research reports. Available outlining techniques allow writers the distinct advantage of focusing separately on small segments of information and of being concerned with only one kind of organizational structure at a time. The advantage of this type of focus is that it helps writers balance the emphasis that needs to be given to each part of the paper. Physician writers usually find informal outlines more useful than formal ones because of their flexibility, and relationships noted in the outline can change as the outline develops and other relationships become apparent. Regardless of outlining technique selected, outlines should not be too detailed, but used simply as a tool for organizing ideas and assisting writers to structure their ideas and concepts by functioning as a scaffolding at the starting point in the writing process. At that point, most writers do not have their ideas in logical order, nor will new ideas come in exactly the right sequence. A free-form type of outline can help put ideas in hierarchical order so writers can see how ideas might fit together, spot weak or missing connections in the developing logic, and be stimulated to generate new ideas on the subject matter. Outlines help writers develop a feel for the proper flow of ideas and sequences, but the physician writer must understand that outlining is considered only a preliminary writing step. Eventually, medical papers must be organized and written in conformity with the formats described in Chapter 5.

Outlining also serves other purposes in the writing process. An outline shows the relationship of thoughts to each other in the development stage of the writing effort and can help demonstrate organizational weaknesses in the author's writing plan. Outlining can also be a useful organizing tool when multiple authors are involved in the writing project, particularly if multiple authors are expected to contribute to the article. In addition, journal editors may use outlines to suggest reorganization of a disorganized article to a physician author who has submitted a manuscript for possible publication. Finally, outlining can be used as a technique to help loosen writer's block. The biggest blocks in medical writing are not associated with a lack of inspiration but are associated with not having adequate data, and not having a clear sense of the topic, the purpose of the writing, or the audience to whom the message of the paper should be directed. If the cause of writer's block is poor organization of data, it may be helpful to construct a rough draft as an outline, written in a casual conversational style.

Types of Outlines

Outline formats can be informal or formal in type. Formal outlines are the kind traditionally taught in English composition classes and are used most often for outlining book chapters or for large commercial writing projects. Informal outlines are less structured and seem to be better suited to the writing purposes of most physician writers.[15]

Informal Outlining Techniques

Mind Mapping or Spoke Wheel Technique

Mind mapping, a technique designed to stimulate a free flow of ideas, is the brainstorming a writer performs with himself or herself before beginning the actual writing process. The writer begins by writing the theme or main topic of the proposed article on a sheet of paper and enclosing it in a circle. Progressively, the writer encloses other main and subordinate points in circles as they come to mind and connects the circles with branch lines. An advantage of this free flow type of outline is that it shows a relationship between ideas without forcing the ideas into a formal structure. These relationships can be changed as the map develops and other relationships become apparent. The map can be rearranged as needed to suit the logic of the main points developed by this technique. Mind mapping is a personal outlining technique and the relationships revealed by the map are those determined by the writer and not those forced on the writer by a structural rigidity inherent in the technique.

Idea (Issue) Tree Technique

Constructing an idea or issue tree as an outline is a way of structuring ideas into a cohesive system which allows a visual representation of the reasoning process.[16] It is a hierarchical array of information elements and subelements, called nodes, connected by branches according to their interrelationship and which, when complete, bears a resemblance to a Christmas tree. In this technique the writer arranges ideas in hierarchical order by:

1. Deciding what pieces of information to include. The information available, the audience for the article, and the purpose for writing the article must be considered in this decision.
2. The writer decides how these pieces of information fit together or are related.
3. Construct the tree with the main topic at the top and related issues and topics branching from it and from each other according to their importance and relation to each other and to other ideas. Seek the logical relationships of the main points on the tree so as to determine the order in which to present the generated ideas.
4. Eliminate dead-end branches and repetitious information elements or subelements.

An idea or issue tree is a technique that permits more versatility than a formal outline whose structure dictates the order of presentation in the writing. An idea or issue tree allows the separation of the problem of structuring ideas from the problem of articulating them.

Index Card Technique

This method of organization is particularly suitable for writing projects that involve extensive research and note taking. Major points, ideas, or items of information are listed on 5 by 8 inch index cards and minor points are listed on 3 by 5 inch index cards. If reference material is added to the cards, include the source and page numbers so that this material is easily retrieved when it is time to assemble the bibliography. When all the notes have been made, group the index cards into piles of closely related points of information, then arrange these points of information in a logical order and in order of importance. Finally, arrange the piles in the sequence in which the writer wishes to present the information in the written article.

IMRAD Format

IMRAD is an acronym for the preferred format for the organization and writing of articles for publication in the biomedical literature (Chapter 5). The acronym stands for Introduction, Materials and Methods, Results, and Discussion, which represent the sections or subdivisions which make up the preferred structure for articles submitted for publication in the biomedical literature. Some experienced physician writers use the IMRAD format as an outlining technique.

Formal Outlining Techniques

Formal outlining, traditionally taught in English class during earlier schooling, is rather rigidly structured in that a predetermined form is required and parallel structures must be used throughout the outline. In addition, formal outlines have a title and a thesis statement, a form of topic sentence, constructed in a restricted and precise fashion and which explains the basic concept and focus of the written material. Formal outlines find their greatest usefulness in outlining book chapters or for outlining large commercial writing projects.[17]

Roman Numeral Format

This formal outline technique makes the assumption that the mass of data or information awaiting treatment by the writer can and should be classified in some way. It first classifies the major ideas according to the topic. Each of the major ideas is then subdivided into divisions. Each major division is then subdivided into its parts, and each part, in turn, is subdivided into smaller details.

Roman numerals are used for major ideas and capital letters for major divisions. Arabic numerals are used for subdivisions of major divisions and lower case letters are used for parts of subdivisions. A formal outline for a hypothetical book chapter could look like this with this technique:

I. Introduction

II. Major Heading
   A. First Major Division
   B. Second Major Division
      1. First Subdivision
      2. Second Subdivision
      3. Third Subdivision

III. Major Heading

IV. Major Heading
   A. First Major Subdivision
      1. First Subdivision
      2. Second Subdivision
         a. First Part of Subdivision
         b. Second Part of Subdivision

V. Summary

Decimal Format

This outline format is similar in design to the Roman numeral format, but uses decimals in place of roman numerals, capital letters, arabic numerals, and lower case letters and numbers. An outline using this technique would follow a sequence such as:

Title
Thesis Statement

    1.
        1.1
        1.2
            1.2.1
            1.2.2
                1.2.2.1
                1.2.2.2
                      1.2.2.2.1
                      1.2.2.2.2

and so on.

There is no writing rule that says any particular outline form or technique must be used or, if used, must be rigidly followed. Each technique can be altered, or even discarded, if that suits the writer's purpose. However, structure is the architectural dimension of writing and remains a crucial component of effective writing. Good organization of the ideas and material remains the key to good medical writing, and outlining is the best strategy available to physician writers for achieving good organization and structure

STARTING TO WRITE

Organizing written notes appropriately and making use of a writing outline allows the writer the opportunity to pull together the data and documentary materials he or she will need to have before actually starting to write. If pieces of clinical evidence such as radiographs or pictures of patients are to be used in the article, written permission to use such materials should be obtained from the concerned patient, physician, or hospital department in advance of beginning the writing effort. If the physician writer plans to use data from another published or unpublished source, permission must be obtained beforehand and full acknowledgment given in the written article. Also at the start, the physician writer should familiarize himself or herself with the manuscript requirements of the journal to which he or she plans to send the completed paper for possible publication. These requirements are listed on the journal's "Instructions to Authors" page. This page informs potential contributing authors as to what type of articles are considered for publication by the journal. It also provides details about manuscript preparation, rules for abbreviations and symbols, use of tables, graphs, and illustrations, abstract requirements, conventions of scientific style, and bibliographic form preferred by the journal. The author is also told how many duplicate manuscripts complete with illustrations the journal will require be submitted. The journal may also require each listed author to sign a conflict of interest statement.

The results of basic and clinical research should be described objectively, accurately, and completely and potential conflicts of interest on the part of any of the authors should be identified. "Conflict of interest," however, is not a precise term and is subject to interpretation and degree. Regardless of how one chooses to interpret the term, it is absolutely essential to the survival of accurate and objective transfer of scientific information that readers be informed of any possibility of author bias. Integral to the concept of scientific inquiry is the inherent right of each and every reader to be able to fully and freely assess the information presented on the pages of peer-reviewed medical journals. Knowledge of the nature of the basis for even the slightest possibility of bias on the part of any of the authors is part of that assessment right. The intent of such a statement is to inform the reader whether or not any of the listed authors have received or will receive benefits for personal or professional use from a commercial party related directly or indirectly to the subject of the article. In addition, authors must state whether or not benefits have been or will be directed to a research fund, foundation, educational institution, or other non-profit organization with which one or more of the authors are associated. Nothing in this statement is meant to imply that these financial arrangements are dishonest, dishonorable, or even wrong. What is wrong is to withhold knowledge of their existence from readers, thus weakening the readers' ability to critically appraise the scientific information presented to them in the paper.[18]

It is also important for the physician writer to think carefully about the authorship of the proposed paper because of the increasing tendency of medical papers to list an inordinate number of authors.[19] The lead name is considered the principal author, but the addition of six to eleven names as co-authors is not uncommon.[20] A type of editorial backlash has arisen against this "writing by committee" and the nonsensical notion that guest co-authorship should be extended to the chief of the service and to everyone who has offered advice, regardless of whether any of them made any intellectual contribution to the work. The editorial policy of many journals now recommends that, normally, not more than six names be listed as authors unless it can be shown that additional authors played a major role in the conception and design of the study and in the analysis and interpretation of the results. The author selected to be the principal author may, or may not, be the most senior of the listed authors. Huth has suggested the following guidelines to assist in determining who should and who should not be listed as an author[21]: (1) an author should have participated in the initiating or planning of a study or have assented to its design if enlisted late in the study, (2) an author should have made some of the reported observations or generated some of the data, (3) an author should have participated in interpreting the observations or data and deriving from them the reported conclusions, (4) an author should have taken part in the writing of the paper, and (5) an author should have read the entire contents of a paper and assented to its publication before it is sent to a journal. Editors of major medical journals believe that a scientific paper is a creative achievement and that co-authorship should imply that the individuals who are listed as authors had been part of that creative process.[22]

Once all the preliminary decisions have been made and the writing is to begin, the physician writer must remember that a scientific medical paper must be organized to meet the needs of valid publication, which means the manuscript must be prepared in the accepted medical journal format (Chapter 5). Medical writing is a process consisting of stages and tasks that are more or less distinct. Unlike other forms of writing, medical writing is highly stylized with distinct and clearly defined component parts. It must, of necessity, be clear, direct, and accurate in its choice of terms and constuctions. The real purpose of medical writing is to disseminate knowledge that will, it is hoped, improve patient care. Because of this purpose, physician writers need to think about answers to two questions as they write:

1. Does this sentence say clearly what I mean or what I want to say? and,
2. If challenged by a reader or an editor, can I support what I am saying with data or some kind of documentation?

The writing itself is the act of joining words into clearly understandable sentences and paragraphs and recording them on a page of some type. In addition to the form and style of medical writing, it is also important for physician writers to appreciate the process of medical writing:

1. Efficiency. This is the process of how one writes. Efficient medical writing dictates that the resulting text be lean because there is limited space available for text in most medical journals.
2. Effectiveness. This is the process of what one writes. Effective medical writing translates into good data presented with clarity in the accepted format.

It is one thing to say, however, that writing is a process of turning vague thoughts into concrete words, sentences, and paragraphs on paper or on a computer screen and quite another to produce a successful and effective piece of writing. Much effort is expended and many writing decisions are made between that simple statement of definition and the production of the finished article. Decisions about writing the paper include such choices as what rhetorical tone the paper should have, what material and information should be included in the paper and, just as importantly, what material and information should not be included in it. Inexperienced writers share a tendency to wordiness and, as a consequence, overwrite by including irrelevant and speculative material, thus producing manuscripts that are much too long. Physician writers should take their time in writing the text and learn to be coldly deliberate in distinguishing important information from the unimportant and irrelevant in preparing medical papers. The author who knows his or her intended journal and audience also knows what and how much to say in preparing the article. An astonishing number of otherwise excellent manuscripts are refused acceptance for publication because they are too long.[6] Physician writers must understand that most medical journals have drastic restrictions on the space they may allot to text in each issue.[23] Some editors try to set a maximum limit of approximately seven printed pages for each article accepted and published. If the point of writing and publishing is to disseminate information, physician writers should appreciate the fact that short papers are more likely to be read than long ones. The nub of the matter is that physician writers must have something worthwhile to say which must be said in a form that has a definite structure, makes its point, and then stops. Successful physician writers avoid the criticism of overwriting by the careful selection of information to be included in the paper and by the use of a crisp and lean writing style in its preparation and presentation.

In addition to a good vocabulary, a feel for good sentence structure, and an ability to string words together in sentences that are pleasing to read, good physician writers are considerate of their readers and keep their needs in mind as they compose the text. Good writers are careful of word selection and avoid words that have possible regional or ethnic differences in meaning, and know to write to the language level of their projected audience. It remains the physician writer's obligation to know and understand all words used and to use words readers will know and understand. The major consideration is to use the correct words so no possibility of reader misunderstanding can occur. Establishing fine shades of meaning is no easy task and adds another degree of difficulty to the writing. Should one aspire to some grace of style, the writing task becomes even more difficult. It is not the writer's obligation to tell readers more than the writer really knows or more than readers want to learn.

Good medical writing is vigorous, clear, and concise with no unnecessary words, sentences, or paragraphs, and places a high value on precision in its prose. The writer must have the ability to organize his or her thoughts and material as an essential prerequisite to starting the writing process. Writing, the very process of putting words down on a page or computer screen, promotes good thinking which, in turn, promotes good writing. Good writing springs initially from creative activity, not from formulas, and requires both a general commitment to writing and candid self-criticism. There is no satisfactory explanation of style, no infallible guide to good writing, nor any assurance that a physician who thinks clearly will be able to write clearly. The writer is required to make clear decisions about what needs to be said and how to say it. Good writers develop an ingrained habit of ruthless word by word criticism of the developing text to be certain the best possible word is used. This is a habit all physician writers should acquire because the ultimate outcome will be to make every sentence not merely capable of being understood, but incapable of being misunderstood.

Physician writers, more than any other group of writers, must avoid ambiguity in their writing. Physician writers need to write clearly and succinctly, using words with the same sort of accuracy a research scientist expects from his or her laboratory equipment. Only standard abbreviations are acceptable in formal medical writing and the full term for which an abbreviation stands should precede its first use in the text unless it is a standard unit of measurement. A good dictionary is indispensable for effective writing and a thesaurus is often helpful. Because all these writing decisions are interrelated and because one leads to or influences another, the habit of writing down ideas about content or structure eliminates a lot of vagueness and reinforces the suggestion that outlining is a helpful preparatory step for writing.

Many physician writers might wonder if it makes a difference in the quality of the final product if the medical paper is written by hand on a yellow legal pad, on a typewriter, or on a computer screen with the appropriate software. It has been shown that it actually makes no difference in the quality of the writing effort if the author works with pen and paper, a typewriter, or on a computer screen through a word processing program. Word processing, while making the physical task of writing easier, appears to have little impact on improving the quality of the written text.[24] At the moment, it seems the critical issue is that the writer use whatever technique feels most comfortable and efficient to him or her in getting the writing task accomplished. However, if longhand is chosen as the writing technique, the text will ultimately have to be typed or a hard copy printed from a floppy disk or diskette using a letter-quality printer. Double spaced typing or printing is required throughout the submitted manuscript, including title page, abstract, text, acknowledgments, references, tables, and legends for illustrations. If the manuscript is typed, white bond paper, 216 by 279 mm. (8½ by 11 inches) or ISO A 4 (212 by 297 mm.) should be used and margins of at least 25mm. (1 inch) provided. The computer's greatest usefulness in the writing process at the present time appears to lie in revising the text. It is an excellent tool for composing, formatting, revising, and polishing the final version of the paper. It seems likely, however, that as more people become exposed to and educated in the efficiency associated with automation, electronic writing will become more common.

References

1. Stewart DC. How to encourage reluctant authors. *The Editorial Eye*. 1990; 13(6): 1-2.
2. Huth EJ. *How to Write and Publish Papers in the Medical Sciences*. Philadelphia, Pa: ISI Press; 1982.
3. Bridwell LS, Nancarrow PR, and Ross D. The Writing Processing and the

Writing Machine. In: Beach R, Bridwell LS. *New Directions in Composition Research*. New York, NY: The Guilford Press; 1984.
4. Daiute CA. *Writing and Computers*. Reading, Mass: Addison-Wesley Publishing Co; 1985.
5. Jorgensen L. Get the writing right. *The Editorial Eye*. 1990; 13(7): 6-7.
6. O'Leary R. The acceptable manuscript. In: Schwager E, ed. *On Medical Communications*. American Medical Writers Association; 1982; Monograph Series 1: 39-42.
7. Haynes RB, McKibbon KA, Fitzgerald D, Guyatt GH, Walker, CJ, Sackett DL. How to keep up with the medical literature: ll. Deciding which journals to read regularly. *Ann Intern Med*. 1986; 105: 309-312.
8. Haynes RB, McKibbon KA, Fitzgerald D, Guyatt GH, Walker CJ, Sackett DL. How to keep up with the medical literature:VI. How to store and retrieve articles worth keeping. *Ann Intern Med*. 1986; 105: 978-984.
9. Haynes RB, McKibbon KA, Fitzgerald D, Guyatt GA, Walker CJ, Sackett DL. How to keep up with the medical literature: V. Access by personal computer to the medical literature. *Ann Intern Med*. 1986; 105: 810-824.
10. Horowitz J. Online searches assist editors and writers. *The Editorial Eye*. 1990; 13(7): 1-3.
11. Medical Subject Headings Section, Library Operations. Medical Subject Headings--Annotated Alphabetical List, 1990. Bethesda, MD: National Library of Medicine; 1990 (available from the National Technical Information Service, 5285 Port Royal Road, Springfield, Va. 22161).
12. Subjects Headings Section, Library Operations. Medical Subject Headings--Tree Structures, 1990. Bethesda, Maryland: National Library of Medicine; 1990 (available from the National Technical Information Service, 5285 Port Royal Road, Springfield, Va. 22161.
13. Haynes RB, McKibbon KA. Grateful Med. *MD Computing*. 1987; 4: 47-49, 57.
14. Horowitz GL, Jackson JD, Bleich HL. Paper Chase: self-service bibliographic retrieval. *JAMA*. 1983; 250: 2494-2499.
15. Leggett G, Mead CD, Kramer MG. *Prentice Hall Handbook for Writers*. 10th ed. Englewood Cliffs, NJ: Prentice Hall; 1988.
16. Semer C. Trees: A New Tool for Writers. In: Boston BO, *Stet! Tricks of the Trade for Writers and Editors*. Alexandria, Va: Editorial Experts; 1986: 105-107.
17. *The Chicago Manual of Style: for Authors, Editors, and Copywriters*. 13th ed. Chicago, Ill: University of Chicago Press; 1982.
18. Gartland JJ. Editorial. Authors, readers, and conflicts of interest. *J Bone Joint Surg*. 1984; 66-A: 1327.
19. Burman KD. Perspective. "Hanging from the masthead." Reflections on authorship. *Ann Intern Med*. 1982; 97: 602-605.
20. Cowell HR. Editorial. Multiple authorship of manuscripts. *J Bone Joint Surg*. 1989; 71-A: 639-640.
21. Huth EJ. Editorial. Authorship from the reader's side. *Ann Intern Med*.

1982; 97: 613-614.
22. Relman AS. Publication and promotion for the clinical investigator. *Clin Pharmacol Ther.* 1979; 25: 673-676.
23. Garrison DS. Trends in authorship in four medical journals reveal some surprises. *Amer Med Writers Assoc J.* 1989; 4(4): 5-8.
24. Lang TA. Word processing and its potential impact on writing process. *Amer Med Writers Assoc J.* 1989; 4(4): 14-17.

5
Medical Writing Formats

Once the physician writer has collected and organized the data and graphics he or she wishes to present, has selected and verified references to be cited, and has determined the order of presentation of the information by use of an outlining technique, he or she is ready to begin the actual writing of the medical paper. In constructing the paper, physician writers should never withhold the most important findings until later in the paper in order to provide a surprise or dramatic climax. While appropriate for mystery and espionage novels, this device has no place in medical writing. Readers of medical papers want to be able to follow the development of the evidence in a logical and orderly fashion and the use of standardized journal formats allows them that opportunity.[1]

Medical journals use conventions in style and format that are widely recognized and understood so that the information contained in the published papers is transmitted in orderly sequence, which assists understanding of the information by journal readers.[2] Regardless of whether one is writing a traditional medical journal article, a case report, or a research protocol, the text must be prepared in the accepted format to be considered seriously by reviewers or editors or to have any chance of being accepted for publication in a reputable journal. Medical journals use standard formats largely because technical prose is difficult in itself and a standard format, which breaks the material into distinctive and manageable parts, makes it easier for both readers and writers to know exactly how the information will be arranged. Readers know what to expect as far as the structure of the paper is concerned and, when the paper is broken into clearly defined sections, can read the parts that are useful or interesting to them. Preparation of any type of medical paper has very little to do with literary skill. The paper will depend on the evidence or data presented for its validity and on its organization, clarity of thought, and use of a common language for its readability.[3] A medical paper, in addition to containing specified kinds of information, requires logic, clarity, and precision in its writing. Scientific writing places a high value on precision in its preparation; the leaner the prose, the better. If the paper or case report is accepted for publication, the critical task of refining a manuscript's spelling, punctuation, syntax, and style is carried out by a copyeditor working for the journal accepting the paper.

THE MEDICAL JOURNAL FORMAT

Medical journal articles are the primary means for the exchange of medical and scientific information. A published journal article documents other medical and scientific literature related to the problem being studied, permits sufficient description of methodology so that the study can be repeated by another, allows for a comprehensive discussion of results, and most important, is subjected to a process of peer review before acceptance for publication.[4] When modern scientific papers, including papers in the medical sciences, are examined, one is struck by a certain sameness about them. This sameness relates to the form or structure of the published papers, not to their content, and derives from the fact that scientific papers are organized in the same way. This organizational format has come to be known as IMRAD, an acronym standing for Introduction, Methods, Results, and Discussion. These specific sections can be further defined as:

1. *Introduction*: What is the problem under study?
2. *Methods:* How was the problem solved?
3. *Results:* What was found?
4. *Discussion:* What do the findings mean?

Although sometimes criticized as too rigid, this organizational format allows scientific papers to be organized in a logically derived sequence that is disciplined and readily recognized and understood by writers, reviewers, editors, and readers.[5] Experienced physician writers occasionally use the *IMRAD* format as an outlining technique to organize their material preparatory to the start of the writing process. Although the *IMRAD* format speaks to the basic content material of a paper, medical literature data base requirements now give added significance to the paper's title and abstract. The complete medical journal format can, therefore, now be said to consist of these component parts:

1. Title
2. Abstract
3. The Introduction section
4. The Materials and Methods section
5. The Results section
6. The Discussion section

In addition, some basic science research papers have a Conclusions section following the Discussion. The majority of published medical papers, however, end with the Discussion section.

There is one cardinal rule physician writers must follow when using this or any other established writing format. When composing text under a specific section heading, the writer must stick to the subject defined by the heading. For example, description of results obtained by the study must be confined to the Results section and not scattered through the Introduction, Results, and Discussion sections. This rule is absolute because readers use the journal format to find the kinds of information in which they have a particular interest. Physician writers, then, make use of the journal format to separate the paper into distinctive sections, each with its own purpose and content. Appropriate use of this writing format makes the information contained in the paper more understandable and accessible to readers.

Each component of the manuscript should begin on a new page, in the following sequence:

1. Title page
2. Abstract and key words
3. Text
4. Acknowledgments
5. References
6. Tables and figures: Each table and figure, complete with title and footnotes, on a separate page
7. Legends for illustrations

Details referable to graphics used with written materials are discussed in Chapter 8.

Before beginning the task of actually writing their papers in accordance with the journal format, physician writers would be well advised to keep in mind the observation of experienced journal editors that the majority of submitted medical manuscripts are overwritten and much too long.[6] Poorly prepared or poorly written papers not only fail to communicate information effectively, but also tend to persuade reviewers and editors that the study being described in the paper was poorly conducted. Physician writers are under no obligation to include every piece of information recorded in their notebooks, but are obliged to include the information or data that support the conclusions the writer wishes to present to readers. Physician writers need to remember that the typical medical paper has never pretended to be more than another little piece in a larger jigsaw puzzle. Most published medical papers are not meant to be final statements of indisputable truths but, rather, tiny tentative steps forward through the jungles of ignorance.[7]

TITLE

The title of a paper is a label used to identify the content of the paper to a reader and must be chosen thoughtfully because it may be included in an abstract, *Index Medicus*, or an on-line medical literature data base. The title should be as informative of the article's content as possible within a reasonable length. The title should also be the fewest possible words that adequately describe the content of the paper. The selected words must attract and inform the reader and identify or classify the paper for indexing and abstracting services. The physician writer should choose a title that will generate reader interest in the paper if seen in bibliographic searches. An uninformative title carries the risk of deterring or misleading possible readers. A title is not a sentence, nor does it need to be. Because it is not a sentence with the usual subject, verb, object arrangement, a title is really simpler than a sentence; however, the order in which the words are presented is important. All words in a title must be chosen with thought and their association with one another managed carefully. The most common errors in defective titles, and the most damaging in terms of reader comprehension, are inappropriate word choice and faulty syntax or word order.

A good title must describe the content of the paper as specifically as possible but, at the same time, in the fewest words possible. Abbreviations, proprietary names, jargon, and unusual or outdated terminology have no place in titles. Indexing and abstracting services depend heavily on the accuracy of the titles of articles included in these services. It is very important that the author provide the right keys for indexing when constructing the title. Words in the title should be limited to those words that highlight the significant content of the paper in terms that are both meaningful to readers and retrievable in bibliographic searches. Key words, whenever possible, should be terms listed in the Medical Subject Headings list from *Index Medicus*.

A few years back, I submitted a paper titled "Orthopaedic Clinical Research. Evaluation of Some Design Strategies and Outcome Measures" to a major peer reviewed orthopaedic journal. The paper described a study that indicated major flaws in study design existed in many published reports of orthopaedic clinical research. Although accepting the paper for publication, the editor pointed out that my selected title was misleading in that it did not specifically describe the content of the paper. The paper was published under the editor's suggested and more meaningful title, "Orthopaedic Clinical Research. Deficiencies in Experimental Design and Determinations of Outcome."[8] The editor was correct in the assessment of my selected title. The word "evaluation" is a neutral term and tells the reader nothing of significance, or what information the reader can expect to gain from reading the article. The reported study identified deficiencies that needed correction and the title suggested by the editor was more accurate and better reflected the content matter of the paper.

The title page of the manuscript should carry the following information:

1. The title of the article;
2. First name, middle initial, and last name of each author with highest academic degree;
3. Name of department(s) and institution(s) from which the work emanates;

4. Disclaimers, if any;
5. Name and address of author responsible for correspondence about the manuscript;
6. Name and address of author to whom requests for reprints should be addressed, or statement that reprints will not be available from the author;
7. Identify the source(s) of support in the form of grants, equipment, drugs, or all of these.

THE ABSTRACT

Abstracts are summaries of published articles which, depending upon the type and purpose of the abstract, are written in a certain prescribed form and length. Abstracts assist readers to select appropriate articles more quickly and allow more precise computerized literature searches. Abstract types of most interest to physician writers are:

1. *Indicative* (descriptive) abstract is the type used mostly for review articles. This form of abstract is written to be a brief description of the content of the article without including results and conclusions, and is constructed from information derived from the background material, the problem reviewed, and the discussion.[9]
2. *Informative* (comprehensive) abstract is the type used for medical journal articles. This form of abstract describes the content of the journal article in brief form and is constructed from information contained in the Introduction, Materials and Methods, Results, and Conclusions section of the accompanying article.[10]

Most medical journals require authors to furnish an informative abstract of the information contained in the paper written in 250 words or less. One of the valuable aspects of preparing an abstract of 250 words or less is the exercise of distilling the most salient features of one's work for the reader. A good abstract provides an overview of the findings in the paper and serves to stimulate reader interest. An abstract, as a summary of the article's major arguments, data, and conclusions, is constructed from answers to the following statements: this is what we studied; this is how we did it; this is what we learned; this is what we believe it means. Abstracts are frequently reprinted in other journals or entered into computerized medical literature data bases and, for these reasons, must be written so they can stand alone and be understandable to readers when read separately from the accompanying paper. Journals requiring the submission of an abstract along with the submitted manuscript place it, if the paper is published, at the beginning of the article between the title and the Introduction.

Some journals, usually those with a major research orientation, may use the term *summary* instead of *abstract*. The *New England Journal of Medicine* now requires abstracts be written in paragraph form with the following paragraph headings: Background, Methods, Results, and Conclusions. The *Journal of the American Medical Association* uses an abstract form that contains the following headings: Objective, Design, Setting, Patients (or Subjects), Interventions (if any), Measurements, Results and Conclusions. In addition to an abstract, some journals require authors to provide, and identify as such, three to 10 key words or short phrases to assist indexers in cross-indexing the article and which may be published with the abstract. If required to furnish key words, physician writers are advised to use terms from the Medical Subject Headings list from *Index Medicus* whenever possible.[1] Journals will not require key words if the entire abstract goes into the computerized data base, but physician writers must remember that MEDLINE cuts the abstract off at the 250 word limit.

An abstract is written to provide an understanding of the article's content when read separately from the accompanying article. Because most journals impose a word limitation on abstract length, they must be written tightly with each word chosen carefully. As summaries of information contained in the body of the papers, abstracts should inform readers in three areas: (1) they describe the problem or question that generated the study, (2) they describe what the author discovered in performing the study, and (3) they tell the reader what the findings mean in terms of relevance to the medical knowledge base or to clinical decision making. The purpose of the abstract is to allow readers to quickly identify the important content material of a paper in order to determine its relevance to their interests. After reading the abstract, readers can then decide whether or not they need or want to read the entire paper. A well written abstract can convince readers of the need to review the entire paper.

Typically, abstracts are limited to a short description of the problem investigated in the study and its solution as proposed by the author. Abstracts of medical papers should follow this organizational scheme in their construction:

1. A topic sentence giving readers some information about the background of the problem investigated and stating the purpose of the reported study.
2. A brief description of the methods used in the study.
3. A summary of the observed results.
4. A conclusion summarized from the Discussion and which, when written, should give readers a sense of relationship to the topic sentence.

Properly written abstracts describe to readers the problem investigated in the study, its solution as proposed by the author, and emphasize the new and important aspects of the results. Abstracts of this type must be informative, must conform to a style and a word limitation, should not cite literature references, and must never give any information or conclusion that is not stated in the paper. Details referable to abstract style and word length are usually given in the Instructions for Authors page of the selected journal. Physician authors tend to write the abstract last so the complete paper can be reviewed for the necessary information. Good abstracts are not easy to write and the technique requires practice. Most authors rewrite their abstracts several times before becoming satisfied with its structure and content. Medical journal editors take abstracts seriously and so should physician writers.

INTRODUCTION

The first section of the text proper is the *Introduction*, a section of considerable importance because it introduces the paper to a reviewing editor and, if published, to readers. This section presents the purpose and scope of the paper, provides background information needed by readers to fully understand the study, and may vary in length from a few sentences to several pages. The main purpose of the Introduction is to tell readers why the study was done and what gap in the knowledge base needed to be filled. If the Introduction does not fulfill this purpose, or if it is so long that it becomes boring to read, or is so short that it fails to convince readers as to the need or the quality of the study, the entire writing effort may be lost. The Introduction is that part of the paper that affords the physician writer the opportunity to tell readers why the particular problem or question was chosen for study, why the reported results of the study are important, and why the paper should be read in its entirety.

The Introduction should supply enough background information to allow editorial reviewers and readers to understand and evaluate the results of the reported study without needing to refer to previous publications on the same subject. References cited in the Introduction should be carefully selected to provide only the most important and relevant background information. In sketching background information in this section to introduce the study to readers, physician writers should bear in mind the amount of information already possessed by the intended readership. If the journal selected to receive the completed paper is an appropriate choice, its readership can be expected to know almost as much about the topic being discussed in the paper as the physician author. The Introduction is not meant to be an opportunity for physician writers to show off a wide breadth of knowledge, but rather the place in the article where the author, in a clear and logically written fashion, brings the reader to a point of understanding in regard to the study being reported. The Introduction is also the proper place in the paper to define any specialized terms or abbreviations the writer uses in the text.

It is important for physician writers, particularly inexperienced ones, to understand and constantly bear in mind during the writing process that the sole purpose of the Introduction is to introduce the article to readers with all possible clarity in thought, language, and sentence structure. The Introduction should first present the nature and scope of the problem being investigated in the reported study. It then should briefly review the pertinent, but carefully selected, literature in order to orient the reader to the direction taken in the reported study. Next, it should state the method of investigation used and, if necessary, the author's reasons for selecting a particular method of investigation. Finally, the

Introduction should give the reader the principal results of the investigation, couched in general terms. Language used in the Introduction should be crisp and precise, and sweeping and nonspecific statements such as, "It has long been known that,etc." must be avoided. A good Introduction ends with a specific Statement of Purpose from the author. This statement is the opportunity for the writer to provide the reader with a brief and clear expression of the purpose underlying the performance of the reported study. Some research journals do not require the submission of an abstract with the manuscript. In this instance, authors of research papers should include the main findings of the study in the Introduction.

Steps in writing an Introduction can be summarized as follows:

1. Present the nature and scope of the problem being investigated in clear and understandable language. Tell readers why the problem investigated in the reported study was considered significant enough to be examined.
2. Review the pertinent literature very selectively and quote only the most relevant studies in order to orient the reader to the direction taken by the reported study.
3. Tell readers the method of investigation used and, if necessary, the author's reasons for choosing a particular investigative method.
4. State the principal results of the investigation.
5. Conclude this section with a specific Statement of Purpose.

MATERIALS AND METHODS

The *Materials and Methods* section takes the problem or question introduced to readers in the Introduction and tells them in specific detail how the problem was solved or the question answered. The Materials and Methods section must contain full and specific details of the investigative methods used in the reported study because the purpose of this section is to provide to readers enough specifics and details of the investigative method to allow a competent worker in the same field to repeat the research if desired. Scientific validity demands very careful writing of this section. The cornerstone of the scientific method requires that reported results be reproducible by others in order to be judged of scientific merit. For the results to be judged reproducible, the author must provide enough detail to allow others to repeat the work and obtain the same result. For this reason, editors and reviewers require physicians writers to be precise about the details of the study and its investigative components in the Materials and Methods section.

Whether or not the reported research or study is ever reproduced by others is immaterial. What is critical to editorial and reader approval is that physician writers approach the task of writing medical papers with an appreciation for scientific integrity, and provide the opportunity in this section for others to reproduce their work.[11] When the completed paper is submitted to a journal and is subjected to peer review by editors, good reviewers study the Materials and

Methods section very carefully. It is understood that honest differences in scientific methods and analysis, interpretation, or judgment of data can occur between author and reviewer and these differences should be respected. However, if there is serious doubt that the research or study could be repeated either because the study design is judged to be faulty or the written reporting of it is confusing, a reviewer is likely to recommend rejection of the manuscript for publication in the selected journal. On the other hand, if another investigator repeats a reported study and obtains results that contradict the initial report, or is unable to replicate the results of a reported experiment or study, the contradiction or inability to replicate should be reported. Scientific integrity requires journals to publish promptly reports of scientific error, contradictory results, and failure to replicate previously reported work.

The Materials and Methods section is the part of the paper in which physician writers must describe in fine detail the research or study that is being reported. To accomplish this goal, this section must address the following points:

1. After the hypothesis underlying the study is stated, the selected study design is described in precise detail. The hypothesis is usually not repeated here in basic science studies but, rather, stated in the Introduction.
2. Subjects (patients, animals, etc.) to be studied must be defined and characterized as fully as possible so as to minimize variations caused by uncontrolled variables. The selected journal may require the author to submit a statement that an Institutional Review Board (IRB) has given permission for human subjects to be studied.
3. Interventions involved in the study (surgical procedures, treatments, drugs, etc.) must be described in detail. Controls and other measures taken to minimize bias must be explained.
4. Measurements, methods, and other observations involved in the study must be defined, described, and justified.
5. Statistical procedures used for the assessment of the observed data must be fully described. It has been noted that conceptual and methodologic flaws abound in the work of medical investigators with limited statistical backgrounds.[12,13] Most physician writers would be well advised to seek assistance from a biostatistician, particularly in regard to study design, sample size, and statistical methods used for evaluating results.
6. In the event animals have been used in the reported study, the selected journal may require an assurance from the author that the protocols for animal studies have been approved by an Institutional Animal Care and Use Committee.

RESULTS

The *Results* section is crucial to the structure of the paper because it presents to readers the new information learned by the author in performing the study. The *Introduction* told readers what problem or question was studied and why; *Materials and Methods* told readers how the problem was solved or question answered and now, in *Results*, readers are told what was found in performing the study. Because of its importance in the total writing effort, the Results section must be written clearly, without verbiage and, most importantly, must be written so the results obtained in the study can speak for themselves without unnecessary embellishment. Although of primary importance to the structure of the paper, the Results section is frequently the shortest segment, particularly if it is preceded by a well written Materials and Methods section and followed by a well written Discussion. The purpose of the Results section is to tell readers what the study design, previously described in detail in Materials and Methods, was able to accomplish or discover. Results simply tells readers what was found in performing the study while discussion of the significance or relevance of these findings is postponed until the Discussion section. The Results section should give readers as clear an answer to the question being addressed by the study as the data will permit, with the writing of the section progressing from old or known information to the new data or information obtained in the study. The writer should tell readers the most important and explicable of the new findings first, with less clearcut results being described last.

Results is the core of the paper because it is the segment in which the data derived from the study is presented to readers. Two points to bear in mind while writing the Results section are:

1. The physician writer should give some kind of overall description of the study or research, thus providing a "big picture" for readers without having to repeat the study details previously provided to readers in Materials and Methods.
2. Only summarized or representative data derived from the study should be presented. Physician writers must avoid presenting data in endlessly repetitive detail. Numerical data can usually be presented more effectively in tables or graphs (Chapter 8). If the data are set up in a table, the text need only point out to readers what differences in data were found or call attention to a lack of statistically significant differences.

Presenting the results of the study in a manner that is acceptable to editors and readers is frequently easier said than done for physician writers. Inexperienced writers, often lacking in writing discrimination, tend to handle the Results section poorly because of a common tendency to overwrite in endless detail. Writing discrimination, a sense of what details should be used and what details should not be used in composing text, means presenting representative bits of data or information to readers, rather than presenting the whole package in repetitive detail. Repetitive determinations are best given to readers in tables or graphs. If only one or a few determinations are to be presented, they can be treated descriptively in the text. Any determinations or bits of data presented in Results, repetitive or otherwise, should be meaningful and germane to the study.

In like manner, any statistics used in describing the results also must be meaningful and germane. The manner in which summary statistics are presented in clinical reports can affect the way physicians make clinical decisions. It has been shown that physicians are more likely to treat patients after reading reports containing statistics on relative change in outcome than one reporting absolute values.[14] It is essential to avoid redundant writing and description of endless detail in constructing the Results section. A frequent fault of inexperienced physician writers in constructing a Results section is the repetition of what is already apparent to readers from examination of accompanying figures and tables. A good way for a beginning physician writer to become familiar with the technique of good Results writing is by studying the construction of articles published in respected peer-reviewed medical journals, such as the *New England Journal of Medicine* and the *Journal of the American Medical Association*.

DISCUSSION

The *Discussion* is the section of the paper in which readers learn the meaning of the findings described in the Results section. The purpose of the Discussion is to tell readers the answer to the question the study posed initially, to discuss the significance or relevance of the results obtained by performing the study, and to relate these findings to previously published studies, pointing out both concurrences and discrepancies with regard to previously reported findings. From a structural standpoint, a good Discussion section begins with the answer to the question which stimulated the study originally. The author next presents the evidence produced by the study which supports both the answer and the author's declaration of its significance. This section ends with a discussion of the significance of the evidence produced and the answer provided by the study results. Physician writers must concentrate in the Discussion section on showing the relationship among observed facts and only discuss the significance of these facts or results. Length of the Discussion section is variable depending upon the complexity of the topic, the amount of evidence to be presented, and the number of points to be discussed.

The Discussion is often the most difficult section of the paper to write well. A common fault of inexperienced physician writers is to extend the implications of the evidence being discussed too far, indulging in speculation not supported by facts generated in the study. Physician writers must take care not to err by trying to extrapolate to a bigger picture than is warranted by the data presented to readers in Results. Readers with a scientific background generally do not appreciate flights of fancy in serious medical articles. What medical journal readers are looking for are firm conclusions supported by credible data or evidence. Another common writing fault in constructing the Discussion section is to make it too long and verbose. Speculative statements to the effect that something "is of wide ranging theoretical and practical importance," or "it is widely believed that," for example, have no place in the Discussion section of a medical paper. Experienced physician writers have learned that the simplest statements written in the clearest language are the best.[15] Verbosity and overuse of fancy technical words are characteristic of poor writing skills and a sign of writing inexperience.

No set rule exists to delineate the length of the Discussion. It should be of sufficient length to give the physician writer the opportunity to convince readers that the arguments supporting both the answer to the question examined by the study and the significance of the results obtained in the study are clear, logical, and reasonable. As is true for the Results section, Discussion tests the physician writer's ability to discriminate among a mass of collected information. What needs to be presented to readers are simply the facts and figures needed to support and justify the conclusions reached by the author. A more serious fault in the Discussion occurs if the interpretation of the findings described in Results obscures the true meaning of the data, or if the physician writer fails to grasp the significance of the evidence gathered in the study. Even though a manuscript may present valid and interesting data, it could still be rejected for publication because of a Discussion section that is considered faulty for any of the reasons mentioned above. From the standpoint of a journal editor, the essential criterion of an article's worth is its validity, and that judgment extends to all its parts.

The essential points of a good Discussion are believed to be:

1. Present the principles, relationships, and generalizations shown in Results. A good Discussion discusses, but does not recapitulate, the Results section.
2. Point out to readers any exceptions or any lack of correlation in the findings of the study and define any unsettled points.
3. Show how the results and interpretations agree, or contrast, with previously published work.
4. Discuss the theoretical implications of the study as well as any practical applications, such as possible clinical relevance of basic research findings.
5. State the conclusions of the study as clearly as possible.
6. Summarize the evidence for each conclusion presented.
7. Discuss the significance of the presented conclusions.
8. Point out possibilities for further study and implications for clinical practice.

CONCLUSION

Although being encountered less frequently, the format for some basic science research papers may end with a *Conclusions* section. The usual medical paper, particularly one with a clinical orientation, does not contain a Conclusions section and ends with the Discussion. If required by a journal, a Conclusions section summarizes the questions asked by the study, the evidence produced by the study, the answers framed by the data produced in the research project, and may elaborate on possible clinical relevance or technical application of the reported results. In the usual clinical paper, this type of final summation belongs in Discussion, thus making the need for a Conclusions section superfluous.

BIBLIOGRAPHY

During the preparation and writing stages, experienced physician writers jot down on index cards each reference they plan to use in the article, and obtain for their files photocopies of the actual articles to be cited in the *Bibliography*. This practice not only allows them the opportunity of referring to the articles as needed, but also allows easy revising of the references into the form required by the journal to which the article is being submitted. Physician writers must exercise great care in amassing references they plan to cite in the body of the paper and list in the bibliography at the end of the article because it is the author's responsibility to verify the accuracy of listed citations. Each reference cited in the paper should be verified in its original printed form and, if possible, a photocopy of the original article retained in the author's file. Having a copy of the original article allows the writer to accurately cite the specific details required in a reference listing. On occasion, observant readers note incorrectly cited references cited in other articles, with the unverified and incorrect citation appearing over and over again.

Medical journals vary in their style of handling references. Some require references to be listed alphabetically according to the last name of the first author, while others prefer references to be numbered consecutively in the order in which they are cited in the text. Do not use *"et al."* in reference to multiple authors but, rather, provide the names of all authors of the article. The form in which the reference is to be written can also vary depending on the form preferred by the particular journal. The exact reference style and form preferred by the author's selected journal can be learned by consulting the journal's Instructions for Authors page. It is appropriate to abbreviate journal names in the reference section according to the style used in *Index Medicus*. A "List of the Journals Indexed" is printed annually in the January issue of *Index Medicus*. The number indicating the cited reference should be placed at that part in the text sentence to which it applies. Physician writers are cautioned against using the so-called "hand waving" reference in which readers, for example, are glibly referred to "Gibbs' classic contribution" without being given any hint as to what Gibbs reported or how Gibbs' results relate in any way to the author's results. If the physician writer believes a reference is worth citing, the reader should be told why.

There are three general rules to follow in compiling a bibliography for a medical article:

1. Always follow the reference style and form preferred by the selected journal as listed in the journal's Instructions for Authors page.

2. List only significant published references in the order preferred by the selected journal. Identify as "in press" papers cited in the bibliography which have been accepted for publication but not yet published. Generally, references to unpublished data, personal communications, abstracts, theses, and other secondary materials are not considered appropriate for inclusion in the bibliography of a paper being prepared for submission to a peer reviewed medical journal.
3. Physician writers must check all parts of every reference cited against the original article to assure accuracy before submitting the manuscript for consideration of publication. It is not a primary responsibility of a journal editor to check the accuracy of references listed in the bibliography of an article submitted for publication. The responsibility for reference accuracy belongs to and remains with the physician writer.

When the writing part is finished, physician writers should check all parts of the manuscript and accompanying graphics for completeness and accuracy before submitting them to the selected journal for editorial review. The package being sent to the journal editor must include the appropriate number of duplicate copies of the manuscript and accompanying graphics along with a letter of transmittal. Details about what information must be contained in the letter of transmittal can be obtained from the journal's Instructions for Authors page. This letter is usually written to the editor by the principal author, but all co-authors may be required to sign it. The journal will require, however, that one author be specifically identified for purposes of correspondence. Most journals require a letter of transmittal to include a statement on authorship responsibility, a statement on financial disclosure, and an agreement from the authors to transfer, assign, or convey to the journal all copyright ownership pertaining to the article in the event the journal publishes the submitted article. When submitting a manuscript, an author should always make a full disclosure in the letter of transmittal to the editor about all submissions and prior reports that might be regarded as prior or duplicate publication of the same or very similar work.

EDITORIAL REVIEW

After the submitted manuscript reaches the journal office, physician writers face the final hurdle in the process of writing medical papers for publication in peer reviewed journals. This is the hurdle of peer review, a process initiated by the journal editor after receipt of the submitted manuscript. In this process, members of the journal editorial board or other reviewers selected by the editor are asked to read and evaluate the manuscript to judge its worthiness and suitability for publication in the journal.[16] The practice of peer review is based upon the social habit of relying on consensus to validate action. The scientific community, including medicine, relies on the peer review process as the acceptable way to judge the validity of the reported work and its study design in order to decide whether the reported results are valid and significant enough to add to the medical literature. The ultimate issue in the peer review process is the quality of the scientific literature and the degree of faith it deserves from readers and researchers. It is absolutely essential to the survival of accurate and objective transfer of scientific information that the highest standards of honorable and ethical conduct be observed in the process of medical writing and its peer review by authors, editors, and manuscript reviewers. In due course, the editorial decision reached by the journal with regard to the submitted manuscript will be forwarded by letter from the journal editor to the author identified as correspondent in the original letter of transmittal. This editorial decision may be acceptance with no particular revisions required; provisional acceptance, or agreement to review the paper again, subject to the author complying with suggested revisions in the text or the accumulation of more data; or rejection of the paper for publication in the selected journal. The second and third of these three editorial decisions are, by far, the most frequent decisions received by physician writers, largely because there is limited text space available in most medical journals. What text space is available is generally allocated to those relatively few articles journal editors determine to be the best of the submissions.

The significance or importance of a medical article submitted for publication in a peer reviewed journal is a difficult and subjective assessment for others than the author to make. The opinions of the author and manuscript reviewer may differ markedly based on their individual experience. Manuscript reviewers are not infallible, and a physician writer whose paper has been rejected for publication has the option to appeal to the journal editor for a review of the editorial decision. Traditionally, reviewer identities are not disclosed to authors of work being reviewed. A reviewer's reasons for recommending revision or rejection of a particular manuscript are usually conveyed anonymously to the author in the decision letter usually written by the journal editor. Before making a written appeal to a journal editor for review of an adverse editorial decision, physician writers would be well advised to make certain they have thoroughly reviewed all the relevant literature in the field so that the importance, or lack of importance, of the contribution can be appreciated in the perspective of previous publications on the same subject.

If the paper is accepted for publication, the principal author will eventually receive galleys or page proof from the journal and will be asked to check them for text and graphics accuracy before the completed work can be sent to the printer. After editorial acceptance of the manuscript, needed copyediting changes in the text are keyed in by a journal copyeditor and the manuscript is formatted into galleys or page proof. Major changes in style, words, or meaning in the manuscript are usually not made by medical editors without author approval. The principal author is asked to check the galleys for content accuracy and return them to the journal in a very short time frame. Text changes in the galleys, other than the correction of inaccuracies or misspellings, are strongly discouraged by journals because of the added expense involved in changing proof and the accompanying printing delay.

THE CASE REPORT

One of the first experiences with medical writing for some physicians is attempting to write and publish a case report. This is particularly true of residents who might wish to begin accumulating a published bibliography. Writing case reports for submission to a journal gives residents an opportunity to improve skills in both critical thinking and writing and an opportunity to learn how to use the medical literature to answer specific questions.[17] If a physician wishes to write a case report, he or she must be certain the case report is written in the accepted format and is submitted to a journal which publishes case reports more or less on a regular basis. Many journals do publish case reports, but most of the major journals publish them only rarely. For many journal editors the case report is regarded as a writing form whose time has come and gone. For years, case reports published in reputable journals were regarded as an effective teaching technique which closely approximated real medical practice. However, more recent advances in medical science and technology have generated such a flood of competing papers that there is simply little space available for case reports in the more prestigious journals. Mainly for this reason, single case reports have become less likely to be accepted for publication in major medical journals. The question facing editors of these journals is whether reports of such cases bring enough new information to readers to warrant giving scarce journal page space to their publication. This does not mean that physicians should not attempt to write and publish case reports, but it does mean that physician writers, so as not to waste time and effort, should be carefully selective about the case to be reported and the journal chosen to receive and, possibly, publish the case report.

Criteria pertaining to acceptability of case reports for publication in journals exist and one or more of the following features characterizes a case report with a high probability for publication[18]:

1. The unique, or nearly unique, case that may represent a previously undescribed syndrome or disease. Observation of a new phenomenon is the kind of creative perception that, in the best of circumstances, contributes to an example or model of change which opens new avenues of investigation for medical scientists.
2. The case with an unexpected association of two or more diseases or disease manifestations that may represent a previously unsuspected causal relationship. For example, a new permutation or combination of clinical conditions might suggest chromosomal proximity of loci, thus advancing genetic mapping.

3. The case with an unexpected evolution suggesting a therapeutic effect or an adverse drug reaction. These are therapeutic or diagnostic observations that promise to fill one or another of medicine's knowledge gaps.

If a physician believes a case in question fulfills one of these criteria and decides to write a case report, the writing must be carefully organized, succinct, and short to have any chance of being accepted for publication without being subject to massive revision at the request of the editor.[19] Long, overly detailed case reports are boring to readers and are unlikely to be accepted for publication. Physicians who wish to write a case report for possible publication would be well advised to keep it to a length equivalent to one printed page in the selected journal. Some indication of the importance editors place on short case reports can be deduced from the observation that some journals title printed case reports as "Brief Reports."

Physicians wishing to write case reports must understand that readers need only five bits of information in the case report:

1. A statement of why the case report is worth reading.
2. An account of the case with supporting data.
3. A discussion of the evidence that supports the author's contention that the case is unique or contains features that are medically unexpected.
4. Possible alternative explanations for the case features should be given.
5. A list of conclusions and a brief note concerning the clinical implications.

These reader needs can be satisfied by physician writers by using the following writing format for case reports:

1. A short introductory paragraph to orient readers to the uniqueness or the unusual nature of the case being reported.
2. The details of the case report or case description are given. Features of the case that justify the decision to write the case report are put in this case description.
3. A brief discussion of the significance of the case ends the case report. The author's argument to support his or her contention that the case is unique or illustrates some unexpected medical feature belongs in this discussion section.

THE RESEARCH PROTOCOL

A *research protocol* is a detailed written plan describing how a proposed piece of research is to be conducted.[20] The most frequent use of a written research protocol is to obtain permission from an Institutional Review Board (IRB), or other review committee, to proceed with a research study involving human subjects (clinical trials, for example), animals, recombinant DNA, dangerous chemicals, or radioisotopes.[21] Depending upon the nature of the research being planned, obtaining IRB approval by means of a research protocol is a necessary first step before writing a grant application to obtain funding for the project. Federal regulations require that all government funded research involving human subjects be approved by an IRB prior to receiving funds. The ethical conduct of research involving human subjects requires physicians to balance the interests of society with the needs of individual patients and, as a consequence, the federal government has imposed the highest possible standards of safety and efficacy for research involving human subjects, new drugs, and medical devices. Regulations of the Food and Drug Administration (FDA) apply to research that tests new drugs and devices on human patients, and these regulations are designed not only to protect patient safety but also to ensure proper study methodology. Most universities conducting medical research in the United States have filed an assurance with the Department of Health and Human Services guaranteeing that all human subjects research conducted by them, whether funded by any source or unfunded, will be reviewed by an IRB according to the same standards and procedures required by the federal government for government funded research.

If human subjects are to be involved in a research study, documentation of informed consent is required. This is frequently the most difficult part of a research protocol for beginning researchers to write well. Consultation with senior researchers on the best way to write the informed consent form is recommended. An IRB will carefully review the informed consent form used by researchers to assure that all of the procedures to be performed on each individual are clearly and accurately described in lay language. All patients in the study are required to sign and receive a copy of the informed consent document and physician researchers are required to maintain files of signed informed consent forms for inspection by the IRB and agents of the FDA as required. Not all medical research projects require IRB or FDA approval, but may need review by some hospital committees or physician monitoring groups. If unsure of the required procedure, a researcher should seek advice from his or her institution's Office of Research Administration or grants officer. Since federal, state, and institutional requirements for documentation and record keeping exist, researchers should also obtain advice relative to the guidelines for submission of the research protocol to the Institutional Review Board. The forms used for the application for IRB approval in most institutions are very similar to the forms used for grant applications, but are usually developed internally.

Research protocols must be written in a precise and organized style and, when written for a new research project, consist of the following component forms:

1. *Cover sheet.* This form provides a brief synopsis of all areas of review necessary, as well as providing for recognition and approval of the project

by the chairs of the involved departments. All investigators and involved department chairs must sign this form prior to submission to the IRB. The writer should provide a summary of the content of the research protocol, a clear Statement of Purpose for the reviewers, and conclude the synopsis with a concise statement of Expected Results.
2. *Abstract.* This form provides space for an abstract of a lengthy protocol or a more detailed description of the research plan for investigator-sponsored, unfunded projects.
3. *FDA and NIH questions.* This form lists important information required by the FDA and NIH and provides a convenient summary of the salient points of the IRB review.
4. *Consent form.* This form duplicates the consent form researchers plan to use and is the consent form human subjects will be asked to sign.
5. *Protocol (research plan).* This form contains a brief written description of the research plan. In some instances, this protocol will be supplied by the research sponsor, such as a drug company. If written by the researcher, the research plan should address these points:
   a. Purpose of the research.
   b. Justification of the research, particularly if the research involves human subjects.
   c. Subject selection and recruitment. The IRB must be assured that sufficient work has been done to justify involving human subjects in the research. The IRB also must be satisfied that no coercive practices are planned to recruit subjects for the research.
   d. Procedures and/or methods. It is important that the procedures or methods proposed in the research protocol show promise of leading to viable conclusions in order to justify initiating the research project.
   e. Data collecting and data management. This is particularly important in relation to the maintenance of confidentiality of patient records.
   f. Statistical analysis.
   g. Potential risks.
   h. Potential benefits.
   i. Risk-benefit ratio. Consideration of (g) and (h) should allow calculation of the risk-benefit relationship. The ratio of potential risks to potential benefits should balance clearly in favor of the subjects involved in the research.
   j. Define the provisions for maintaining subject confidentiality.
   k. The subject's financial responsibilities, if any.

Once the research protocol is written, the researcher must make certain the required numbers of each form in the protocol are submitted to the Institutional Review Board. A researcher can usually develop a grant application from a well written IRB approved research protocol (see Chapter 9).

References

1. International Committee of Medical Journal Editors. Uniform requirements for manuscripts submitted to biomedical journals. *N Engl J Med.* 1991; 324(6): 424-428.
2. Huth EJ. *How to Write and Publish Papers in the Medical Sciences.* Philadelphia, Pa: ISI Press; 1982.
3. Zeiger M. *Essentials of Writing Biomedical Research Papers.* New York, NY: McGraw-Hill, Inc; 1991.
4. Plaut SM. Preparation of abstracts, slides, and presentations for scientific meetings. *Clin Res.* 1982; 30: 18-24.
5. Day RA. The origins of the scientific paper: the IMRAD format. *Amer Med Writers Assoc J.* 1989; 4(2): 16-18.
6. O'Leary R. The acceptable manuscript. In: Schwager E, *On Medical Communications.* Amer Med Writers Association. 1982; Monograph Series 1: 39-42.
7. Ziman JM. Information, communication, knowledge. *Nature.* 1969; 224: 318-324.
8. Gartland JJ. Orthopaedic clinical research. Deficiencies in experimental design and determinations of outcome. *J Bone Joint Surg.* 1988; 70-A: 1357-1364.
9. Mulrow CD, Thacker SB, Pugh JA. Proposal for more informative abstracts of review articles. *Ann Intern Med.* 1988; 108: 613-615.
10. Ad Hoc Working Group for Critical Appraisal of the Medical Literature. A proposal for more informative abstracts of clinical articles. *Ann Intern Med.* 1987; 106: 598-604.
11. Buckwalter JA. Medical researchers must be ethical. *Amer Acad Orthop Surg Bull.* 1990; 38(3): 27-29, 31.
12. Colton T. The "power" of sound statistics. *JAMA.* 1990; 263(2): 281.
13. Eastman JD, Smith EO'B, Klein ER. Medical writers and editors should learn fundamentals of statistical principles. *Amer Med Writers Assoc J.* 1990; 5(4): 14-17.
14. Forrow L, Taylor WC, Arnold RM. Absolutely relative: how research results are summarized can affect treatment decisions. *Am J Med.* 1992; 92: 121-124.
15. Woods D. Good English is good medicine. *Can Med Assoc J.* 1981; 125: 624-629.
16. Ingelfinger FJ. Peer review in biomedical publications. *Am J Med.* 1974; 56: 686-692.
17. Petrusa ER, Weiss GB. Writing case reports: An educationally valuable experience for house officers. *J Med Educ.* 1982; 57: 415-417.
18. Riesenberg DE. Editorial. Case reports in the medical literature. *JAMA.* 1986; 255(15): 2067.
19. DeBakey L, DeBakey S. The case report: 1. Guidelines for preparation. *Int J Cardiol.* 1983; 4: 357-364.

20. Woodford FP. ed. *Scientific Writing for Graduate Students*. Bethesda, Md: Council of Biology Editors, Inc; 1986.
21. Clinical Research: An Overview. Profile. Thomas Jefferson University Hospital Medical Staff. February 1989; 1-4.

6

Revising and Rewriting

Revising and rewriting what has already been written is an exercise physician writers should carry out in a continuing fashion during the entire writing process, making certain that what has been said is said with accuracy, clarity, brevity, and as much grace as possible. Later drafts of written materials generally read better than earlier drafts because good writers think hard about what they have written and create, by this thinking, ideas for better organization and structure, clearer sentence construction, or more appropriate word choice as the writing progresses.[1] However, there are two specific occasions in the creation of publishable medical manuscripts when revising and rewriting become deliberate and conscious steps in the writing and publishing process. The first occasion is when the physician writer edits his or her work before submitting the manuscript to the selected journal for editorial review and possible publication. The second occasion is the revising and rewriting required in response to specific suggestions for revision contained in the decision letter from the journal editor, following completion of editorial review by the journal's editorial board. It becomes a matter of personal choice whether the revising and rewriting is done on a computer screen using cursor or mouse or on a printed or typed hard copy of the manuscript using a pen or pencil. Most physician writers at the present time find it easier to revise and rewrite using paper and pen or pencil because this method permits the author to make a variety of notes and colored marks not permissible with most on-line editing programs now available. Another advantage of pen and paper is the ability to carry them around, which allows the author to work on revisions when away from the computer screen.[2]

REVISION BEFORE SUBMISSION

Revision is the process whereby a writer edits his or her own work before submitting the manuscript to a selected journal for possible publication. Editing one's own work, it is believed, represents the most constructive way of sensitizing a writer's mind to the nuances of language and logic. Physician writers must guard against the temptation of falling in love with their own words and some physicians, unfortunately, never develop the emotional distance needed to edit their own words effectively or polish them beyond a certain point.[3] When approaching the task of revision, physician writers would do well to remember the literal meaning of the word *revision* is "seeing again." Those physician writers who can revise their own material effectively have learned to critically review what they have written from the viewpoint of a reader. Revision has to do with change, specifically with finding those particular changes that bring about improvement in writing style and a better fit for sentences and individual words.[4] For example, after finishing the first draft of this section of the chapter, the last sentence in the first paragraph, page 96, read "If the writer, and colleagues who have read it, believe the paper is poorly written, poorly organized, or both, there should be no hesitation on the physician writer's part to reorganize and rewrite the paper instead of tinkering with it in an effort to respond to fix it which is an effort which almost never succeeds." On rereading this section, it was clear this was a poorly constructed, awkward, and vague sentence and was revised to read "If the writer, and colleagues who have read the manuscript, believe it to be poorly written, poorly organized, or both, the physician writer should reorganize and rewrite the manuscript instead of tinkering with it in a vain attempt to fix something beyond repair."

Another purpose of revision is to ensure that the organizational structure of the manuscript is correct so that it has proper balance. Revising is a regular part of the writing process and has to do with improving structure, style, and organization and is accomplished by simplifying the text, fixing grammatical errors, identifying and correcting gaps in the logical flow of ideas or in the interpretation of data, or reorganizing any concepts that seem awkwardly presented. Physicians do not have an excess of time in which to read and rarely will waste it on poorly organized or poorly written papers. It does not matter how pleased an author might be to have converted all the right data into sentences and paragraphs; it matters only whether a large majority of the reading audience accurately perceives what the author had in mind.[5] Almost all writers have to revise and rewrite their material several times before becoming satisfied with the final draft, and few physician writers are so expert they can produce what they are after on the first try. Revising and rewriting is an excellent and highly recommended exercise for physician writers because it usually makes the difference between a mediocre and a good medical paper. It has been said there is no good writing, only good rewriting-- that what is worth setting down at all can be done twice as well in half the number of words--only it takes twice as long to do it. Original writing, like tapping a maple tree, is tedious business, but the really slow work, and the hard sugar, come in the boiling down of the sap.[6]

Good medical writing flows together easily and does not seem awkward when read. The sheer awkwardness of expression exhibited by some competent physicians when they try to communicate on paper is unfortunate. There is no exact way to predict the forms that awkward writing can take except to say that awkwardness in medical writing stems, largely, from a failure on the part of physician writers to understand that words in a sentence should fit together comfortably and should speak to each other. Words should work together through consistency of content, through the order in which they are arranged, and even through punctuation conventions that bind them. A concern for grammatical accuracy is part of the commitment made to writing and a writer's assurance of efficient communication.[7] Physician writers need to keep in mind that words can be put together in more than one way.

Examples:
The passive and active voice: The grant application was written mainly by the department chairman. The department chairman wrote most of the grant application.
Converting an overly long sentence to a shorter one: The investigators met at the end of the day to revise their grant application because the funding source returned it with the comment that it was too long and was written in a confusing and convoluted style and advised them to rewrite it before considering resubmission. The investigators met to shorten, clarify, and rewrite their grant application in accordance with the criticisms and suggestions received from the funding source.
Using a subordinate clause: I will send a reprint of the article to whoever writes to request it.
Using a prepositional phrase: The proposed treatment is experimental in addition to being expensive. Other prepositional phrases include "as well as," "along with," and "by the way of."

The qualities that define graceful prose for medical writing include not only accuracy, clarity, and brevity, but also the ability to produce prose that does not bore or irritate readers. The fact that good medical writing is crisp, lean, and objective does not preclude it being composed with grace and style and a sense for pleasing word selection and fit. Graceful prose carries the reader along a line of thought in which paragraphs are linked so that readers do not start a new paragraph wondering how it relates to the one just finished. Physician writers should use all the skills they can muster in reviewing a completed manuscript for paragraph length and structure, paragraph linkage, sentence structure and variety, and the details of word choice and usage.[8] If possible, obtain help from colleagues who possess writing and editorial skills to assist in the task of manuscript review.

The work of revising a manuscript or research protocol should follow an organized sequence and should be carried out in a thorough and efficient manner. It is through exercises in revising and rewriting that physician writers build a technical proficiency in verbal techniques and aesthetic sensitivity so essential to developing a sense of fit for words and sentences. A lot of writing and rewriting experience helps physician writers develop the lean, crisp, and pleasing style that characterizes good medical writing. Successful revision can be described as a productive dialogue between the writer as a *writer*, and the writer as a *reader*, an exchange in which the needs of the reader are paramount. If the writer, and colleagues who have read the manuscript, find the reading easy and understandable, the chances are good that other readers will also. If the writer, and colleagues who have read the manuscript, believe it to be poorly written, poorly organized, or both, the physician writer should reorganize and rewrite the manuscript instead of tinkering with it in a vain attempt to fix something beyond repair.

The self-editing process is, by necessity, a slow, critical, and objective rereading of the entire manuscript, sentence by sentence, paragraph by paragraph, and section by section in a conscious effort to clarify the writing and improve the organization of the written material. Sentences and paragraphs should be reviewed to make certain that gaps in the text are bridged by appropriately chosen transition words. Possessing an eye for textual and structural detail is a valuable skill to have for this self-editing exercise. Medical writing is improved by shortening sentences and words, correcting grammatical errors, simplifying the vocabulary, and cutting out verbiage. The purpose of this self-editing process, then, is to improve the final product by reviewing the text, the organizational structure of the manuscript, and the fit and appropriateness of the graphics in a critical and objective manner to make certain the final product has proper balance and achieves the purpose for which it was written. A general outline that has proven useful for guiding the work of revision of medical manuscripts before submission to journals consists of the following steps:

1. After writing the first draft of the manuscript, let it sit for a week or two and do not look at it. Then, reread the first draft and revise it for content and structure. Physician writers should be aware that many medical journals require that all numbers less than 100 be spelled out, with the exceptions of numbers that begin a sentence, percentages, degrees, gauges, and numbers expressed as decimals.
2. Circulate the second draft to all co-authors, if any, and other interested colleagues for comment and suggestions.
3. Circulate the third draft to the same people after the suggested changes have been made.
4. After all suggestions for revision have been considered, do final revision of the writing style in an attempt to make it interesting and pleasing to readers.

In addition to content, structure, and writing style, physician writers should use the self-editing or revision process to take a hard look at the manuscript's credibility, proportion, and structural progression. Credibility in a manuscript comes from two sources: the authenticity of the material itself and the conviction, generated by the writing, that the author speaks the truth. Credibility, then, arises from a combination of facts correctly used and a coherent argument clearly constructed. The criterion of proportion as applied to a completed manuscript measures three things: (1) the scope of the topic or the ground covered in the manuscript, (2) the thoroughness with which the topic is covered, and (3) a realistic appraisal of the sense of proportion and balance in the completed manuscript. For example, a physician writer who attempts to discuss all the diseases affecting the human nervous system in a manuscript of twelve to fifteen pages would produce a manuscript that not only lacked credibility, but would also have serious problems with proportion and balance. A good sense of balance and proportion would also induce the author to eliminate superlatives, overreactions, and overstatements written into the text. Physician writers also need to look at the text from the standpoint of progression to ensure that the organizational structure of the manuscript is built in proper proportion and follows the appropriate format for the type of manuscript being produced, be it a journal article, a case report, or a research protocol.

Providing answers for the following questions when reviewing completed manuscripts and responding in a positive manner to the answers help physician writers perform more thorough revisions of their manuscripts:

1. Does the completed manuscript fulfill the purpose for which it was written?
2. Is the content of the manuscript accurate and complete?
3. Is the organizational structure of the manuscript correct and clearly presented?
4. Are the data, facts, and conclusions developed in a coherent manner?
5. Are the data, facts, and conclusions presented clearly and in proper order?
6. Are the points the physician writer wishes to make presented to readers in a clear and understandable manner?
7. Is the writing style pleasing to read?

Most physicians tend to overwrite; consequently, almost all medical manuscripts can be improved by a shortening process that deletes all nonessential background material and other data, and excises wordiness, buzzwords, jargon, and redundancies in words and ideas.[9] Consider this sentence in the preface of a popular pediatrics textbook: "As in previous editions, this text is directed to and intended for those physicians who devote the major part of their professional lives to the care of children." In the context of that sentence, "directed to" and "intended for" have the same meaning and one phrase or the other should be deleted to eliminate the redundancy. The readability of a manuscript can be improved by replacing unduly long sentences with shorter ones, by correcting double negatives, and by converting as many single negatives as possible into positives. Single negatives can slow the reading process by requiring the reader to conceive of the positive before negating it. Converting a single negative into a positive, however, may require substituting a different verb.

Examples:
Double negative: The Faculty Senate rejected a proposal that would have altered the provisions of the faculty practice plan. Corrected: A proposal to alter the provisions of the faculty practice plan was rejected by the Faculty Senate.
Single negative: There were no technicians or animals in the laboratory when the explosion occurred. Converted to a positive: The laboratory was vacated before the explosion occurred.

The language of the manuscript can be made more comprehensible to readers by replacing complex words with simpler or shorter ones, by eliminating redundancies and unnecessary word, phrase, and clause qualifiers, and by guarding against digressions and secondary ideas being wedged into sentences.[10] If possible, a writer should not begin a new sentence with the same word used to end the preceding sentence. Passive verbs should be replaced with active verbs wherever possible. Noun strings, combinations of nouns grouped together as if they were adjectives, should be avoided or unpacked. For example, "health care delivery system evaluation planning activity" is a noun string. Linking verbs should be eliminated because they contribute to weak language. Linking verbs are verbs that function chiefly as connections between a subject and a predicate complement and include "be," "appear," "seem," and "become." For example, instead of writing "this result appears to be an affirmation of," say "this result affirms." Good editing by physician writers clarifies the language, making it more concise, correct, clear, and consistent. Consistency in language provides logical connections between the ideas and parts of any thoughtfully written and edited medical manuscript.

While revising the text, physician writers should also reassess the proportionate value of each table, graph, diagram, illustration, and reference, bearing in mind that most inexperienced physician writers tend to make excessive use of graphic materials. Only those graphics absolutely essential to the message a physician writer wishes to convey should be submitted with the completed manuscript. Medical journal editors have to be especially sensitive to the relationship between tables and figures on the one hand and the accompanying text on the other. Likewise, physician writers must understand not only that graphics should be selected and designed to communicate the bulk of the data and information to readers, but also that accompanying text should be written to carry the reader from one such piece of information to another. Understanding this relationship is a necessary prerequisite if physician writers are to develop a full sense of the appropriate balance between graphics and text. Each table and figure that can be discarded allows that much more space for descriptive paragraphs in the text. Although references are printed in small type, each reference fills its own small area and duplications cut down on the total space available in the journal for text.

The work of revising and rewriting a manuscript is not complete until the following are accomplished:

REVISING AND REWRITING 99

1. All is said in the manuscript that has to be said and no more is said than is needed for the message to be understood by readers.
2. All elements of the manuscript are in correct sequence and every detail is made as clear as possible for readers.
3. All persons listed as co-authors have read and approved the final version of the manuscript.

After the work of revising and rewriting the manuscript is complete, physician writers must make certain the final form of the manuscript is properly prepared for submission to the selected journal. The final manuscript is prepared for submission in three steps:

1. Review the manuscript requirements of the selected medical journal as listed on the journal's Information for Authors page and confirm that these requirements have been met.
2. Review the final version of the manuscript and accompanying graphics to make certain all the needed elements are in place and that these elements are presented in accord with the requirements of the selected medical journal.
3. Have the manuscript typed or printed from a word processor, with all text double spaced. If printed from a word processor or computer, a laser or other letter-quality printer must be used.

Revision in Response to Editorial Suggestions

The decision letter received by a physician writer from a journal editor is notification of the editorial decision made on the submitted manuscript by the journal's editorial board after completion of the peer review process. The editorial decision announced in the letter can be, in order of decreasing likelihood, rejection of the manuscript for publication, provisional acceptance of the manuscript predicated upon completion of suggested revisions, or acceptance of the manuscript for publication without major change. Key to the editorial decision is the determination by reviewers and editors of the value of the submitted manuscript to the scientific literature of the field to which it applies, and the knowledge that reviewers and editors try to salvage submissions they believe to be valuable. When it is appreciated that a periodical like the *New England Journal of Medicine* turns down more than 85 percent of the unsolicited articles received, the need for prior thought in the planning, care in the design, and skillful execution in the writing of the manuscript becomes apparent.[9]

The editorial decision letter may notify the author of provisional acceptance of the manuscript predicated upon completion of suggested changes and revisions. The practice of most medical journal editors is not to revise or rewrite submitted manuscripts themselves, but to require the submitting author to do the work. If a submitted manuscript is believed to be in need of revision or rewriting before it can be considered worthy of publication, the submitting author is required to make the requested changes. The decision letter will outline the work to be done and the manuscript changes required, including an explanation of any errors and deficiencies noted in the text or graphic materials, and will give practical suggestions for improving the manuscript. If a major reorganization of the manuscript is believed to be needed, the responding editor may indicate the scope of the suggested changes in an outline form. Physician writers may be asked to tighten the language of the text by weeding out wordy constructions, untangling convoluted sentences and unpacking noun strings, eliminating repetitious material, translating jargon words and phrases, and deleting duplication of tabular and graphic material.[11] The decision letter may state the work seems not to be totally original, seems to duplicate other material recently published, or does not make its points with accuracy and clarity and may, therefore, ask the author to provide further clarification or information or even additional data.

The author may be requested to reorganize the manuscript in order to sharpen its focus for the benefit of readers. In some medical manuscripts readers have to wade through several sentences and even paragraphs of peripheral background information before learning the point of the article. A better plan for physician writers is to learn to begin the manuscript with a piece of positive information or some type of impact statement designed to catch the interest of readers. For example, a published article describing the benefits of using ultrasound in the evaluation of the infant hip leads off with the following two sentences: "At the ---- Hospital, real-time sonography has been an accepted method for evaluating the infant hip since 1984. Our hospital is a regional referral center for infants suspected of having congenital dislocation and/or dysplasia of the hip and more than 700 patient examinations are performed each year." The reader finally encounters the following sentence twelve lines from the end of this five page article: "Examination of the hip with real-time ultrasound provides an effective alternative for detecting congenital hip subluxation, dislocation, and/or dysplasia." Because the author's purpose in writing this article was to bring to the attention of the journal's readers the value of ultrasound in the detection of congenital hip subluxation, dislocation, and/or dysplasia, the article would be better focused to catch reader interest and its message would be strengthened if it was reorganized to lead off with the information contained in the last quoted sentence, instead of having it buried near the end of the article. The information contained in the original two opening sentences more properly belongs in the description of the patient population studied in this clinical research effort. In the article just quoted no such reorganization was apparently requested and the article remains in the medical literature as a good example of poor information transfer. If reviewers believe weaknesses in the author's logic or organization of the material exists, the physician writer may be asked to perform a major restructuring or rewriting of the material in order to make the manuscript suitable for publication.

In addition to editorial requests for more information, more data, or for text or organizational revisions in the submitted manuscript, authors may be told that flaws exist in their use of statistics. Conceptual and methodologic flaws abound in the work of those inexperienced in statistical methods and techniques and statistical errors tend to make editors and reviewers suspect the validity of the whole study.[12] Research methodology has strict criteria and physician writers who are inexperienced in statistical techniques and statistical analyses should get help from experts in the field before submitting their work to the peer review process.

An astonishing number of otherwise excellent manuscripts are refused publication because they are too long; many more are returned to their authors with a request to shorten them by one-half to two-thirds. Editors of medical journals agree that most manuscripts submitted to them for consideration of publication are overwritten. In that regard, it has been noted that almost never is a manuscript returned to a physician author with an editorial request to lengthen it.[9] The response of some physician authors to editorial criticism that their submitted manuscripts are too long is not to delete any of the ideas or exclude nonessential facts and data but, rather, attempt to crowd the same amount of information into fewer pages. Revising a manuscript down to proper or acceptable length is a difficult task which usually requires almost a complete rethinking of the writing effort. It may be that the scope of the subject matter covered in the manuscript is too broad and diffuse, needing to be more finely focused. It may be that more background and introductory material is included than is necessary, offering more than the reader needs to know in order to fully understand the message contained in the manuscript. It may be that too many facts and details that are not germane to the message it contains are included in the submitted manuscript, or reviewers may believe the conclusions expressed by the author are faulty. Often the principal reason for excessive length of submitted manuscripts is that the text rambles or the author's writing style is loose and verbose and needs conversion to a writing style that is brief, concise, and crisp. This type of writing style conversion is often difficult and even impossible for some physician writers to achieve. If that is the situation, such physician writers would be better advised to seek help from colleagues known to possess good writing skills, rather than waste time in fruitless efforts to achieve a result that might be beyond the capability of their own writing skills. In revising submitted manuscripts for length in response to an editorial request, physician writers should bear in mind that space available for text in most medical journals is limited and most medical journal editors try to set a maximum length of approximately seven printed pages for each article accepted.

Occasionally, inexperienced physician writers may feel hurt and resentful at some of the suggestions for revision made by reviewing editors, but these feelings are rarely justified. Such feelings arise more out of bruised egos than out of instances of error on the part of editorial reviewers. When mulling over editorial criticisms and suggestions for improvement that might be contained in an editorial decision letter, physician writers need to remember that while writers, understandably, are concerned with the *content* of the manuscript, editors are concerned with the *expression* of that content in the manuscript and are, therefore, reader conscious. A medical journal editor's goal is to provide for the reader an ease of understanding of printed words and thoughts. For their part, readers should be able to depend on consistency in editorial style, usage. and format to assist in this understanding of an author's intentions and interpretations. Although physician writers and medical journal editors share the common goal of trying to produce the best final product possible, each approaches this goal from differing perspectives. In approaching the task of revision in response to editorial criticisms and suggestions for change, physician writers must understand that medical journal editors are not advocates for authors but, rather, advocates for readers. Good medical journal editors are not obsessed with commas, spacing around headings, or parallelism, but are concerned about their readers and their ability to understand printed words and thoughts as effortlessly as possible. A true medical professional should be able to recognize good editorial advice and criticism, accept it graciously, and act on it accordingly.

References

1. Huth EJ. *How to Write and Publish Papers in the Medical Sciences.* Philadelphia, Pa: ISI Press; 1982.
2. Smith T. On-line vs on-paper editing. *The Editorial Eye.* 1989; 12(8): 2-3.
3. King LS. *Why Not Say It Clearly. A Guide to Scientific Writing.* Boston, Mass: Little Brown and Company; 1978.
4. Day RA. *How to Write and Publish a Scientific Paper.* 3rd ed. Phoenix, Ariz: Oryx; 1988.
5. Gopen GD, and Swan JA. The science of scientific writing. *Amer Scientist.* 1990; 78(6): 550-558.
6. Garland J. Annual Oration. The New England Journal of Medicine and the Massachusetts Medical Society. *N Engl J Med.* 1952; 246: 801-806.
7. Barnes GA. *Write for Success. A Guide for Business and the Professions.* Philadelphia, Pa: ISI Press; 1986.
8. Cheney TAR. *Getting the Words Right: How to Revise, Edit & Rewrite.* Cincinnati, Ohio: Writer's Digest Books; 1983.
9. O'Leary R. The acceptable manuscript. In: Schwager E, ed. *On Medical Communications.* American Medical Writers Association; 1982; Monograph Series 1: 39-42.
10. Radovsky SS. Medical writing. Another look. *N Engl J Med.* 1979; 301(3): 131-134.
11. Woods D. Good english is good medicine. *Can Med Assoc J.* 1981; 125: 624-629.
12. Eastman JD, Smith EO'B, and Klein ER. Medical writers and editors should learn fundamentals of statistical principles. *Amer Med Writers Assn J.* 1990; 5(4): 14-17.

7

Presenting Conferences and Talks

Presenting a medical conference or delivering a professional talk before a live audience can be a powerful and persuasive form of medical communicating. If properly prepared and adequately presented, it provides the speaker with an opportunity to transfer knowledge from his or her mind directly to the minds of the listening audience. Physicians who wish to be more effective in commanding the attention of listening audiences in order to move them toward the position advocated by their message can accomplish this by learning and using the techniques developed for this powerful form of medical communicating. In contrast to medical writing, presenting medical conferences and talks to listening audiences allows a greater freedom of personal expression in how the material is organized and presented because *content, organization,* and *delivery,* the major elements of this form of medical communicating, are less restrictive than the elements required for medical writing. Some physicians might view this form of medical communicating with fear and trepidation because it involves direct interaction with a live audience, whereas audience interaction with medical writing is more indirect and distant. If the physician presenting a conference or delivering a talk is adequately prepared, there need be nothing frightening about appearing before a live audience, because this form of medical communicating is based on conversation, the most familiar form of human communication.[1]

Good oral presentations by physicians can fulfill the purposes of informing, persuading, and even entertaining. Giving good talks, however, is not simply a matter of giving information to listening audiences. Information presented in a talk will be best served by a simply presented, logically organized format. The use of first rather than third person pronouns and the active rather than the passive tense will contribute to a smoother, more informal style. The effect of the talk, and any benefit derived from it by the audience, will depend greatly on the speaker's personality, motivation, and style of delivery while on the podium or at the lectern.

In addition to having something worthwhile to say, it is important for speakers to be able to project to the audience a sense of being poised and comfortable at the lectern while all eyes are focused on them. Complete control of an audience's attention comes not only through the words uttered by a speaker but also through the speaker's appearance, posture, body language, and enthusiasm. Although what a speaker looks like should never overshadow what he or she has to say, it is nevertheless true that a good appearance by a speaker can help make the message more convincing to an audience.

Although few physicians are naturally gifted speakers, most can master techniques to enable them to speak with authority and confidence. As physicians gain experience with this form of medical communicating, most develop an individual speaking style appropriate to his or her own personality. A distinction which is worth noting has been made between an experienced speaker and a good speaker. It is said that an experienced speaker is one who goes on making the same mistakes, but with increasing confidence. A good speaker is one who asks friends and critics to tell him or her what was wrong with the presentation so that mistakes can be corrected.[2]

The ability to present effective medical conferences or deliver good professional talks rests on the principles of good organization and preparation, as well as knowing something of the type and interests of the listening audience and their familiarity with the subject matter of the presentation. Organization and preparation are largely dependent upon having sufficient time to research and plan what has to be said, followed by organization and production of what is to be said. Ideas to be presented in conferences or talks must be developed logically and delivered clearly, so the listeners have no difficulty understanding what is being said and are able to absorb the message being presented by the speaker. Unlike readers of journal articles, listeners do not have the luxury of rereading a printed page in order to better understand what is being said.

The best way for physician speakers to control nervousness or stage fright is to be confident that he or she is well prepared, not only as far as the text for the presentation is concerned, but also by rehearsal and practice of the oral delivery. When involved in more formal speaking occasions before relatively large audiences, physicians would be well advised to speak from a prepared text. For most presentations to small or medium sized audiences, it is quite appropriate to speak from notes or use slides or overhead projections as an outline for the delivery. These are not fixed rules and physicians should use whatever technique seems most comfortable to them. Knowledgeable physician speakers tend to let the nature of the occasion and size and type of audience be the primary determinants of how the content material for a medical conference or professional talk is to be presented.

Regardless of whether the decision is to use a prepared text, notes, or speak from slides or overhead projections, the physician's style of speaking and delivery should be factual and objective without being dry, boring, and uninteresting to the audience. This is where the personal style of the speaker plays a large role, with judicious and natural-appearing use of appropriate humor, the occasional gesture, and avoidance of appearing to be pretentious or lecturing the audience are all aspects of effective style and delivery. Medical conferences and professional talks have an underlying serious purpose of disseminating useful and relevant information to listeners; therefore, the physician's speaking style and form of delivery should reflect this serious purpose. A speaking style and form of delivery appropriate for a company sales meeting or a religious revival meeting, for example, would not be appropriate for a presentation to a medical or other professional audience. Medical conferences and talks are generally presented to professional audiences who have a general knowledge of the subject matter to be discussed and an interest in learning more about it. Although such audiences are composed of peers, individual members of the audience may have differing levels of background knowledge about the subject to be discussed. A medical conference or talk must always address the needs and interests of the entire audience, if it is to be effective and useful to them. Medical conferences and talks should be designed to present pertinent information, motivate the audience to accept and use the information presented, and keep the audience involved and interested until the presentation is completed. The main points or premises made in the presentation can be supported or illustrated by the use of case histories or other pertinent clinical examples, statistics or other data, quotations from authorities in the same or related subject areas, and audiovisual aids of various types. Because listeners have difficulty retaining large amounts of information given in a talk, experienced speakers know to limit the number of main points presented and to repeat them for emphasis during the presentation.

MEDICAL CONFERENCES

Physicians may be asked to organize and present a medical conference as part of a continuing medical education effort sponsored by a hospital, a medical school department, or a professional organization. It is common for residents as part of their graduate medical education experience to be required to organize and present medical conferences. Medical students may be asked to participate in these conferences and even, although less likely, may be assigned the task of organizing and presenting such an effort. The key to organizing and presenting a successful and effective medical conference is good communication between the person responsible for initiating the idea for the conference and the one assigned the responsibility for organizing and presenting it. Good communication between these key persons ensures that both are working toward the same objective for the planned conference.

The following suggestions are offered as guidelines to physicians, residents, or medical students who might be asked to organize and present a medical conference or to participate in one.

I. The first step should be to consult with the person responsible for initiating the idea for the conference, be it a department chair, director of medical education, chief of service, or chief resident physician, in order to define clearly the educational goals and objectives of the proposed conference. It is critical to a successful outcome of such a conference that all involved persons understand, agree on, and accept the defined goals and objectives for the proposed conference. It is at this early point in conference development that conference presenters should obtain specific information and instruction from the conference developers about the scope of material they are expected to cover, the specific points that will need to be emphasized, how much time is to be allotted for the presentations, and information as to the expected size and nature of the audience.

II. Physicians who are preparing material for presentation at a medical conference will find the use of an outlining technique helpful in the organization of the material to be presented (Chapter 4). Once properly organized, the material itself should be prepared and presented according to the following structural format which is considered the most appropriate format to use for formal oral presentations:

   A. *Introduction.* This section should be brief and contain only material pertinent to the educational objectives of the conference. As part of the introduction, presenters should tell the audience what material they are planning to cover and what points they are planning to make.

   B. *Body of Talk.* This section contains the bulk of the material to be presented, in addition to whatever supportive or illustrative material is to be used. Physician presenters must learn to be discriminating in the selection of the number and types of slides and other illustrative materials used. Experienced physician presenters know to use only those graphic materials that complement and broaden the impact of the oral presentation.

   C. *Conclusion.* This section is the place where the presenter reviews the main points in the material just presented and explains to the audience the relevance and significance of these points to the main subject matter around which the conference has been developed.

   Preparing and delivering the presentation according to the introduction, body, and conclusion format gives structure and direction to the presentation. The introduction sets up the topic of the presentation for the audience. The body is used to explain the main points of the presentation and provides the audience with supporting evidence for the points of view taken by the presenter. The conclusion is used to tie the main points of the presentation together and should be given in such a way as to leave the audience with a sense of closure and direction.

III. In preparing material to be presented at a planned medical conference, physicians should review the prior work done and reported in the literature on the topic to be covered in the conference. As part of the introduction section of the presentation, speakers should refer briefly to pertinent past work in order to bring the audience up to date on the topic and indicate to them the direction they, as presenters, are preparing to go with the material. It is just as bad to assume an audience knows more than they do as it is to assume they know less than they do. Knowing just how much introductory material to present can be a difficult judgment for inexperienced physician presenters to make. Audiences are bored if too much prior work is presented in too much detail, and may not understand the message of the presentation if too little prior work is discussed. Discrimination on the part of physician presenters and the ability to select from a sometimes large menu only those items particularly relevant to the discussion at hand are needed prerequisites in order to perform well in this part of the presentation.

In preparing material for presentation to live audiences at medical conferences, physicians must take special care to prepare their remarks so that all members of the audience can understand and follow the development of the points being made by the presenter. It is not uncommon for some physician speakers, particularly those possessing some type of specialized knowledge, to assume a level of awareness among members of the audience higher than actually exists, particularly if medical students and physicians from other specialties are in attendance. It has been noted on more than one occasion at academic medical centers that resident physicians are often guilty of forgetting to speak to the information needs of medical students who might be in the audience. Those physicians who do not take special care to prevent this from occurring during their presentation usually lose the attention of this segment of the audience and rarely regain it during the presentation.

IV. Physician speakers will find the following suggestions helpful for guiding the delivery of the presentation.

A. Physicians should tell the audience at the beginning of the presentation what material they are planning to cover and the points they plan to make.

B. Presenters should cover the material and the points they wish to make in a clear, organized, and succinct manner and in the allotted time period. Successful accomplishment of this goal by physician speakers requires good organization of the material to be presented and practice in the technique of oral presentation. Nothing is worse to a professional audience than a poorly organized, poorly prepared, and rambling speaker who has no regard for time allotments.

C. Presenters should prepare sufficient material to occupy the time period allotted to them, but must be certain to complete their presentations within the allotted time period. A presentation at a medical conference is concluded by reviewing with the audience the main points made during the presentation, and by explaining to the audience what the presenter believes the significance or relevance of these main points is in relation to the topic or subject matter of the medical conference.

PROFESSIONAL TALKS

The opportunity to present a medical talk to a professional audience can run the gamut in personal exposure and audience size from a medical staff meeting to a more formal presentation before a large audience at a national meeting of a professional organization. Regardless of the size of the listening audience, the location of the setting, or the prominence of the meeting, success in the endeavor depends upon having good material to present, good organization and preparation of the material to be presented, and a pleasing style of delivery of the material at the time the talk is presented.[3] The prominence of the presentation is usually directly related to the size of the audience. Presenting a talk at a national or regional medical meeting is a challenge and a responsibility and deserves a quality effort from physician speakers. Presentations for major meetings should be written out, practiced for delivery and timing until perfect, and illustrated with carefully selected slides that are professionally produced. For some meetings, physicians may be asked to provide a written abstract of the talk for publication in the meeting program. It can then be said there are four strategies involved in giving a talk at a major meeting: (1) writing the text, (2) appropriate preparation, including practice in delivering the talk and becoming familiar with the facilities and equipment available for the use of the speaker, (3) delivering the talk, and (4) preparing a written program abstract, if required.

Writing the Text

Organizing and writing the text for a medical talk follows quite a different format from that used for organizing and writing the text for a paper that is to be submitted for publication in a journal. Unlike text for published medical articles, text that is to be delivered orally must be written for the ears of listeners. It must be delivered by the speaker in such a way that the important points to be made in the talk can be heard, understood clearly, and remembered by the audience. Therefore, papers written for publication are rarely interchangeable with papers intended for oral delivery, and vice versa. There is a specific difference in structure, content, and delivery between spoken and written material, and neither can be satisfactorily substituted for the other without substantial rewriting.[4] Preparation of a talk should concentrate on communicating the highlights of the study to be reported in a well paced, well organized, and easily understandable fashion. There is neither time nor need in a professional talk to include all the information derived from a study that would be included in a paper submitted for publication. Physician speakers need to bear in mind that scientific presentations do not carry the same weight as a paper published in a peer reviewed medical journal, nor do they require the same need for a stylized format in their presentation. The reading of a formally prepared manuscript, complete with headings, makes for a rather cold, stilted delivery, which will not communicate the desired information to listeners as well as a more freely flowing conversational style.

Text that is written to be delivered in a talk must be constructed quite differently than text for a written article because writing for a live audience means writing for the ear, not writing for the eye. This is accomplished by writing in so-called "listenable packages," using an uncomplicated organizational scheme, simple declarative sentences, and single direct statements. Simple statements are used most effectively to introduce an important point or to sum up for the benefit of the audience. How the text for a talk should be written will also vary, depending upon the nature and presumed knowledge base of the expected audience. In order to prepare the text properly, physician speakers should know in advance whether they will be speaking to a lay audience, an audience of medical students, residents, and familiar faculty persons, or to an audience of knowledgeable professionals as will be encountered when giving a talk at a regional or national medical meeting.

When writing text for a talk, physicians should try to write an opening that gets the attention of the audience quickly and focuses it on the message to be delivered. Consider, for example, the effectiveness of the opening two sentences Daniel Webster used when he arose in the Senate on March 7, 1850, to join the debate on the Clay Compromise. He began, "I speak today for the preservation of the Union. Hear me for my cause." Using long or unusual words in a medical talk to impress listeners is futile because the attention of the audience tends to wander as they ponder the meaning of the long or unusual words. Simplicity, repetition, and alliteration in writing the text, in addition to vocal cadence and tone modulation to prevent a lecturing delivery style, are more effective in oral presentations than long tortuous sentences and complex words. Some physician speakers seem to love neologisms and, in amazing displays of rhetorical ignorance, contrive to use their new words both as nouns and verbs in the same talk. Regardless of how knowledgeable speakers may be about their subject matter, those who fail to impose structure on their text and, consequently, ramble when delivering it, dilute the message that is being given; therefore, usually losing the attention of the audience. An interesting exercise to perform to illustrate the deadliness of rambling is to record a talk given to a professional audience entirely from slides, and without a written text. Then, attempt to edit the tape to prepare a text for publication. More often than not, the tape will be filled with gratuitous asides, irrelevancies, discontinuity, repetitions, and shouted requests to the projectionist to identify a slide number because the speaker has lost count.[2]

An outlining scheme that can help physician speakers organize material in preparation for writing the text for a medical talk has the following steps:[6]

1. Lead off with a statement of the problem which is the subject of the talk.
2. Outline the solution.
3. List examples and evidence of positive results from the solution, including statistics, facts, and other supportive and illustrative material.
4. Summarize, or briefly restate points 1, 2, and 3.

Once the material has been appropriately organized by an outlining technique, the text for the talk can be written following one of two structural formats. Physician speakers can select the *IMRAD* format used for journal articles (see Chapter 5), or the format of introduction, body, and conclusions, which is described in the section on Medical Conferences and which is the format selected most frequently by physician speakers. With this latter format, the introduction is used to set the topics and goals of the presentation. The most important part of the introduction is an explicit, logical explanation as to why this particular study was done. On occasion, speakers may need to speak to their background or research efforts in relation to the topic being discussed. The body of the talk should follow up on the goals set for the presentation in the introduction, explaining to the audience the reasons for these goals and providing them with information supporting the primary topic. This section, the longest part of the talk, is the section in which the data and supporting evidence for the premise of the talk is given to the audience. When presenting statistical information, speakers should simplify the numbers in the spoken part of the talk and provide the specifics in accompanying slides or overhead projections. The conclusion section is used to summarize and amplify the main points made by the speaker during the body of the talk. These main points should be restated in a clear and forceful manner in the conclusion section, thus driving these points home to the audience.

Physician speakers should compose their text according to one or the other of these two structural formats. The introductory part of the text should refer briefly to pertinent prior work in the area of interest to bring the audience up to date on the topic before indicating to them the direction the talk is going to take. Speakers should tell their audiences at the beginning of the talk what material is to be covered and what points are to be made. Good physician speakers do not assume audiences know more than they do or less than they do, but attempt to prepare their texts so the audience can be carried along intellectually as the talk progresses and the ideas develop. The prepared material and the important points to be made should be presented to the audience in a clear and succinct manner, within the allotted time period. Listeners have but a finite capacity for absorbing detailed factual information in a brief period of time. Speakers must possess sufficient discrimination to be able to select the most salient information derived from the study and be able to present it to listeners in a comprehensible way.

Speakers should conclude their talks by reviewing with the audience the points that were made and by explaining their meaning or relevance to the practice of medicine, so as to leave the audience with a sense of closure and direction. Speakers should signal the approach of the ending of a talk to the audience by using phrases such as: "In summary," or "In conclusion." Such phrases tend to sharpen the attention of listeners to focus on what the speaker is about to say. The most effective presentations end with a clear, concise summary of the conclusions derived from the study.

Audiovisual aids used most frequently in medical talks are 35mm slides, overhead projections, videotapes, and movie film (see Chapter 8). Slides are usually shown from a single projector with the speaker acting as both narrator and slide changer. Videotapes and movie film can be shown, but are more expensive to produce and more difficult to project and, as a consequence, are not used as often as 35mm slides in medical talks. If a talk is worth giving, it is worth giving from a prepared text, using just enough slides to keep the attention of the audience focused and to illustrate the major ideas the speaker wishes to present, and doing all this within the allotted time period. Physicians who have to prepare a text for oral delivery before an audience of any size would do well to reflect on the words contained in a memorandum sent to young reporters by Edward R. Murrow, a renowned World War II journalist: "First, you tell them what you are going to tell them. Then, you tell them. Then, you tell them what you told them."[7]

The best way for physicians to make effective oral presentations is to speak from prepared texts. Once the text is written, it should be typed or printed on a letter-quality printer in large upper and lower case letters with double or triple spacing. Double or triple spacing allows for easier reading and provides space for the addition of handwritten notes or personal speaking instructions. Sentences in the typed or printed text should be complete on a single text page and not be carried over from a preceding page. Speakers should not hesitate to underline words or phrases to remind themselves to project these words with added emphasis during the delivery. Speakers often write notes to themselves about their delivery style, such as "slow down," in or along the text page margins. Notations can also be added to the text page about audiovisual aids, such as when in the course of delivering the talk slides should be projected.

Even though the text is typed or printed, physician speakers should not simply read the prepared text to the audience but, rather, learn the technique of speaking effectively from prepared texts. The ability to project oneself in a favorable light to an audience and the ability to speak clearly implies to listeners that the speaker possesses the ability to think clearly. One of the best ways for a physician to project that image to an audience is to learn how to deliver a prepared talk in a pleasing and effective manner. It is not enough for physician speakers to have good data to present to listening audiences. In addition, they must learn how to communicate their information to listeners in an effective fashion. A critical review was undertaken of one-third of the scientific presentations at the 1974 Annual Meeting of the Association for Academic Surgery. The purpose of this review, one of a very few such published exercises, was to determine the frequency with which scientific presentations failed to transmit information effectively to listeners. The data demonstrated that more than 50 percent of the surveyed presentations failed to transmit scientific data effectively.[8]

Preparation

Little data or anecdotal evidence exists to indicate whether physicians who are scheduled to give medical talks before professional audiences spend much time preparing for such an event, or even rehearsing the talk before giving it. Regardless of the answer, the only way to ensure a polished and professional performance is to practice the presentation in such a way that immediate feedback on the talk's effectiveness and the presenter's style of delivery and sense of timing can be given to the physician speaker. If it is important enough for the physician to stand up in front of a group of people and have them listen to his or her presentation, then it is important enough for the physician to present his or her message in the best possible light. The better prepared the physician is for the presentation, the better will be the presentation and its reception by the audience. It is critical to the success of such a presentation that physician speakers be calm and in control of the situation during the delivery of the talk, It is equally important that physician speakers appear to be clear, confident, and convincing to audiences. Good preparation puts the physician speaker in direct control of the presentation, functions as a confidence builder, and contributes to a personal sense of comfort as the speaker approaches the lectern.

Speech anxiety is experienced by all speakers, particularly when faced with an unfamiliar or an especially large audience. The best way for physician speakers to combat speech anxiety and stage fright is to be certain they are fully prepared and well rehearsed which should expand their confidence in their presentation, style, and speaking skill. There is no reason for physicians to fear this kind of experience, particularly if they have a prepared text before them which they themselves wrote. Other helpful hints to physician speakers in regard to speech anxiety are: (1) Physicians should remember they would not have been selected or invited to speak at the meeting if someone had not considered their ideas to be of value and, at least for the occasion of the talk, they are regarded as experts in the field. Recognition of that fact should induce an attitude of positive thinking in physician speakers who should also appreciate that their nervousness, if any, will be much more obvious to themselves than to the audience, (2) A physician speaker's natural fear of the unknown can be markedly diminished if he or she researches the type of audience expected, room layout, and program specifics in advance of the presentation, (3) Physicians should prepare the text well and rehearse delivery of the talk with particular attention to style and timing of the delivery. When speakers realize early on during a presentation that the talk seems to be going well, nervousness usually disappears. (4) Text for a talk should not be memorized. Physician speakers should learn how to speak from a prepared text, from an outline of key words and points, or from slides alone if the physician possesses total familiarity with the subject matter.

Once the text for the talk has been typed or printed, physician speakers should practice delivering the talk. Rehearsal gives the presenter a feel for the cadence and timing of the presentation. Effective practice does not mean simply reading the text aloud to oneself but, rather, making use of one of several effective practice techniques that are available. The most effective practice techniques contain a feedback loop that allows mistakes and weaknesses in either the text or style of delivery to be identified and corrected well in advance of the time for the formal presentation. The practice technique that provides the most feedback information is to have someone videotape the performance while the speaker delivers the talk in a practice session. This provides the physician speaker an opportunity to assess his or her appearance and sense of poise and comfort at the lectern, as well as providing an opportunity to assess the impact of the talk and the speaker's delivery style. If videotaping is not feasible, the next best practice technique is to rehearse the talk with a tape recorder and then listen to how it sounds. Another effective technique is to deliver the talk by microphone from a lectern to an associate sitting somewhere in the empty seats in the back of the room. This practice technique provides speakers with instant and helpful feedback on delivery, speaking tone and style, timing, and microphone technique.

Among the items physician speakers should consider as they assess the feedback from a rehearsal or practice session are:

1. Was the talk delivered clearly enough to be easily understood by listeners?
2. Did the important points made in the text of the talk come across clearly?
3. As a speaker, did the physician sound interesting, convincing, and in control of the situation?
4. Was the pace of the delivery appropriately quick, without appearing to be rushed?
5. Was the pace and volume of the delivery sufficiently varied? Speakers should move quickly through well understood material, but more slowly through new and possibly more complex information. Main points to be emphasized in the talk should be delivered slowly and forcefully.
6. Did the speaker remember to pronounce medical and technical terms in full, rather than refer to them by using abbreviations?
7. Did the speaker pause often enough during the delivery, or did the pauses

come just once in awhile? Were the pauses placed appropriately between paragraphs and main points, but not in the middle of sentences or ideas?
8. Did the speaker look at the audience enough during the presentation and did his or her gestures appear relaxed and effective?
9. Was the speaker guilty of using unnecessary verbal fillers such as "um-," and "you know?"
10. Did the talk come through as clear and convincing, and was it delivered with pleasing vocal cadence and voice modulation?
11. Ask for any other suggestions for improvement from the listeners at the practice session.

If the audience size is expected to be more than forty-five people, speakers will need to use an amplifying system which makes microphone practice essential because using one correctly takes practice. It would be helpful for the speaker to know the type of microphone available for the talk and its location. If the facility to be used for the talk provides a fixed microphone set on a lectern or table, it should be adjusted to an appropriate height so the speaker does not have to hunch over to speak into it. A fixed microphone should be kept six to eight inches from the speaker's mouth. Speakers should never be so close to a microphone that their voices are too loud or so far away from the microphone that they can not be heard clearly by all members of the audience. Both an overly loud speaking voice and a low, barely audible one associate negatively with the audience's reception of the speaker's message.

If the speaker is to use a hand-held microphone, he or she should practice with it to learn the proper distance from the mouth for effective voice amplification. Practice with this type of microphone allows a speaker to become comfortable with its use and familiar with the proper distance between microphone and mouth. Lavaliere microphones are frequently provided at large regional and national meetings. This is the most useful type of microphone to have because the speaker does not have to be concerned about the distance between microphone and mouth and it provides the speaker a greater degree of freedom to point out salient points on slides or overheads.

If travel to a distant city is required for the presentation, physician speakers would be well advised to carry both their text and slides with them. Checked baggage has a nasty habit of getting lost. If scheduled to give the talk in an unfamiliar place, physician speakers would be wise to go there well ahead of the start of the program to check the facility and equipment available for the use of the speaker.[4] Physician speakers should notice if a lectern with a speaker's light is provided, as well as whether the lectern sits on the floor or sits on a podium. Early examination of the facility allows the speaker the opportunity to give his or her already numbered and arranged slides to the projectionist and become familiar with the mechanism that is to be employed to project and change slides during the talk. This is part of good talk preparation and guards against the speaker having to ask the embarrassing question from the lectern and in front of an expectant audience, "How does this thing work?"

Points to Remember About Delivering a Talk
1. With a typed or printed and appropriately marked text in front of you, the circumstances governing the talk should be under your total control.
2. Speak in a voice that is loud enough to be heard easily by the entire audience; speak clearly and pronounce words distinctly; use a speaking cadence that is geared to the time period allotted for the presentation.
3. Time the talk carefully so that you make effective use of the allotted time, but never exceed the time allotted to your presentation. Exceeding your allotted time is bad speaking manners and may result in having your microphone turned off by the moderator, if one is present. Exceeding your time limit may infringe on the time allotted to speakers who follow, thus possibly causing them to lose time from their own presentations.

Delivery

The impact of a message that is delivered orally is enhanced if physician speakers appear natural and at ease to the audience during the delivery of a talk. The appearance of being natural and at ease at the lectern is often referred to as stage presence. When used in reference to physician speakers, possession of stage presence correlates positively with the speaker's knowledge of the subject being discussed and the adequacy of the physician's preparation for the particular talk about to be given. A physician speaker's ability to establish and maintain eye contact with the audience while delivering the talk, combined with good stage presence, helps the audience forget the speaker is reading a prepared text. Speaking naturally, being well prepared, and having worthwhile information to share are the greatest assets physician speakers possess. Physicians should practice and work to develop a warm and friendly speaking style and avoid a lecturing or droning speaking style by making use of the vocal techniques of speech cadence and voice modulation. Audiences tend to react negatively to lecturing tones and positively to warm and pleasant speaking styles. Physician speakers should speak slowly and present what they have to say in a calm and reasonable manner and, above all, should not digress to distracting or confusing side issues. Deliberate pauses during the oral presentation can be used to good effect by speakers because short pauses in the delivery tend to heighten the audience's understanding of the message. Speakers should not be afraid to smile or use an occasional graceful gesture. Some physicians have an easy and natural sense of humor and know how to use it effectively. Trying to be funny, however, seldom works and is generally considered to be out of place in the presentation of a serious medical talk.

As important as good delivery is for an effective presentation, the critical element for most medical talks is the content of the talk, not the stage presence or personal foibles of the speaker. Physician speakers must remember that good speaking style alone can not replace substance because, as far as medical audiences are concerned, the message of the talk usually is the important element, not the person delivering the message. Physician speakers would be well advised to do nothing at the lectern that would tend to draw attention to themselves and away from the content of the talk. This includes dressing conservatively and trying to look as neat as possible. Do not pace, fidget, or rock back and forth while at the lectern, but try to stand as still as possible so that attention is not drawn to the speaker and away from the content of the talk. Nervous speakers can eliminate some purposeless, nervous gestures by gripping the sides of the lectern, but must be careful not to convey a sense of their nervousness to the audience by appearing to be holding on to the lectern for dear life. Speakers should not look at their wrist watches during the presentation because this movement only serves as a distraction for the audience. A better strategy for speakers who are concerned about keeping within their allotted time is to place the wrist watch on the lectern where the speaker and no one else can see it.

Eye contact between the speaker and the audience is an essential feature of a good oral presentation. Eye contact establishes rapport with an audience, rivets their attention on the speaker, increases the speaker's credibility, reinforces the message of the presentation, and helps dispel a perception that might be held by the audience that a prepared text is simply being read to them. Audiences react negatively to speakers who can not or will not establish eye contact with them. An effective speaker establishes eye contact with an audience immediately and maintains it by looking at various members of the audience, one at a time, for five to ten seconds each. Maintaining eye contact with an audience through the entire presentation is essential to an effective performance and is a technique employed by all good physician speakers.

In addition, good speakers have learned to memorize the opening lines of their text so they can begin the talk without glancing at their text or notes and continue to look up at the members of the audience as often as possible during the delivery of the talk. A helpful technique to use during delivery of the talk is to run one finger down the text lines while speaking. The advantages of doing this are to ensure that the speaker's place in the text is not lost while looking up at the audience and to help dispel any impression held by them that the prepared text is simply being read to them by the speaker. Audiences like to see speakers for a few moments before the room lights are dimmed or turned off for the viewing of slides. Far too many physician speakers issue the command, "Lights off and first slide on, please," immediately after being introduced to the audience. A more desirable technique would be to not begin showing slides until eye contact has been established with the audience and presentation of the talk has begun. Also, speakers should not end their talks in the dark. Summation points may be projected on a slide, but the concluding sentence or paragraph should be delivered with the room lights on and with the speaker again in eye contact with the members of the audience.

The text for a talk should be typed or printed in large print with wide margins and placed on the lectern in front of the speaker. The text pages may be marked appropriately by the speaker by underlining words or phrases that need to be emphasized during delivery and by marking in the text page margins when slides are to be projected. If it is necessary to dim or turn off the room lights in order to view the slides, the speaker should keep the lectern light on. Speakers should never be completely in the dark during the showing of any audiovisual aids, but always be illuminated by the lectern light. A disembodied voice carries very little authority for an audience. Speakers should remove paper clips and staples from the text pages, should number the text pages, and make certain the pages are in the correct sequence before going to the lectern to deliver the talk.

Points to Remember While Delivering a Talk
1. Use your nervous energy constructively. Project your voice and your message to the person at the back of the room.
2. Look at the audience as much as possible when giving the talk; eighty percent of the time is believed to be a realistic goal. Do not try to look at everyone at once. Focus on one person for a few seconds, then on another person in a different part of the room, and so on. Strong eye contact with the audience suggests to them that speakers who follow this practice possess confidence and control.
3. Make any gestures, such as using a pointer, above the top of the lectern and in full view of the audience. Do not tug on your clothing while speaking.
4. You can move away from the lectern if the need arises if you are wearing a lavaliere microphone. However, do not just wander around the floor or the podium in a purposeless fashion.
5. For a positive and forceful conclusion of the talk, memorize the last sentence of the text. Deliver it with the room lights on and while looking at the audience. Pause, then, for a few seconds after you have finished speaking and continue to look at the audience. Thank the audience for their attention, gather up your notes, and sit down.

The best advice for physician speakers to follow is to come to the lectern fully prepared and with a well organized and rehearsed talk. Instructions regarding speaking style and delivery and the showing of slides will assist in adding to the professionalism of the presentation but, in no way, will substitute for preparation and organization.

Program Abstract

Abstracts prepared for talks to be given at meetings, and which may be printed in the meeting program, are informational abstracts similar to those prepared for journal articles (see Chapter 5). This type of abstract describes the content of the talk in brief form and is constructed from information contained in the introduction, materials and methods, results, and conclusion sections of the text. Physicians must remember that program abstracts are frequently limited to 300 words or less because of space limitations in the printed program.

The writing of program abstracts must be done very carefully so the important points to be made in the talk are clearly apparent to the program reader. Good program abstract writing requires a brief, direct, and uncluttered writing style.

Chapter 9 contains a fictional National Institutes of Health grant application titled "Testosterone, Weightlessness, and Bone Mass in Male Rats." This fictional grant application is used in Chapter 9 to illustrate grant writing technique to readers. Figure 1 illustrates how a program abstract for this same material might look if "Testosterone, Weightlessness, and Bone Mass in Male Rats" was presented as a talk at a major medical meeting.

Introduction

TESTOSTERONE, WEIGHTLESSNESS, AND BONE MASS IN MALE RATS. JOHN Q. PUBLIC. SOUTHNORTH UNIVERSITY SCHOOL OF MEDICINE, METROPOLIS CITY.

Male astronauts subjected to prolonged weightlessness develop osteoporosis. A known relationship exists between hypogonadism and bone mass in females. This study was done to determine if a relationship exists between hypogonadism, weightlessness, and bone mass in male rats.

Methods

Study population consisted of 160 young mature male Wistar rats, of which 80 were randomly selected and rendered hypogonadic by surgical castration 4 weeks prior to beginning the study. Rats from the non-castrated group (Group A) and from the castrated group (Group B) were randomly assigned in aliquots of 20 from each group to 1 of 4 exercise models and made to perform the assigned group task for 24 weeks. The 4 exercise models were (1) normal cage activity used for control group, (2) a specially constructed swimming tank simulating weightlessness, (3) an 8 percent sloped running track, and (4) a velcro weight pack averaging 60 percent of body weight worn constantly plus exercising daily on a 45 degree inclined treadmill. Rats sacrificed after 24 weeks and bone density measured by digital radiography and mechanical bone strength by three-point bending stress. Measurements obtained in the 2 groups of rats in the 4 exercise models were compared to each other and to known average values for male rats.

Results

Results indicate castration alone has only a small effect on bone mass in males rats but greatest loss of bone mass noted in castrated rats exercised in the weightlessness model. Mean bone density for this rat group averaged 357.7 hounsfield units as compared to 252.5 in the non-castrated weightlessness group, 275.3 units in the castrated control group, and 267 units in the normal population. Breaking point measurements in these 4 rat groups were 3.7, 6.2, 7.1, and 6.8 newtons respectively.

Conclusions

Castration plus simulated weightlessness seems to have a synergistic effect greater than the sum of individual effects. This suggests a relationship between testosterone, weightlessness, and bone mass in male rats.

Fig 1.--Example of a program abstract.

References

1. Staheli LT. *Speaking and Writing for the Physician*. New York, NY: Raven Press; 1986.
2. McClenahan J. And now, may we have the first slide? *Phila Med.* 1986; 82(8): 301.
3. Kern RA. How to present a scientific paper before a large audience. *Ann Intern Med.* 1952; 37: 618-624.
4. Meadow R. Speaking at medical meetings. *Lancet.* 1969; 2: 631-633.
5. Plaut SM. Preparation of abstracts, slides, and presentations for scientific meetings. *Clin Res.* 1982; 30: 18-24.
6. Gruber F, Keane RM, Cooper G, Mazor B. *How to be a Good Speaker.* New York, NY: Research Institute of America, Inc.; 1986.
7. Gastel B. *Presenting Science to the Public.* Philadelphia, Pa: ISI Press; 1983.
8. Kraft AR, Saletta JD, Moss GS, Herman CM, Tompkins RK. A critical appraisal of the effectiveness of scientific presentations. *J Surg Res.* 1976: 20: 377-379.

8

Graphics for Written and Spoken Material

Graphics is the term used for both the *artwork* chosen by authors to illustrate, clarify, or support material presented in written texts, and the *visual aids* chosen by speakers to amplify or clarify points made in spoken texts. The use of well planned, simple, and memorable graphics will enhance the impact of any presentation. Beautiful graphics can now be produced using a computer and an appropriate software program. Graphic materials can enhance the effectiveness of both written and spoken texts if they are carefully selected, appropriate for the expected audience, complement the message being delivered in the text, and are used in an amount that provides a correct balance between text and graphics. For most medical writing purposes, the choice of graphic materials includes tables, graphs, diagrams, and photographs. Medical journals label graphs, diagrams, and photographs as *figures*, while *tables* retain their own designation.

Audiovisual aids used most frequently with spoken material are 35mm slides, overhead projections, videotapes, and movie film. These different kinds of graphic materials are not necessarily interchangeable. Tables, graphs, and drawings produced in sufficient detail to allow leisurely study in a published article, for example, are unsuitable for slides to be used in a talk. Situations arise in medical writing and speaking where a particular kind of graphic is more appropriate to use than other kinds and part of becoming a good medical writer or speaker is knowing when such situations occur and knowing what kind of graphic to select.

The idea governing the appropriate choice of graphics to use with written material is that organization of the material being presented to readers depends upon the process of perceiving relationships. In some instances, such relationships are so complex that they are difficult for both writer and reader to understand until they are expressed in graphic form.[1] The idea governing the appropriate choice of graphics to use with spoken material differs from the choice for written material in that graphics used with spoken material function mainly as assisting devices to amplify specific points made by speakers while delivering their talks. Such points made by speakers should be able to stand alone without the support of graphic material, but the effect or impact of the specific points on audiences can be enhanced by the support of carefully selected audiovisual aids. Graphics chosen for use with spoken material should be simple and direct and not so complicated their use might divert the attention of the audience from the content of the talk.[2]

GRAPHICS FOR WRITTEN MATERIAL

The function of tables, graphs, diagrams, and photographs, the graphics appropriate to use with written materials, is to help authors understand the data or information they are presenting to readers so that relationships which are either too difficult or too cumbersome to express in narrative form can be expressed more clearly to readers in graphic form.[3] Conversely, poorly conceived and constructed tables and figures can turn readers off, making it more likely the accompanying article will not be read in its entirety or, if read, will not be clearly understood. To summarize, properly constructed graphics selected to use with written material have two principal purposes:

1. To clarify ideas the writer wishes to present to readers and,
2. To present relevant data or information in a condensed form.

Properly designed tables and figures often need very little accompanying explanation. Tables and figures, if constructed correctly, should be sufficiently focused and contain enough information to allow them to stand alone without repeating information given in the text. Well conceived and designed tables and figures relieve the text of the pressure to present data, allowing more space for the text to comment on the data's significance. Tables and figures work best when they are well integrated with the text. Whenever possible, physician writers should attempt to write the text of their papers around the evidence to be conveyed to readers in the tables and figures, instead of writing the text first, then appending tables and figures to the finished text. If a paper can be written around the tables and figures, it gains in clarity and requires less words in its writing.[4] Like prose, tables and figures convey their messages clearly only if their purposes are fully appreciated by physician writers. The purposes of tables and figures are to show results of the study being reported, reveal comparisons or changes, indicate trends and relationships, and, if possible, indicate why the data are significant. In general, shapes and trends are better portrayed in graphs and exact values in tables.

Because a frequent use for tables and figures is to support the author's conclusions, each table or figure, when possible, should be a single unit of communication, completely informative in itself. Each table and figure must be sharply focused so it reveals its purpose and results at a glance. Whenever possible, each table or figure should make one point only and lead the reader to a single conclusion. The purpose of a graphic is to communicate a message to readers. If the graphic material is too complicated in its design, or if it is presented in excessive numbers, the message being communicated risks becoming garbled.

Tables and figures that physician writers plan to use in their articles should be given the same care and attention in their design as the other components of the manuscript. Each table and figure used in the article must be cited in the text in consecutive order.[5] In providing legends for tables and figures, the written name should be used for the quantity plotted and then its dimensions should be presented in parentheses, for example, Time (Days). Abbreviations such as *mg*, *cm*, and *hr* do not take periods. During manuscript preparation, data included in tables and figures should be checked repeatedly for accuracy, not only in relation to the data itself, but also in relation to the accompanying text. Physician writers must be sensitive to the proportional value of each table, illustration, footnote, and reference. Like the critical appraisal and reappraisal given to words in the development of text, physician writers must take special care to determine how essential each element of the graphics presentation is to appropriately communicating the article's main message. Experienced physician writers understand that the impact of graphic material is strengthened if used sparingly and selected carefully so that an appropriate balance is achieved between text and the accompanying tables and figures.

It is important for physician writers to understand that the author of a medical manuscript does not necessarily have freedom of choice over the number of tables and figures used in a published paper. Some journals set limits on the number of tables and figures acceptable to them, but others do not. Advice referable to tables and figures is given in the Information for Authors page of the selected journal. The editorial cost of preparing and printing tables, graphs, and illustrations is high and, if the data or information can be adequately handled in the text or if any of the figures duplicate other material, most journal editors will delete the graphic material they believe to be duplicative or consider unnecessary for reader comprehension. Although an author is under an obligation to present enough data in the paper to enable an interested and qualified reader to regenerate his or her raw data or, at least, a population of values with the same statistical characteristics, journal editors look askance at large numbers of accompanying figures and tables filled with raw data. Novice physician writers invariably include more tables and figures with their manuscripts than most medical journals will either need or want. With experience, physician writers should develop the sense of discrimination necessary to achieve proper balance between text and graphics.

At some point between the first draft and the final version of the paper, a decision will have to be made about the number and type of graphic materials to be included in the finished manuscript. At this point, the physician writer will need to make a final decision on questions such as which tables are really necessary, which tables would be better replaced by graphs, and which tables should be discarded in favor of summarizing the data in the text? Certain types of data, particularly of the sparse variety or the type that is monotonously repetitive, do not need to be brought together in either a table or graph. The purpose for which the graphic is intended should determine which type of graphic is selected. It is generally agreed that:

1. If the data show pronounced trends or makes an interesting picture, use a graph.
2. If the numbers just sit there with no particular trend evident, a table would be the better choice.
3. A generally useful guide for physician writers to follow is to use no more than one table or figure for each 1,000 words of text. For most articles, this works out to be no more than one table or figure for each four pages of manuscript text. Obviously, this is not an absolute rule and a great deal of editorial judgment goes into selecting the final number of tables and figures to be published with any article.
4. The cardinal rule that must guide the physician writer when considering the use of graphic materials is to present the data in the text, or in a table, or in a graph, but never present the same data in more than one way in the same article.[6]

Tables

Tables provide a method of structuring and presenting data or information to readers in support of statements or conclusions provided in the text.[7] The correct function of a table is to illustrate or support a statement or conclusion from the text, but not duplicate material already given in the text. A table can be used to display data when the data themselves are important to the reader or to summarize facts that would be too cumbersome to write out in prose. The most frequent use of tables in place of text in published clinical articles is to summarize patient data in a review article or a case series analysis. In order to construct good tables, physician writers must be able to appreciate the needs of readers, must be able to present tabular data in a form that is understandable to readers and, whenever possible, produce tables pertaining to only one topic. In turn, readers should be able to understand each table and its title without having to refer to the text. Reader comprehension is enhanced when tables have a logical and uniform structure. Most journals have a preferred form for tables which is explained in the journal's Instructions for Authors page.

Tables should contain only data or numbers that are significant to the purpose of the article and which, for reader clarity, would be confusing or too lengthy to present in the text. Commensurate with reader clarity and understanding, physician writers should strive to use as few tables as possible in the preparation of their manuscripts. Because tables are more expensive to typeset than text, editors are prone to ask authors to eliminate tables they consider editorially unnecessary to the clarity of the paper's message. In addition, the use of too many tables in proportion to the length of the text may produce difficulties in the layout of pages in the journal. Tables should not be used when the data can be summarized in the text with a few sentences, or when the relationship of data to each other or to a time sequence can be expressed more clearly in a graph. Two good reasons exist for not constructing tables unless repetitive data must be presented:

1. It is neither good science nor good writing to regurgitate reams of data just because it exists in a physician writer's notes. Only data samples and break points need to be listed in a table.
2. The cost of publishing tables is higher than publishing text and editors will delete tables they consider unnecessary to the clarity of the paper's message.

Constructing Tables

Tables can be as simple as a single listing of facts set off from the text or as complicated as a complex arrangement of data with multiple variables. Tables that deal with technical material, however, are usually constructed with the six major parts shown in Figure 2. Horizontal lines are used to serve as boundary markers for the entire table and sometimes may be used to separate categories of data in the data field of complex tables. It is considered useful to provide double horizontal lines at the bottom to indicate the end of a table. Most medical journals and style guides advise that tables be constructed without additional horizontal or vertical lines because lines increase reader difficulty with scanning groups of data in the table. Whenever possible, construct tables so they can be read in the same direction as the text. Having to turn the page around to read a table can be annoying to readers.

Each table should be constructed on a separate sheet of paper and numbered consecutively in the text. The title announces the purpose of the table and should be brief, provide a clear indication to readers of the table's content, be double spaced, and be placed above the table. If orienting information for readers must be included, it should be given in the title of the first table only and not repeated in the remaining tables. The variables go in the box head and the stub and the data being reported goes in the data field. A third variable can be introduced in the box head and data field by use of additional columns called spanners. Spanner heads and field spanners are always underlined in the table.

A useful rule of thumb is to give the control or normal values first, either in a column toward the left of the table or in the top row of figures. Each column head may have a short or abbreviated heading, provided each heading accurately describes what lies below. Units of measurement used in the stub and column heads in the box head are indicated in parentheses. Units of measurement may

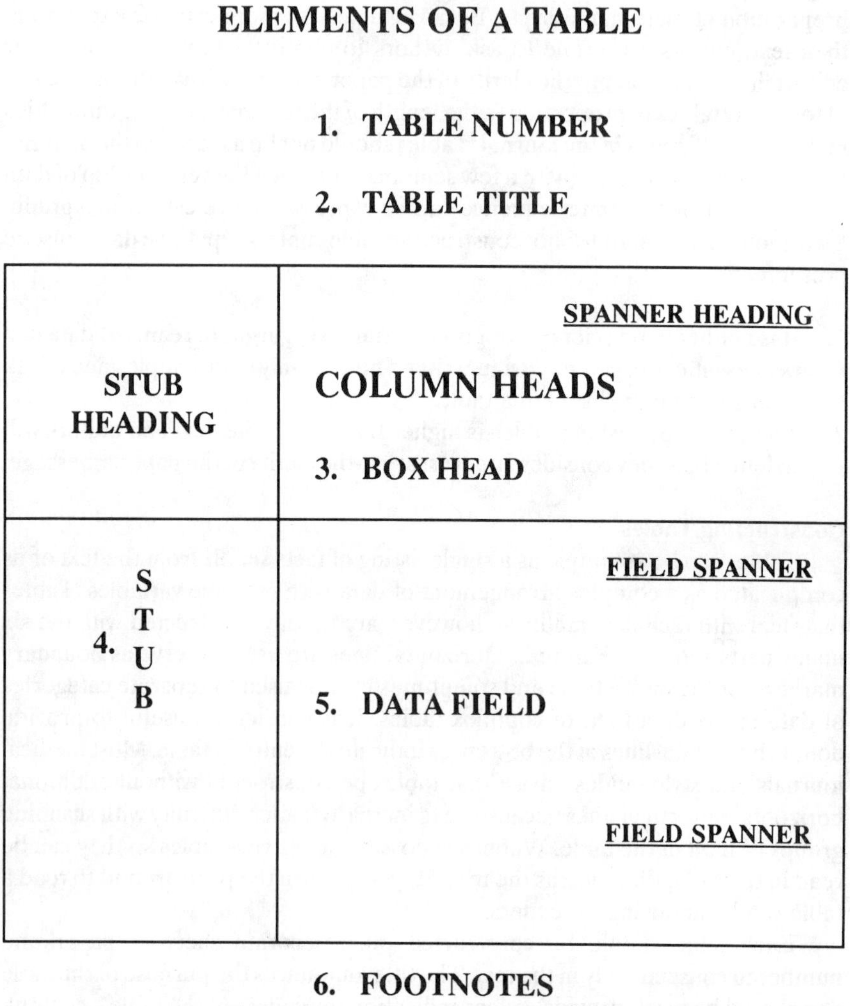

ELEMENTS OF A TABLE

1. TABLE NUMBER

2. TABLE TITLE

STUB HEADING	SPANNER HEADING
	COLUMN HEADS
	3. BOX HEAD
4. S T U B	FIELD SPANNER
	5. DATA FIELD
	FIELD SPANNER

6. FOOTNOTES

Fig 2.--Elements of a table.

be abbreviated as long as the abbreviations remain consistent throughout the table. Unless otherwise stipulated by the selected journal, the metric system should be used for measurements. Any explanatory material that must be included in tables should be given in the footnotes, not included in the headings. Footnotes, if used, should be written carefully as they are an extremely important part of tables. Footnotes are used to cite sources, explain abbreviations, and give more information about the table as a whole. For example, any discrepancy between the number of patients reported in a text and analyzed in a table would be explained to readers in a footnote. Multiple footnotes in the same table are identified by lower case letters or asterisks.

Graphs

Graphs are used to show trends in the data and illustrate comparisons as clearly as possible. Their purpose is to promote understanding of the results of the reported study and suggest interpretations of their meaning.[1] A main objective for a physician writer in constructing a graph is to make certain it is clear, concise, and accurate. Graphs, like tables, should be free-standing, self-supporting structures which do not have to depend on the surrounding text to make them clear. Graphs are constructed on separate sheets of paper, are labeled as figures, and, like tables, are numbered consecutively in the text. However, in contrast to tables, legends for graphs are placed below the graph. Graph legends function as titles and are used to orient readers toward the interpretation and meaning of the graph, and as a mechanism to explain symbols and images used in the graph. Graph legends are required to be double spaced and written on separate sheets of paper. Some journals stipulate a maximum word length for graph legends. Some journals require graphs be submitted as 5 by 7 inch glossy black-and-white photographs, while others prefer the original drawings. Several commercial software programs are available which, when used with a computer, are capable of producing publication quality scientific graphs. The selected journal's Instructions for Authors page will inform the writer of the journal's preference with regard to graph submission. Footnotes are rarely used in graphs because extra information needed for graph clarification would be included in the legend. Many kinds of graph forms exist, but the most useful ones for scientific work are plotted curve graphs and histograms.[8]

Constructing Graphs
Plotted curve graphs can be constructed as either arithmetic line graphs or semi-logarithmic line graphs.

- *Arithmetic line graphs* show a trend in the data over time and are particularly useful in summarizing trends or interactions between two or more variables. An arithmetic line graph portrays comparative fluctuations only when the quantities compared have similar values. Equal spaces in the graph represent equal amounts of change in arithmetic line graphs (see Figure 3).
- *Semi-logarithmic line graphs* are used to show relative rate of change. This type of graph, portraying proportional and percentage relationships, is useful because it shows both relative changes in the data and absolute amounts. Relative change for both large and small quantities can be compared. This type of graph is useful to show relative changes when baseline quantities differ greatly. Semi-logarithmic line graphs are also

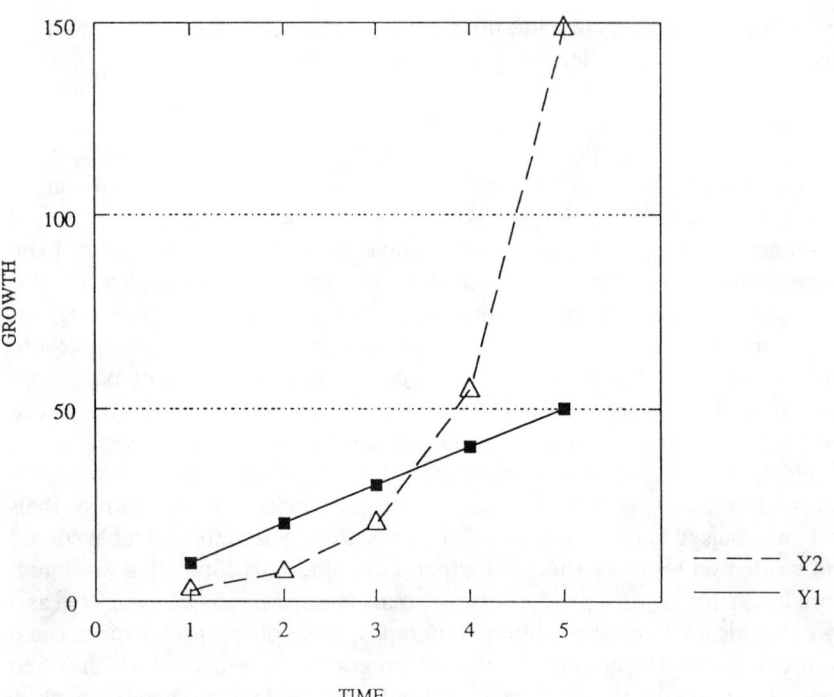

Fig 3.--Graph with arithmetic scale.

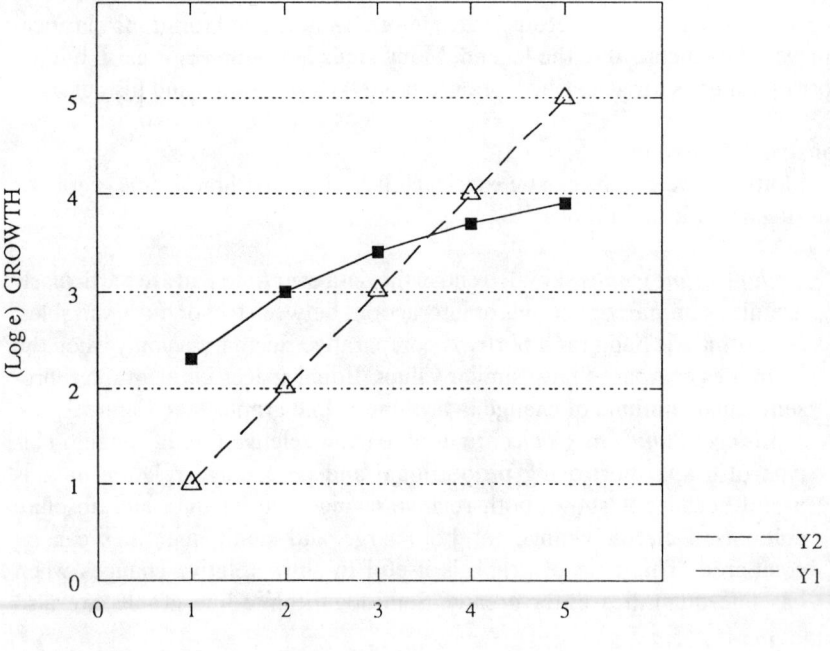

Fig 4.--Same data on logarithmic scale.

useful to compare relative changes of variables expressed in different units. Equal spaces in the graph represent equal amounts of relative change in semi-logarithmic line graphs (see Figure 4).

The horizontal axis of a *plotted curve graph* is the x-axis (*abscissa*). The independent parameter, such as time, is always plotted on the x-axis. The vertical axis of a plotted curve graph is the y-axis (*ordinate*). The dependent parameter, such as a factor being measured in the study, is always plotted on the y-axis. It is a publishers' convention that axis lines be twice as thick as data lines. Both the x and y axes must be labeled and the units of measure indicated. Axis labeling should be simple, clear, and done with a minimum of letters. Tick marks may be used in axis lines to indicate a break in the scale. When constructing a plotted curve graph, it is well to remember that the shape of graphs can be determined almost arbitrarily by appropriate choice of scale. This makes it important to consider the format of the selected journal to assist in determining proper scale so resulting graphs would best fit into the journal pages. Often the best orientation of a graph on the printed page is to construct the y-axis as the long axis of the graph.

Data points should always be shown on the curves. Five to ten data points generally suffice to show the essential trends of most functions. Symbols used in graph construction to indicate data are: filled and open circles, filled and open squares, and filled and open triangles. It is believed that six different symbols are all one graph can handle before becoming too confusing for readers.[9] Physician writers are cautioned never to extrapolate a line or curve outside the points observed without informing readers of the extrapolation. Graph lines or curves should be labeled individually if possible. It is permissible to use an arrow to match the lines with the labels. If this proves to be technically difficult, a graph key may be placed in the lower right hand corner of the data field to identify what is being measured (see Figure 5).

Histograms, a form of vertical column graphs, are diagrams or graphs in which the values found in a statistical study are represented by vertical columns, bars, or rectangles. This type of graph can be used when comparing magnitude or emphasizing differences in one variable at different time periods. Histograms should not be used to indicate a trend in the data because the plotted curve graph better fits that purpose. Physician writers are cautioned not to include more than three groups of data in histograms because too much data results in cluttered and unreadable graphs (see Figure 6).

Bar graphs, a form of horizontal column graphs, are useful to illustrate differences between many items at one specified time. Bar graphs should not be used to compare differences in one item over a period of time because histograms better fit that purpose.

Other types of graphs include other forms of *column graphs*, *pie charts*, and *pictorial charts*. These forms of graphs are used more in popular writing than scientific writing because they provide a relatively small amount of information while occupying a relatively large amount of space which is at a premium in most medical journals.

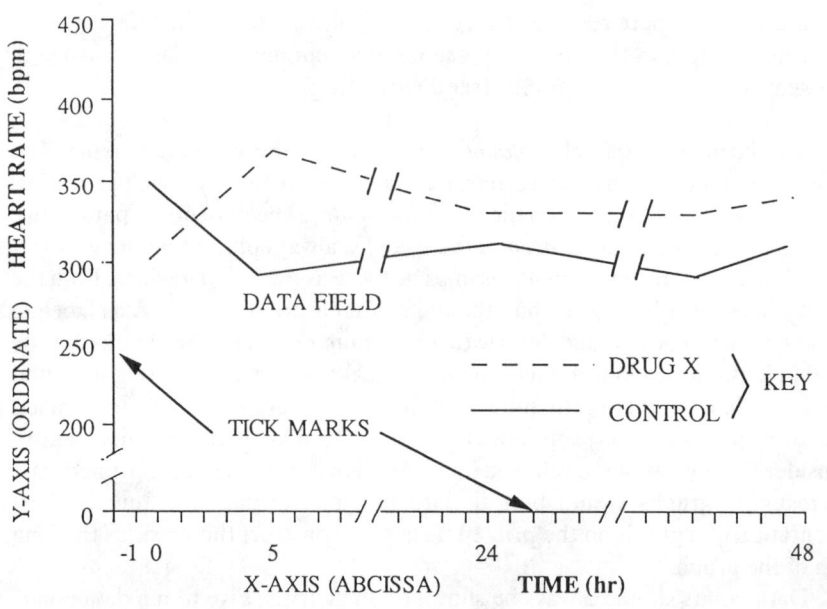

Fig 5.--Arithmetic line graph showing effect of orally administered drug *x* on mean heart rate of conscious dogs.

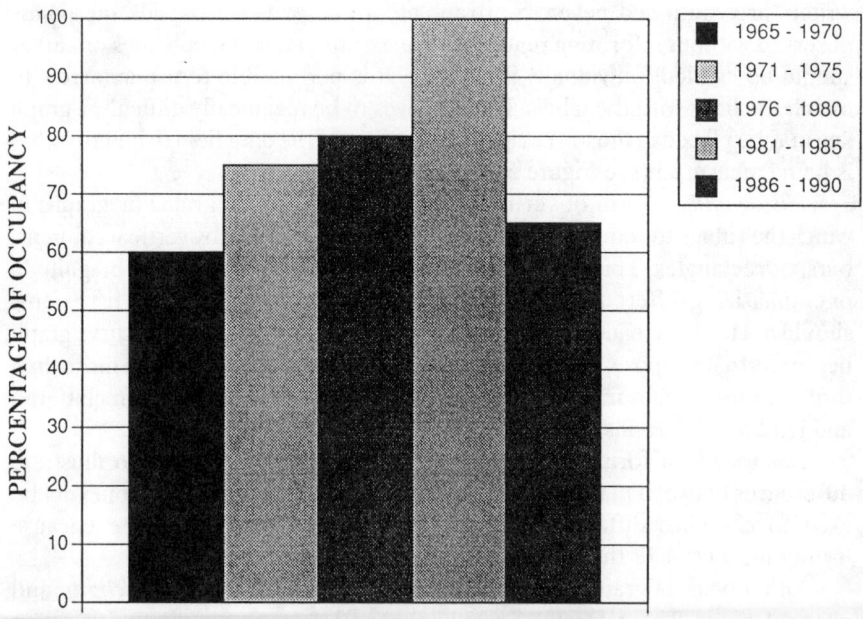

Fig 6.--Year occupancy rates at City General Hospital.

Illustrations (Diagrams, Photographs)

Illustrations are used to clarify technical information given in the text or phenomena observed by authors when neither a verbal description nor another graphic form would suffice in giving readers the information physician writers wish to convey. Diagrams are sometimes useful as summarizing devices or for illustrating more complex relationships, such as spatial configurations, pathways, processes, and interactions. Like graphs, illustrations are labeled as figures and all figures, regardless of type, are numbered consecutively as they appear in the text. Each illustration should be provided with a double spaced legend on a separate page. Illustrations should be drawn in a professional manner and photographed. Freehand or typewritten lettering is not acceptable to most journals. In certain kinds of research reports, authors will need to decide whether diagrams or photographs give more information to readers. This decision should be made with the advice of senior investigators and professional technical experts.

Sharp, glossy black-and-white photographic prints of original drawings, roentgenograms, and other materials, usually 127 by 173mm (5 by 7 inches) but no larger than 203 by 254mm (8 by 10 inches), are required by journals. Color illustrations will not be used by most medical journals unless the journal editor believes the color conveys information not available from black-and-white prints. Letters, numbers, and symbols used in graphic materials should be clear and even throughout and of sufficient size to be legible when reproduced for publication. Photomicrographs must have internal scale markers visible on the print. Symbols, arrows, or letters used in photomicrographs should contrast with the background for better reader comprehension. Titles and detailed explanations belong in the legends for illustrations, not on the illustrations themselves. Authors are cautioned not to write on the back of submitted tables or figures. Instead, write the figure number, name of principal author, a short version of the manuscript title, and an arrow indicating the top of the figure on a gummed label and affix the label to the back of the graphic material. Figures that are being submitted to a journal with the manuscript should not be mounted on cardboard, bent, or attached to other material by staples or paper clips.

Inexperienced physician writers tend to submit far too many illustrations with their manuscripts. Journal editors always consider the manuscript as a whole and will look at submitted illustrations with a critical eye. Editors evaluate the text and submitted graphics to reinforce, but not duplicate, each other. Editors will determine to keep or delete an illustration based upon a proper appreciation of the value of the illustration to the message presented in the text. Editors also take into account the fact that photographs become halftones in the printing process and the costs of halftone reproductions are high. If a physician writer wishes to reprint a diagram or illustration from another printed source, written permission must be obtained from the original author and the original source must be cited in the legend accompanying the reprinted figure. If photographs of persons are to be used as illustrations, either the persons in the photographs must not be identifiable or use of their photographs must be granted by written permission. Most things relating to written material can be adequately described by words used in the text. Some other things, however, are better described by an illustration. It is the fine line of balance between these two decisions that guides an experienced physician writer in selecting appropriate illustrations to include with the submitted manuscript.

GRAPHICS FOR SPOKEN MATERIAL

The function of 35mm slides, overhead projections, videotapes, and movie film, the graphics appropriate for use with spoken material, is to act as assisting devices to amplify specific points made by speakers when delivering their talks. These audiovisual aids are used to complement and enhance the message the speaker presents vocally and, as such, must be carefully selected in order to perform this task appropriately. Novice speakers not infrequently tend to overuse audiovisual aids and suffer the danger of losing the attention of audiences because of discontinuity. A sense of discrimination and balance is just as important for physician speakers in selecting the proper type and number of audiovisual aids to use as visual graphics as it is in selecting the proper words to use in the text of the talk. Audiovisual aids used with spoken material are helpful in amplifying and emphasizing the message to be delivered in the text of the talk, but are not as critical to the content of the spoken message as are the graphics used with written material. Physician speakers should compose the text for their talks in such a manner that, in the event of an unexpected equipment breakdown making it impossible to present audiovisual aids, the meaning of the spoken message can be conveyed to listeners entirely by means of the words in the text.

Slides

The visual aid used most frequently in medical conferences and talks are 35mm slides. The correct function of slides is to complement a talk in the same way that pictures enhance the effect of an advertisement.[10] Good slides can present data and information to listeners in a much more understandable fashion than can words from a speaker. Slides have their greatest usefulness as visual graphics if they:

1. Contain only enough information on each slide to clarify one major idea.
2. List the information on the slide horizontally with light type against a darker background. Most viewers find lower case letters easier to read on a slide than capital letters.
3. Are readable in the last row of a large auditorium, and
4. Show something that can not be explained as well without the slide.

Some physician speakers, because they are so familiar with their own work, do not use prepared texts but give organized and skillfully managed talks solely from slides, frequently projected on multiple screens. This is not a recommended technique for most physician speakers to attempt because only a small percentage of physician speakers can do it successfully and well. Also, it takes a very experienced and sophisticated speaker to get a meaningful message across while, simultaneously, filling multiple screens with constantly changing slides. For most physician speakers, this is an adventure that should not be undertaken. Sometimes there is a very fine line between a useful scientific message and confusing chaos.[3]

Slides prepared and used by physician speakers frequently contain too much data or information, are prepared in print sizes that are barely readable, and are projected on the screen for too short a time for full audience understanding. It has been estimated that only about 40 percent of slides shown at most major medical meetings are readable and self-explanatory.[11] Seven adjectives have been listed as being characteristic of good slides.[10] If more than two of the adjectives in the following list do not apply to a physician speaker's slides, it is believed the slides should be discarded and redone:

1. Appropriate. Tables and graphs used in published articles usually are inappropriate for use as slides to be shown during a talk.
2. Accurate. Speakers must make certain that data and information to be projected on slides is correct and no misspellings are present on the slide.
3. Legible. Choose upper and lower case consistently. Use upper case for titles and lower case for text. It is more arresting to use bullets or asterisks in summary slides than the more formal 1, 2, and 3.
4. Comprehensible. So much information should not be put on a slide that the speaker has to apologize for showing it. Such slides should be discarded and redone because viewers get no useful information from them.
5. Well executed. As often as possible, slides should be designed to be shown horizontally (landscape) rather than vertically (portrait). A viewing screen may cut off one end of a vertically designed slide when it is projected. Graphs that are to be projected as slides should be drawn on unlined paper. Graph paper should not be used in slides because the lines are confusing and distracting to viewers.
6. Interesting. This means the slide should be interesting to viewers, not just interesting to the speaker.
7. Memorable. Rarely achieved but the effort to attempt to create a memorable slide is worthwhile.

Good 35mm slides begin with thoughtful consideration of the data or information to be projected and good technical preparation of the slides themselves.[5] The following points are important in good slide preparation:

1. Physician speakers would be well advised to work with an expert in the preparation of slide material. Beautifully constructed slides can be made using computers and a graphics software program.
2. Limit title slides to five words or less. A title slide should supplement, not duplicate, data or information to be presented on the slides to follow.
3. The best slides are simple in both design and content. The ideal slide uses bright contrasting colors, covers one idea, features only one headline, and includes no more than seven lines of type. Using more than seven lines of type results in a cluttered appearing slide.
4. The layout of the slide should be simple with plenty of open space on the slide. Space between lines of type on the slide should be at least the height of a capital letter.
5. Do not project a slide containing a crowded and busy table or graph. Two or more simpler or less complicated slides are better than projecting one that is complicated in design. Audiences rapidly lose interest in slides that are too busy or too complicated in design.
6. Slides are useful for projecting graphs because the significance of data can be understood more readily by audiences if projected in the form of a graph rather than in the form of a table. Graphs projected on slides should be drawn on unlined paper, be simple in design, use rounded numbers, and contain as few captions as possible. Generally, it is easier for audiences to remember a pattern of lines than individual data points in a table, or even the speaker's words.
7. It is not considered necessary to make extensive use of color slides for every medical conference or talk. White lettering on a blue background is attractive and easy to read. For simplicity, plain, sharp black lettering on a white background is also easy to read. Color slides can be used selectively to supply emphasis when needed.
8. Make duplicate slides if there is a need to project the same slide at different times during the presentation.

Physicians can make their own 35mm slides using a computer and appropriate graphics software programs. The most useful software programs currently available for this purpose are: (1) Basic Graphics which is a program that should be adequate for general use. This program will handle the text and chart material that need to be shown as 35mm slides for most medical conferences and talks; (2) Advanced Graphics which is a program that allows the inclusion of design and drawing abilities not found in the Basic program. The advanced program is more technically difficult to use than the basic program and needs more hardware (speed) requirements. Clip art for the computer is another graphics possibility for physicians to use. Clip art is any artwork that is saved on a computer and can be brought into a word processing or graphics program. A clip art program allows physicians to add a graphic touch to 35mm slides. Most of the clip art programs currently available, however, are directed to business uses, but clip art programs for medical uses are being developed.

At most medical meetings, slides are shown from a single projector with the speaker serving the dual roles of narrator and operator of the remote control button to change the slide when needed. Slides should not be projected on the screen until they are needed in the talk, otherwise their presence on the screen diverts attention away from the speaker and the material being presented. Once the speaker has explained the contents of a slide to the audience and the slide has served its purpose, it should be taken off the screen. Slides that take attention from the speaker and the content of the talk for too long a period of time detract from what the speaker is saying. Because there is no agreed upon proper length of time for a slide to remain on the screen, it becomes a matter of experience and judgment for the speaker to make that determination. It is believed, however, that if a slide is not understood by the audience in about four seconds, it is a bad slide and should be redesigned.

Physician speakers should identify by name and program each slide they plan to use in the presentation. Slides should be numbered sequentially, placed in a carousel tray in correct order, and given to the projectionist in advance of the time scheduled for the talk to be presented. Speakers should make certain each slide to be projected is free of finger prints and smudges, is not upside down in the tray, and is slotted in the tray in the exact order in which each slide is to be projected during the talk. Physician speakers should note in the margins of their prepared texts the order and place for each slide to be projected so the talk and the slides used to complement the talk can be delivered to audiences in an orderly and synchronous fashion and within the time period allotted for the presentation.

Other Graphics

Overhead projections are best suited for viewing by smaller audiences in smaller meeting rooms. If overhead projections are used, it works best if each overhead is mounted in a frame. Mounting overheads in frames makes it easier to change the overhead during the presentation, and speakers can use the frame space for written notes. Videotapes and movie film can be shown, but are more expensive to produce and more difficult to project. Consequently, videotapes and movie film are the least used of the audiovisual aids available for medical talks.

If physician speakers wish to hand out printed material to audiences, it is best to hand it out after the talk has been given, otherwise the material will distract the audience during the presentation. One exception to this advice is the handing out of a talk outline which, if distributed before the talk begins, may clarify the presented information for listeners, particularly if the information to be presented is complex, or if the message to be delivered is complicated and involved.

References

1. Katz MJ. *Elements of the Scientific Paper*. New Haven, Conn: Yale University Press; 1985.
2. Tufte ER. *The Visual Display of Quantitative Information*. Cheshire, Conn: Graphics Press; 1985.
3. McClenahan J. And now, may we have the first slide? *Phila Med*. 1986; 82(8): 301.
4. Simmons D, ed. *Charts and Graphs: Guidelines for the Visual Presentation of Data in the Life Sciences*. Baltimore: MTP Press; 1980.
5. Foote MA. Incorporating slides can enhance and improve almost any presentation. *Amer Med Writers Assoc J*. 1989; 4(4): 11-13.
6. International Committee of Medical Journal Editors. Uniform requirements for manuscripts submitted to biomedical journals. *N Engl J Med*. 1991; 324(6): 424-428.
7. Macgregor AJ. *Graphics Simplified: How to Plan and Prepare Effective Charts, Graphs, Illustrations, and Other Visual Aids*. Toronto: University of Toronto Press; 1979.
8. Anderson PJ. Scientific Illustrations Committee of the Council of Biology Editors. Illustrating Science: Standards for publication. Bethesda, Maryland: Council Of Biology Editors; 1988.
9. Woodford FP, ed. *Scientific Writing for Graduate Students*. Bethesda, Md: Council of Biology Editors; 1986.
10. Evans M. The abuse of slides. *Br Med J*. 1978; 1: 905-908.
11. Kraft AR, Saletta JD, Moss GS, Herman CM, Tompkins RK. A critical appraisal of the effectiveness of scientific presentations. *Clin Res*. 1982; 30: 18-24.

9

Grant Writing

Grant writing requires a particularly precise and organized style because the purpose of applying for a grant is to ask someone for money to support a proposed research project. Two issues are paramount in writing grant proposals: having something worthwhile to say to the funding source, and saying it clearly.[1] Money to support research projects can come from varying sources including departmental or institutional funds, foundations of many types, and government sources such as the National Institutes of Health (NIH). All funding sources, regardless of type, have specific and often different purposes, goals, and special interests which are fundamental to their reason for supporting research projects. The first requirement facing a grant applicant is to make certain the content and emphasis of the research, as defined in the grant application, matches the purposes, goals, and special interests of the funding source from whom money is being requested. Before awarding research funds, most funding sources will require answers to three basic questions: (1) who the investigator is, (2) what the investigator wants to do, and (3) how much money is needed to do it. Answers to these and other questions make up the content material relating to the proposed research that is contained in the body of the grant application. How well and how persuasively this content material is presented to grant reviewers reflects the writing and organizational skills of the grant writer.

Because the demand for research money far exceeds the supply, applicants increase their chances of success by submitting interesting, well organized, and well written proposals. Grant writing calls for straightforward, concise language that incorporates appropriate technical terms.[2] The application must focus on a solid objective and be supported by a clear and concise plan for its accomplishment. Trying to pursue multiple hypotheses or solve all possible problems in a single application seriously weakens the effort. Diffuseness in organizing and writing the grant application and lack of focus in its research plan are major reasons why some grant requests are not approved and funded. Successful applications clearly and persuasively describe what questions, issues, or hypotheses are to be addressed, what the investigator or others have done before in leading up to the project, how the work is to be carried out, and for how long support will be needed to bring the project to a definitive conclusion in a reasonable time frame.[3] Resources allocated by educational, governmental, or philanthropic organizations for the performance of specific scientific work should be only used for that purpose unless the granting agency gives specific permission for a reallocation of the resources.

The writing of the grant application must follow exactly the instructions and guidelines for the format and content of the proposal as stated by the granting source. The style and format of good applications combine good writing skills with a clear writing style. The content of successful grant applications starts with a good idea and approaches the answers to the proposed questions with good science. The underlying good ideas and good science contained in an application must come from each investigator's creativity and skill. Hypothesis-generated research that is directed toward an important mechanism of action is often most successful. Demonstrating the capability for successfully accomplishing the proposed research is the responsibility of the applicant and must be demonstrated in the strength and persuasiveness of the grant application. The application must contain enough preliminary data to satisfy even the most skeptical grant reviewer that the applicant has the ability to carry out a full-scale project. Previously published research, preliminary data obtained with small grant funds or seed money, and identification of appropriate collaborators are helpful elements. The application must deliver a clear message to grant reviewers that the proposed project as described in the application can be done and is worth doing. A successful and well written application provides the grant reviewer with a clear focus of the hypothesis and research plan and an appreciation of the logical and scientific approach needed to accomplish the goals of the research project as proposed by the applicant.[4]

In grant terms, the lead researcher is called the *principal investigator* who, in addition to being the lead researcher, carries the responsibility for making certain the application is written with great care and follows the instructions issued by the funding source. A poorly worded description of the project, an error in addition of the budget, or an unclear graph of preliminary results could lead to a rejection of the application. The principal investigator of a basic science or clinical research project is also responsible for proposing, designing, and reporting the research. The principal investigator may delegate portions of the work to other individuals, but this does not relieve the principal investigator of the responsibility of his or her conduct. Inexperienced grant writers should seek advice about content and budget of the application from one or more experienced investigators. The principal investigator, and the proposal writer if different persons, must be involved with the budget process so questions about how the budget relates to the proposed research can be answered appropriately.

The applicant must be certain the budget is completely justified and commensurate with the scope and relevance of the proposed project. Grant reviewers are too sophisticated not to recognize and reject inflated budgets. On the other hand, a budget that is too modest may suggest to a grant reviewer that the applicant has poor judgment. The applicant must be certain appropriate indirect costs are included in the budget figures. *Indirect costs* are additional sums added to the budget request to support administrative and maintenance costs incurred by the grantee's institution. These costs add a fixed percentage of the budget for the research project to the total financial request. The size of the percentage to be added for indirect costs is determined by the applicant's institution.

Grant applicants should plan enough time to be able to write multiple drafts and to receive critical preliminary reviews from colleagues and experienced grant writers prior to the deadline for submission of the grant request to the funding source. Generally, sources of data can be cited in the body of the proposal, but footnotes and unsupported assumptions are to be avoided. Send the original proposal and include copies only if the funding source requests them. Extravagant proposal packaging should be avoided. An unusual proposal format or packaging style risks focusing more attention on the form of the proposal than on its content and risks suggesting to the proposal recipient that the applicant has a tendency to waste money. If the submitted grant application is rejected for funding, the rejection notice may come with a request for more data, a specific objection, or a suggestion for a revised approach. An applicant whose grant request is rejected initially should plan to respond to the criticisms or suggestions offered by reviewers and resubmit the application. The chances of receiving funding appear to improve each time an application is improved and resubmitted.[5] Most grantmakers tend to regard tenacity in grant applicants as a virtue.

FOUNDATIONS

There are approximately 24 000 private foundations that give money to support projects. However, foundations are of varying size and have differing purposes, goals, and special interests that dictate for whom and for what purposes funds are awarded. For that reason it is of particular importance that applications to foundations be tailored to reflect these special interests. Foundations solicit research proposals on subjects of special interest to them and may consider unsolicited proposals from grant applicants. Some foundations are willing to take a chance on innovative projects, while others have special funds to support proposals submitted by different minorities. Approximately 4800 of the total of 24 000 private foundations provide 80 percent of all foundation money for approved projects.

Total giving from foundations is about $4 billion per year, of which about 5 to 6 percent of this sum is related to research in medicine or the life sciences.

Persons seeking grants from private foundations and other grantmakers such as health related institutions like the American Cancer Society, or the Arthritis Foundation, among others, often must present their ideas in the form of a written proposal. However, the focus of the proposal must fall within the solicited foundation's current areas of interest if there is to be any hope of receiving funding. In some instances the foundation program staff will work with a grant applicant to sharpen the proposal or its focus or to broaden its area of coverage.

Relevant information about funding capabilities and special interests of foundations can be obtained from the Foundation Center, an independent national service organization established by foundations to provide an authoritative source of information on private philanthropic giving. The New York, Washington, D.C., Cleveland, and San Francisco reference collections operated by the Foundation Center offer a wide variety of services and comprehensive collections of information on foundations and grants. The Foundation Center maintains the *Foundation Grants Index,* which is one of the first tools a grant seeker should use to identify foundations that might be interested in funding the grant seeker's project. Potential grant applicants can ask the Foundation Center for a COMSEARCH printout. This will set in motion a search of the *Grants Index* database to identify foundations with interests similar to the interests expressed by an applicant.

After appropriate foundations have been identified, the applicant should request information about guidelines for grant applications from selected foundations. While few foundations have printed grant application forms, it cannot be assumed that each foundation will issue the same instructions for the format and content of the grant application. Most foundations will ask for a brief letter in which the applicant identifies himself or herself, describes the research plan, and specifies the amount of funding being sought. The applicant may or may not be requested to submit a more formal written proposal along with the letter. The Robert Wood Johnson Foundation, for example, asks applicants to provide the foundation with a letter, not to exceed four pages, describing the project, its objectives, and a number of other pieces of information as described in their application guidelines. A full proposal may then be requested, based on that letter. If so, the applicant will be given instructions regarding what information the proposal should contain, and how to present it. For a modest charge, the Grantsmanship Center in Los Angeles will send interested persons a booklet entitled "Program Planning and Proposal Writing," which gives instructions on proposal writing and proposal content for use in instances where foundations and other funding sources provide no specific guidelines.[6]

Regardless of how the proposal is structured, the criteria used by most foundations in evaluating a grant application include: (1) the excellence of the proposal, (2) the judged ability of the applicant to carry out the work to a definitive conclusion, and (3) the adequacy of the laboratory, institution, or other facilities where the work is to be carried out. Some foundations require successful applicants to submit financial reports quarterly, detailing how the awarded grant money was spent before allocating the next quarter's funds.

THE NATIONAL INSTITUTES OF HEALTH (NIH)

One of the main functions of the National Institutes of Health (NIH) is to grant funds to outside investigators in support of biomedical research.[7] The purpose of these grants is to facilitate the pursuit of a scientific focus in the area of the investigator's interest and competence. The majority of NIH awards are in the form of investigator-initiated research project grant applications (coded RO1 by NIH), regardless of whether the application is for support of basic or clinical research, but other types of grant awards also exist.[8] There is a constantly changing list of grant awards developed at NIH, and information regarding them can be obtained from the Division of Research Grants at NIH or through the office of sponsored programs at the applicant's own institution. For example, the current FIRST awards, which have different review criteria than the regular RO1 grants, are considered excellent grant opportunities for young investigators.

Original and innovative proposals that are supported by good science have the best chance of being approved and funded. NIH grant proposals must be hypothesis driven, not methodology or technique driven. A good research idea based on a meaningful hypothesis is the cornerstone of a successful NIH grant application. It is important to define the rationale for developing the hypothesis that may be based on the applicant's publications, the publications of others, or on preliminary data to be given in detail in the application. The hypothesis should be such that it can be proved or disproved by the proposed experiments. Before embarking on the arduous task of writing an NIH grant application, investigators must realize they will be competing against some of the best scientists in the country for a share of the biomedical research money allocated to NIH by Congress.

Applying for NIH funding is a difficult, demanding, and time consuming process because the NIH application form (Grant Application Form PHS 398) imposes very strict guidelines on its structure and format. In addition to good science, applicants for NIH funding must present a well organized and well written grant proposal.[9] The application itself is strictly constrained as to page length so close attention to detail is required. If the application is for a clinical study, statistical support is essential, and the experimental plan must document methods for patient accrual and numbers of patients required to meet specific statistical objectives.[10] It is also important to demonstrate sound procedures for data collection, management, and analysis. Applicants for NIH grant awards should be aware of the significant amount of time involved in the turn around of a grant at NIH between submission, review by the initial review group, and receipt of the summary statement or pink sheet. An additional nine months can be the cost if an approved grant has to be revised and resubmitted. A great deal of lost time can be prevented, therefore, by not submitting hastily prepared applications but, rather, applications that are well thought out, well organized, and well written.

Brevity, clarity, and organization are essential components of successful NIH grant applications. Such an application focuses on a solid objective and is supported by a clear and concise plan for accomplishing the specific aims. Successful applicants present proposals that address important questions that need answering, and are resolvable in a reasonable time frame in an appropriate research environment. In addition, the research proposes a hypothesis that is capable of being tested. The research description is written clearly in logical sequences and is totally understandable to grant reviewers. Although NIH is not likely to fund purchases of routine laboratory equipment that it believes should be provided by the sponsoring institution, it frequently funds the purchase of equipment that is documented in the proposal as essential to the research project and not readily available in some other nearby laboratory. If approved and funded, grants are awarded for periods of two to five years, depending upon need or excellence of the proposal. Most grant awards are for three years. Grants can be renewed but the grantee must file for renewal, including submission of a progress report demonstrating satisfactory progress during the previous grant period.

It is admittedly difficult for young or first time applicants to obtain approval and funding of their proposals at NIH. If a weak hypothesis, weak science, or a poorly written grant proposal are eliminated as causes of rejection, the major remaining reason for rejection is that the investigators have not yet established a research track record nor have established their research credibility at NIH. The way out of this dilemma is to get seed money from some other source to support a pilot study to develop preliminary data that can then be used to bolster the investigator's claim to NIH that the proposed work can be done. Such an investigator should design a pilot project and apply for a relatively small amount of money (seed money) from his or her home institution or other sources, such as specialty medicine or specialty oriented funding sources. The investigator should then perform the pilot study, present the results at a national meeting, and attempt to get the results published in an acceptable journal. Potential applicants would be advised not to apply to NIH for funding unless and until the applicant has prior data, publications, or has established criteria to prove he or she can do the work proposed in the application and will not waste the taxpayers' money. Because credibility and experience must be established before asking NIH for large sums of money, most young and first time applicants, even with the required preliminary data, seem to be better regarded if their first applications contain a modest budget in the range of $70 000 to $100 000.

The NIH Grant Application Review Process

There are usually three review cycles or rounds per year, each consisting of two stages: the initial scientific peer review stage and the subsequent council or

GRANT WRITING

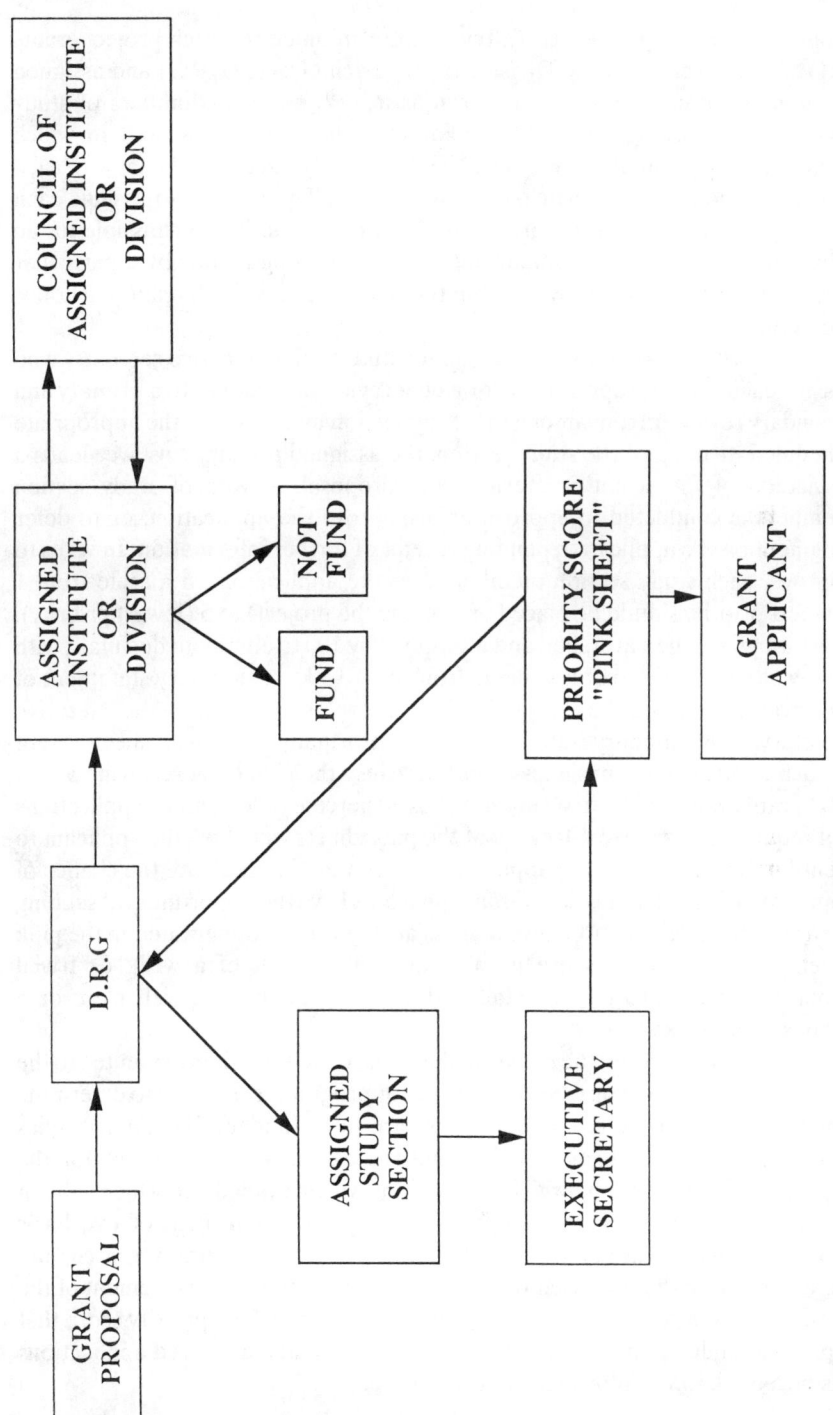

Fig 7.--NIH grant proposal process.

program review stage (Figure 7). Investigator-initiated research project grants (RO1s) are received by the Division of Research Grants (DRG) and assigned to an appropriate review panel known as a *study section*. Members of study sections are working scientists familiar with the field of research in which support is being sought. On request, NIH will supply a grant applicant with a list of current members of particular study sections. The DRG also assigns each grant application to an appropriate institute or division. It is permissible for an applicant to submit an accompanying letter requesting review by a particular study section, institute, or division, but the DRG is under no obligation to honor the request.

Each study section is staffed by an institute-based executive secretary who assigns each received application for a peer review assessment to a primary and secondary reviewer from among the study section members. At the appropriate scheduled meeting of the study section, the assigned primary reviewer leads a discussion of the scientific merit of the proposal. A vote of study section members is conducted to approve or disapprove the application, or to defer judgment on the application pending receipt of further information. In votes to approve, each study section member rates the application on a scale from 1 (highest priority should be placed on funding the project) to 5 (lowest priority). The ratings are then averaged and multiplied by 100 to eliminate decimals, with the resulting priority scores ranging from 100 to 500. A summary statement of the review, including the assigned priority score, is prepared by the executive secretary. This summary statement, known informally as the pink sheet, is sent to each applicant as a progress report. Because the chance of receiving a new NIH grant award on the first submission is 30 percent or less, many applications will require resubmission. Review of the pink sheets will allow the applicant to identify what changes in the application are required to improve the chance of approval for the resubmission. Grant applicants have the opportunity of sending a letter of rebuttal if they believe there is an error in anything stated in the pink sheet. A poor priority score is most often the result of a weak or trivial hypothesis, an inadequately detailed description of the research plan, or a proposal that lacks focus.[11]

The application and the results of the initial review are then presented to the advisory council of the institute or division for program review and to determine which of the approved grant applications are to be funded. The council relies heavily on the study section review and the assigned priority score for the application in determining which applications will be funded and which will not be funded. The council reviews approved applications in light of two basic considerations: the availability of institute funds for extramural research, and the contribution the proposed research would make to the advancement of the mission of the institute or division if it were performed. The priority score that separates funded approved applications from unfunded approved applications has become known, informally, as the *payline*.

Writing an NIH Grant Application

Applications to NIH for investigator-initiated research project grants (RO1s) are made on Grant Application Form PHS 398, available on request from NIH or from the research grant administrator in the applicant's sponsoring institution. This form is used also for Research Career Development awards and Institutional National Research Service awards. The application package contains specific instructions for every step in the process of writing the application and these instructions must be followed exactly. Writing for an NIH grant requires a clear, brief, and to the point style because of the detail requested, and the page and space limitations imposed on the grant writer. For example, the title of the proposed research project must not exceed 56 typewritten spaces including spaces between words and punctuation, and subsections A through D of Section 2 (Research Plan) must not exceed 20 pages.

The application form consists of three sections, with the first two sections containing multiple subsections. *Section 1* establishes the level of expertise and credibility of the principal investigator and contains the following subsections: (1) Face Page, Description and Key Personnel, Table of Contents, (2) Detailed Budget for First 12-Month Budget Period, (3) Budget for Entire Proposed Project Period, (4) Budgets Pertaining to Consortium/Contractual Arrangements, (5) Biographical Sketch--Principal Investigator/Program Director, (6) Other Biographical Sketches, (7) Other Support, and (8) Resources and Environment. Section 1 is designed to assemble the essential database concerning the investigator, the institution in which the investigator plans to perform the research, the environment and resources available to the investigator for the conduct of the proposed project, and the required budget. The budget must be compiled realistically and honestly with each budget item justified.

Section 2 is devoted to details of the research plan and is the section grant reviewers examine most critically. Section 2 contains the following subsections: (A) Specific Aims, (B) Background and Significance, (C) Progress Report/Preliminary Studies, (D) Experimental Design and Methods, (E) Human Subjects, (F) Vertebrate Animals, (G) Consultants/Collaborators, (H) Consortium/Contractual Arrangements, and (I) Literature Cited. The research idea and its background rationale are developed in the first three of these subsections. Often the difference between approval and disapproval of a grant application relates directly to the strength or weakness of how the research plan is formulated and described. Information given in the Experimental Design and Methods subsection to support the proposed hypothesis must be well focused and contain sufficient detail to permit grant reviewers to judge the applicant's knowledge of potential problems that may arise in carrying out the proposed experiments. A part of this subsection should supply details on how the investigator plans to deal with problems in methodology. The investigator who addresses in the application potential problems that might arise during the course of the research, and gives details on how he or she plans to deal with them, shows a foresight that usually impresses reviewers. In addition, the experimental design must provide convincing evidence to grant reviewers that the applicant can develop the necessary flexibility and alternate procedures to meet these problems should they arise, and also must contain a logical schedule for completion of the project. The accompanying instructions caution the grant writer not to scatter literature citations throughout the text, but rather to list them at the end of section 2.

Section 3 is the Appendix, which is devoted to supplementary background information designed to strengthen the research proposal. Background material documenting preliminary studies, supplementary background graphs, diagrams, tables, and charts directly pertinent to the application go in the Appendix. If the application is for renewal of an awarded NIH grant (called Competing Continuation and Supplemental Applications by NIH), copies of publications, manuscripts accepted for publication, patents, invention reports, and other printed materials that have resulted from the project since it was last reviewed competitively are included in the Appendix. All graphs, diagrams, tables, and charts must be drawn in black ink. Photographs, oversized documents, or materials that cannot be photocopied also are to be submitted in the Appendix.

Because of their particular importance to the strength of an NIH investigator-initiated research project grant application, grant writers must pay special attention to the writing of the Description in Section 1 and Specific Aims, Background and Significance, Progress Report/Preliminary Studies, and Experimental Design and Methods subsections of Section 2. Examples showing how the Description, Specific Aims, Background and Significance, and Experimental Design and Methods subsections might be written are provided. The provided examples were written only for the purpose of illustrating a writing style and form for these particular subsections. The content matter of these examples is deliberately preposterous and concerns a fictional NIH grant application titled "Testosterone, Weightlessness, and Bone Mass in Male Rats." This fictional application proposes the erroneous hypothesis that the taking of supplemental testosterone by male astronauts would eliminate the osteoporosis that can accompany the prolonged weightlessness involved in space flights.

Description Subsection

Description is, in effect, an abstract of the proposed research study and must be concise enough to explain the study to a reader and short enough to fit in the rectangular space measuring 7½ inches by 5¼ inches that is provided on the form. The grant writer must present the application's long-term objective and specific aims, make reference to the health relatedness of the project, and concisely describe the methodology for achieving these goals. Summaries of past accomplishments and the use of the first person should be avoided. The Description is meant to serve as a succinct and accurate description of the proposed work when separated from the total application package and read as an isolated segment by some external person such as a grant reviewer.

Example (Description):

Reports from NASA and Skylab describe demineralization with subsequent loss of bone mass in male astronauts subjected to prolonged weightlessness. The mechanism of action is unclear. A pilot study evaluated the effect of castration, the effect of exercise (with one exercise group simulating weightlessness), and possible interaction between castration and exercise in male Wistar rats.

The results suggest that castration itself may have a effect on all groups but the data strongly suggest the effect seems especially large in the group with simulated weightlessness. Castration plus simulated weightlessness seems to have a synergistic effect greater than the sum of individual effects. A relationship seems to exist between testosterone, weightlessness, and bone mass in male Wistar rats that could have relevance to the U.S. space program. The pilot study results support the need for a larger study to include both bone density measurements and three-point bending bone strength measurements in its design. Based on results of the pilot study, it is estimated that 20 animals per group would give a power of 80 percent to detect a difference between subgroups of approximately 20 percent (density) and 10 percent (strength).

Specific Aims Subsection

Specific Aims is the subsection in which the grant writer, within a recommended length of one page, has to state the broad, long-term objectives of the proposed research, and outline what the research described in the application is intended to accomplish. The hypothesis upon which the proposed study is based, and the logical scientific questions required to test the hypothesis must be included. The aims of the research project must be focused and clearly stated. The scope of the proposed work should be capable of being accomplished within the proposed grant period.

Example (Specific Aims):

Reports from NASA indicate male astronauts subjected to prolonged weightlessness are prone to develop bone demineralization with subsequent loss of bone mass. These effects define osteoporosis, a condition in which decreasing bone density weakens bone, causing a susceptibility to fracture. Osteoporosis is the leading cause of fractures in postmenopausal women and older persons of both sexes, and the mechanisms of action for the disorder in these groups of individuals are well understood. What is not presently understood is why healthy young males subjected to prolonged weightlessness develop osteoporosis.

It is apparent that a direct relationship exists in females between hypogonadism as measured by decreasing estrogen levels and bone mass. Studies show that estrogen plays a vital role in maintaining bone mass in females. Studies also show that supplemental estrogen therapy restores depleted bone mass, provided other variables, such as dietary calcium, vitamin D, and exercise, are controlled. No comparable data exists for males.

The purpose of the proposed study is to test the hypothesis that a relationship exists between hypogonadism, as measured by a decreased testosterone level, weightlessness, and bone mass in male Wistar rats. The experimental approach is to measure and compare bone density and bone strength as determined by digital radiography and three-point bending stress among a group of normal and a group of castrated rats subjected to one of four exercise models, one of which simulates weightlessness, for a total study period of 24 weeks.

Background and Significance Subsection

Background and Significance is the subsection in which the grant writer, within a two to three page limitation, must sketch the background of the proposal, evaluate existing knowledge, and identify specifically the knowledge gaps which the proposed project is intended to fill. This is the subsection in which the grant writer presents the importance of the proposed research and defines the "big picture." However, the grant writer must be careful not to present an overly ambitious scope of work for the current project period. This subsection is the place where the grant writer must document an understanding of the relevant and current questions in the area of the proposed investigation and make clear to grant reviewers that successfully completing the proposed experiments will make a meaningful contribution to the knowledge base of the subject in question.

Example (Background and Significance):

Previous studies have reported that the female sex hormone, estrogen, plays a vital role in maintaining bone mass in females. The two female groups at greatest risk for the development of osteoporosis are postmenopausal women and young athletes with exercise induced amenorrhea. Studies in both groups have shown conclusively that supplemental estrogen therapy restores depleted bone mass, provided other variables such as dietary calcium, vitamin D, and exercise are controlled. For a number of years the assumption that exercise prevents osteoporosis in both sexes has been a widely held belief by most authorities in the field. In 1984, the National Institutes of Health Consensus Development Panel recommended a program of modest weight-bearing exercises for the possible prevention of osteoporosis in both sexes. In addition to the salutary effect of weight-bearing exercise noted on bone mass, dynamic loads applied to bone have been shown to increase both bone formation and bone mass in both sexes.

It is apparent that a relationship exists between hypogonadism as measured by decreased estrogen levels and bone mass in females. It is also apparent that a relationship exists between bone mass and aging, weight-bearing exercises, and dynamic bone loading in both sexes. No studies to date have explored in depth the relationship between weightlessness, hypogonadism as measured by decreased testosterone levels, and bone mass in males. In view of the Skylab findings demonstrating a relationship between prolonged weightlessness and bone mass in male astronauts, it seems that a pivotal question to address is whether a relationship also exists between hypogonadism as measured by decreased testosterone levels and bone mass in males subjected to a weightless environment.

The principal investigator recently completed a small pilot study designed as a preliminary testing of the hypothesis stated above. The study population consisted of 16 sexually mature young male Wistar rats. Of these 16 rats, 8 were rendered hypogonadic by surgical castration 4 weeks prior to the start of the experiments. Serum testosterone levels averaged 0.005 ml in the castrated group as compared to 2.75 ml in the 8 non-castrated rats at the start of the experiments. All rats were fed the same diet for the 12-week study period. Bone density measurements of the right hip were made by digital radiography in all rats prior to the start of the study.

The rats were randomly assigned in aliquots of 2 from each group to one of four exercise models and made to perform the task assigned to the particular model group for 12 weeks. Bone density measurements of the right hip were obtained by digital radiography at the completion of the study. The values obtained from each exercise model were compared with each other and with the average values for normal male rats documented by Wesson in the *Journal of Analytical Anatomy*.

The four exercise models were:

1. Normal cage activity used for the control group;
2. A specially constructed swimming tank used to simulate weightlessness;
3. An 8 percent sloped running track; and
4. A velcro weight pack averaging 60 percent of body weight was worn constantly by this group in addition to exercising daily on a 45-degree inclined treadmill.

The results of the pilot study indicated that exercise in the absence of castration did not have a substantial effect on bone mass in male rats. In all exercise groups, castration itself may have a small effect on bone mass in male rats. The data strongly suggested, however, that loss of bone mass seemed especially large in the group of castrated rats exercised in the special swimming tank which simulated weightlessness. The mean bone density as measured by digital radiography for this group of rats averaged 357.5 hounsfield units as compared to 252.5 units in the non-castrated swimming rats, 275.3 units in the castrated control group, and 267 units in Wesson's normal rat population. Castration plus simulated weightlessness seems to have a synergistic effect greater than the sum of individual effects. These results suggest a strong relationship exists between testosterone, weightlessness, and bone mass in male rats and support the need for a larger study to include both bone density measurements and three-point bending bone strength measurements in its design.

Progress Report/Preliminary Studies Subsection

Progress Report/Preliminary Studies is the subsection in which the grant writer has six to eight pages to provide an account of the principal investigator's preliminary studies pertinent to the application and any other information that will help establish the experience and competence of the investigator to pursue the proposed research project to a definitive conclusion. Enough completed work should be described to convince grant reviewers that the project has an excellent chance of succeeding, and that the investigator has the skills and experience to do the work. Titles and complete references to appropriate publications and manuscripts accepted for publication may be listed. Sets of other background materials must be included in the Appendix.

If the application is for renewal of an awarded NIH grant, this subsection is designed to supply the progress report demonstrating satisfactory progress during the previous grant period. Copies of publications, manuscripts accepted for publication, patents, invention reports, and other printed materials that have resulted from the project since it was last reviewed competitively are to be included in the Appendix.

Experimental Design and Methods Subsection

Experimental Design and Methods is the subsection in which the design of the proposed experiments and the methodologies that will be used to meet the proposed objectives are described and is, perhaps, the most important part of the entire application package. It is the evaluation of this subsection of the application by grant reviewers that contributes the most in voting for the priority score. In a well-written Experimental Design and Methods subsection, a grant reviewer obtains a clear focus of the hypothesis and research plan and an appreciation of the logical approach needed to accomplish the goals of the research project as proposed by the applicant. It is critical to the final priority score rating of the proposed project that this subsection be written with extreme care and a great deal of thoughtful planning. This subsection of the grant application must be particularly well focused and organized so as to convince a busy grant reviewer that the applicant can do what is proposed, possesses the technical skills and research background necessary to perform the proposed experiments, and can reach the described objectives. Many experienced grant writers spend more time on this subsection than any of the others, and often begin work on this subsection first so as to minimize or avoid the frequent criticism that the described research plan lacks focus. Although no specific page limitation is imposed on this subsection, the combined total for subsections

Specific Aims, Background and Significance, Progress Report/Preliminary Studies, and Experimental Design and Methods may not exceed 20 pages.

An important part of conducting research is thorough planning and the grant application must be written so that a clear research plan is conveyed to grant reviewers. This requires the grant applicant to propose a high quality scientific approach to answering questions posed by the hypothesis. The research should proceed in a step-by-step logical sequence that is documented in a work schedule. Each described experiment should be responsive to a specific aim of the research and fit into a reasonable overall approach. The applicant must give and justify the rationale for the particular experimental methods selected. The technical protocols will require sufficient descriptive detail to assure grant reviewers that the research will achieve valid results. The applicant must be able to convey a clear definition of the assumptions and limitations of the planned research, and identify problems or pitfalls that might occur during the course of the research, and the planned solutions should they arise. It is also important that the statistical aspects of the application be addressed correctly in this subsection.[12] The precision and accuracy of the proposed methods must be clearly and carefully defined. Statistical power calculations should be used, when appropriate, to determine the number and type of experiments.

Example (Experimental Design and Methods):

The determination of bone mass involves measuring bone density and mechanical bone strength. The technique of digital radiography measures bone radiodensity in hounsfield units. Because x-ray penetration is inversely proportional to bone mass, the higher the number of hounsfield units, the less dense and more osteoporotic is the bone measured. The validity and clinical relevance of digital radiography as an accurate tool for measuring bone density has been established. Three-point bending records bone strength in newtons by measuring mechanical resistance of bone to breaking. The lower the number of newtons to break point the weaker is the bone measured. In-vitro studies have demonstrated the validity of using three-point bending stress as an accurate measurement of bone strength in both normal and osteoporotic bone. Wesson, using digital radiography and three-point bending stress, has documented average bone density and bone strength determinations in mature male Wistar rats.

Based on the results of the pilot study, it is estimated that 20 animals per group would give a power of 80 percent to detect a difference between subgroups of approximately 20 percent in bone density and 10 percent in mechanical bone strength. Based on the above statistical determination, the study population will consist of 160 sexually mature young male Wistar rats. The subgroups will be exercised in one of the four exercise models for a total period of 24 weeks. One-half of the study population (80 rats) will be randomly selected and rendered hypogonadic by surgical castration 4 weeks prior to the start of the experiments. The pilot study demonstrated that 4 weeks was sufficient time to decrease testosterone serum levels to negligible levels (0.005 ml.) All rats will be fed the same diet for the 24-week study period.

The 80 young mature non-castrated male Wistar rats (Group A) and the 80 young mature castrated male Wistar rats (Group B) will be randomly assigned in aliquots of 20 rats from each group to one of the four exercise models and made to perform the task assigned to the particular group for a total time period of 24 weeks.

Group 1. (20 rats, Group A; 20 rats, Group B). These rats will be allowed normal cage activity for 24 weeks and will function as the control group.
Group 2. (swimmers, 20 rats, Group A; 20 rats, Group B). These rats will swim for one hour daily in a specially constructed swimming tank that simulates weightlessness. Prior testing of the tank demonstrated that rats in the tank carry approximately 5 percent of body weight on their tails. Total test period will be 24 weeks.
Group 3. (runners, 20 rats, Group A; 20 rats, Group B). These rats will run for one hour daily on an 8 percent slope for 24 weeks.
Group 4. (weight lifters, 20 rats, Group A; 20 rats, Group B). These rats will wear a velcro weight pack averaging 60 percent of body weight and will exercise on a 45-degree inclined treadmill for 30 minutes at 0.25 miles per hour daily for 24 weeks.

All rats will be sacrificed at the end of the 24-week study period. Digital radiography will be used to measure radiodensity of the right hip and three-point bending stress will be applied to the proximal left femur to measure bone strength. The measurements obtained in the two groups of rats in the four exercise models will be compared to each other, and to the averaged normal values of 267 hounsfield units for radiodensity and 200 newtons for bone strength as reported by Wesson, and conclusions drawn.

The final step in the application process is to complete the checklist. The checklist is for the use of NIH staff and will be detached from the application package by staff upon receipt and assignment of the grant application by DRG. Mail or deliver to the Division of Research Grants the complete and signed typewritten original of the application, six signed, exact, clear, single-sided photocopies, and the Appendix in one package. Pay particular attention to the application receipt dates printed in Grant Application Form PHS 398. These receipt dates are selected to correlate with the three yearly grant review cycles conducted by NIH.

References

1. Merritt DH. Grantsmanship: an exercise in lucid presentation. *Clin Res.* 1963; 11: 375-377.

2. DeBakey L, DeBakey S. The art of persuasion: logic and language in proposal writing. *Grants Magazine*. 1978; 1: 43-60.
3. Balch CM. Ten principles for writing grants. *Amer Coll Surg Bull*. 1987; 72(9): 17.
4. DeBakey L. The persuasive proposal. *J Tech Writing and Commun*. 1976; 6: 5-25.
5. Williamson D. The grant game. Princeton Alumni Weekly. February 22, 1989: 16-21.
6. The Grantsmanship Center, 650 S. Spring Street, PO Box 6210, Los Angeles, Ca. 90014.
7. Executive Office of the President, Office of Management and Budget. Catalog of Federal Domestic Assistance. Published annually. Washington, D.C. 1992
8. Zinner MJ. Obtaining NIH grants. *Bull Amer Coll Surgs*. 1987; 72(9): 16-17.
9. Niederhuber JE. Writing a successful grant application. *J Surg Res*. 1985; 39: 277-284.
10. Wyngarden JB. The clinical investigator as an endangered species. *N Engl J Med*. 1979; 301: 1254-1259.
11. Cuca JM. NIH grant applications for clinical research: reasons for poor ratings or disapproval. *Clin Res*. 1983; 31: 453-463.
12. Eastman JD., Smith EO'B, Klein ER. Medical writers and editors should learn fundamentals of statistical principles. *Amer Med Writers Assoc J*. 1990; 5(4): 14-17.

10

Communicating with Patients

Successful patient care, be it in an outpatient or inpatient setting, is highly dependent upon an appreciation of the rights and responsibilities of both parties involved in the physician-patient interaction, as well as on effective communication between physicians and patients. To be effective, communication with patients must convey concern, compassion, and information on the part of the physician because the object of the communication is a concerned patient, a fellow human being apprehensive about his or her own state of health.[1] The ability to help patients requires that physicians demonstrate an understanding of the human aspects of disease. A principal function for a clinician is to give substance at all times to this universal reaching out for help and hope. Physicians and patients have different roles in this interaction, in addition to having unique responsibilities to each other. If these different roles and responsibilities within the clinical encounter are not understood and respected by physicians and patients, conflicts in communication between both parties may arise which often lead to dissatisfaction with the results of the clinical encounter. Effective physician-patient communication helps improve patient compliance with medical recommendations and the outcomes of medical care and, in the aggregate, saves time for both participants in the clinical interaction.

Previously healthy people can suddenly become ill and be plunged, totally unprepared, into an unfamiliar and frightening world of modern high technology medicine, a world in which the direction of their lives and the impact of their own unique personality is subordinated and diminished somewhat for a period of time by the frightening environment in which they find themselves, and by the medical authority exercised by physicians. It must be recognized and understood by physicians that illness creates an abnormally sensitive emotional state in many patients. If hospitalized, patients suffer loss of privacy and control of their lives and are isolated from their usual support systems and people. The intensity, emotional content, and connection to fundamental aspects of life involved in hospital encounters give hospitals a somewhat fearful connotation in the consciousness of most patients. Regardless of whether the scenario for this unsettling clinical experience is an outpatient or inpatient setting, it is how the scenario plays out that determines whether or not there will be problems with physician-patient communication. If a sick person is unaware of the rights and duties of being a patient, his or her communications are liable to be inept and to evoke aberrant responses from physicians and nurses. In turn, physicians by virtue of their professional education, personality, and work setting take control of medical care delivery situations but, at the same time, tend to markedly and consistently underestimate patients' level of comprehension about their own medical condition. American patients, by contrast to others, seem to be extraordinarily well informed and demanding purchasers of medical services. An American patient is more likely to have read relevant medical information in the newspapers and to have seen it on television, to have his or her own preferences about diagnostic procedures and treatment options, to obtain a second opinion, and to engage in medical malpractice litigation.[2] A better understanding of how conflicts between patients' rights and responsibilities and the medical authority of physicians could contribute to weakening of physician-patient communication should help physicians avoid such conflicts and become better communicators.[3]

Parsons defined the four essential aspects of the "sick role," sometimes called "Parsons' Postulates," which speak to the rights and responsibilities of patients.[4] First, depending on the nature and severity of the illness, the sick person is exempted from some or all of his or her normal responsibilities. Second, the sick person can not help being ill and can not get well by an act of decision or will. Third, the sick person is expected to want to get well as soon as possible. Fourth, the sick person is expected to seek help, usually from a physician, and cooperate with that help in an effort to get well. Physicans, on their part, must appreciate the origin, responsibility, and consequences of their medical authority in order not to abuse it.[5] Authority exercised appropriately by physicians in medical care situations can be therapeutic and is associated with positive patient responses. Authority exercised by physicians in a thoughtless and insensitive fashion, on the other hand, can have a negative and distressing effect on physician-patient communication. Medical authority is believed to combine three types of authority, sapiental, moral, and charismatic authority. *Sapiental* authority means the right to be heard that is derived from knowledge or expertise. *Moral* authority stems from physicians doing what is expected of them as physicians and their concern with the good of the patient. *Charismatic* authority is the right to control and direct derived from a God-given grace. This element of physician authority reflects the original unity of religion and medicine in the ancient world, and which still persists in some parts of the world. It is the element of charismatic authority that colors what we, as physicians, refer to as the art of medicine and bedside manner. It was charismatic authority the Swedish physican-author, Axel Munthe, had in mind when asked the question: "What is the secret of success?" His answer: "To inspire confidence. The doctor who possesses this gift can almost raise the dead."[6]

Patients consider confidence a desirable trait for physicians to possess and want to believe their own physicians are omnipotent in medical matters. Wise physicians, however, realize that the realities of modern medicine with its attendant uncertainties make confidence tempered by honesty and sincerity a better course to follow. Patients tend to be the losers when overconfident physicians, by ignoring these uncertainties, promise them more than they or medicine can deliver. Medicine has traditionally presented itself, both to individual patients and to society, as an activity in which its practitioners are virtually incapable of error, and long years of education and hospital training tends to induce a self confident pose in most physicians. The truth of the matter is that many gaps in the knowledge base of medicine exist and many clinical decisions made for patients rest on an uncertain knowledge base because of these gaps. It is this uncertain knowledge base underlying modern medicine that often makes it impossible for physicians to know with certainty which among several courses of action, or inaction, will produce the best, or even an acceptable outcome for patients. Physicians should neither ignore these uncertainties in a false sense of confidence nor be paralyzed into inaction by them. Medical uncertainties affecting clinical decision making exist and this fact needs to be acknowledged by physicians and accepted by patients. In areas of clinical uncertainty, wise physicians use their best clinical judgment to guide patients in an honest and sincere fashion. This allows the selection of a course of action for patients based on forthright input from physicians and an expression of preference by patients.

Physicians who are able to communicate well with patients react intuitively by combining common courtesy with common sense, but a background in counseling and interviewing skills is both helpful and desirable. Characteristics that are important to good personal communicating are empathy, trust, honesty, validation or respecting each other's right to communicate, and caring. A crucial part of the bond between a physician and a patient is complete trust in the physician's honesty and sincerity. Two additional characteristics of importance to physician communication abilities are recognition of the importance of listening and the use of gentle humor to neutralize or alleviate stress. Patient compliance with physician suggestions is improved when the patient is treated as a distinct individual by a physician who understands the requirements of good physician-patient communication and shows interest, attentiveness, and empathy toward the patient. The most central aspect of the physician-patient relationship is the willingness and the ability of the two parties to talk freely and openly with each other. The medical profession clearly recognizes the importance of confidentiality in promoting full discussion and the law has historically protected physician-patient communication, understanding that confidentiality is needed for effective medical care.[7] Physicians should, in order to acquire a better understanding of the dynamics of a physician-patient interaction, treat patients as they themselves would want to be treated in a like situation. The weakness of that advice is that, if the physician has never been seriously ill and been through the experience of sickness as a patient, it is very difficult for him or her to truly understand the sick role. A better way to approach the physician-patient encounter is to understand, appreciate, and accept the rights and responsibilities of both parties in this type of social interaction and act accordingly. Understanding how communication should work under appropriate circumstances should facilitate a cooperative relationship between both parties. Each party in this relationship expects, or at least hopes, the other party will act in certain specified ways, according to each one's rights and responsibilities. The more each party fails to meet the expectations of the other party the more the relationship is weakened. Physicians know, but need to be reminded from time to time, that medicine is still an area in which one physician, by bringing together the qualities of a knowledgeable and skillful clinician and a warm, caring, and supportive humanist, can make a real difference for a sick patient and for the entire profession.

In order to treat patients successfully, physicians must be willing and able to share information with them about diagnosis, treatment, including self-care, and prognosis of their medical condition. The content matter of some communications, such as eliciting compliance with a medical treatment program or obtaining informed consent for a surgical or other invasive procedure, is more traditional to a physician-patient interaction but other communications, such as discussing pain, suffering, and even death with patients, are more emotion-laden and more difficult for physicians to carry out. Conveying relevant information to patients in a clear and understandable fashion is usually associated with three beneficial outcomes to the interaction: (1) it allows patients to give informed consent to the proposed treatment, (2) it enlists patients in the treatment process, and (3) it enables patients to cooperate with the process as treatment progresses.[8] Present day patients are surprisingly well informed about many medical matters and resent physicians who do not give them information about their medical problem in a clear and logical fashion, and who do not provide them with sufficient time to discuss details of their own health status. A survey of residents of rural and urban communities in Pennsylvania found that a majority of older people receive most of their health information from print media with only a minority reporting they received health information from their physicians.[9] Physicians need to realize that the increased time spent in providing explanations to patients and patients' families is usually more than made up in increased efficiency of the provided care. Patient resentment against a physician's inability or refusal to effectively communicate details of patient management to them has been the generating stimulus for many malpractice suits against physicians. In addition, many patients are disenchanted by what they regard as the careless, callous, thoughtless, or nonexistent psychosocial attitudes exhibited toward them by their physicians. For the outcome of a physician-patient interaction to achieve its maximum potential, physicians should possess some knowledge, proficiency, and understanding of interviewing skills and psychosocial issues as these relate to the patient's health and ability to effectively communicate problems and needs to the physician.[10] An ability to evaluate the patient within the context of his or her own family and community increases the physician's ability to gather important diagnostic and therapeutic information. In addition, physicians must possess sufficient communication and interpersonal skills to be able to convey emotion-laden information to patients and their families with sensitivity and understanding. Neither the physician's depth of knowledge nor interviewing skills will be sufficient to provide effective and compassionate care unless the physician's attitude during the clinical encounter conveys to the patient the sense that addressing the patient's needs ranks above all other considerations.

When meeting new patients, physicians should introduce themselves and, if other than the attending physician, indicate their status to the patient, be it medical student, resident, fellow, or other.[11] It is important for physicians to make every effort to see patients with minimal delay. Long waits for physicians after the designated appointment time or interruptions during the visit devalue the importance of patients' time and worries. A simple apology for significant lateness or unavoidable interruptions acknowledges that the delay or interruption is the physician's problem or a result of unavoidable circumstances and not an indication of the patient's lesser status.[12] The use of medical jargon, appearing hurried or giving patients the sense of begrudging them adequate time to be heard, or conveying the perception of a pretentious, condescending, or paternalistic attitude on the part of the physician are the most commonly encountered barriers to effective communication between physicians and patients in face to face encounters.[13] In speaking directly to patients, physicians should always address them by name and not use that paternalistic and patronizing phrase, "and how are we today, Mrs. Jones?" when Mrs. Jones is a single apprehensive patient and not a group of people.[14] Patients and their families often become resentful because they are given little diagnostic, therapeutic, or prognostic information by their physicians or because their physician provides inadequate time or little effort to communicate with them in a meaningful way. Such failures in physician communications with patients frequently result in confusion, negativism, anxiety, lack of compliance with treatment programs, and law suits. A good physician communicator understands that the fruits of well considered conversations with patients and patients' families are understanding and motivation, peace of mind, and confidence in the physician.[15] If physicians fail to grasp the importance of exhibiting good communication and interpersonal skills with their patients, and the need to function, first and foremost, as patient advocates, they risk further lessening of their professional image in the public's view. Loss of political support by patients for medicine's values risks opening the door to profound social changes affecting the delivery of medical care.

PHYSICIAN-PATIENT INTERACTIONS

The term, *clinical encounter*, is used in its generic sense in this chapter, and is applied to any professional interaction between physicians and patients. The term, *diagnostic interview,* is used in a more specific sense to refer to the initial interaction between a physician and a new patient, in either an outpatient or inpatient setting.

THE CLINICAL ENCOUNTER

The *clinical encounter* is any professional interaction between a physician and a patient and can occur in a variety of settings. The clinical encounter is considered the cornerstone of effective medical care because it focuses on direct service to others, the principal reason most people choose medicine as a career. The interaction in a clinical encounter is an interpersonal relationship that should occupy the physician's full attention because it involves supplying medical help to a fellow human seeking that help. This relationship, in which one participant seeks and needs help and the other participant can provide that help, makes the clinical encounter a very different kind of social interaction from any other involving two persons. Clinical encounters, in addition to providing professional assistance for specific health problems, should be associated with a subjective process that is sensitive and emotionally supportive and includes an understanding of the patient, his or her personality, and his or her distress.[16] Regardless of whether the requested help is for advice, reassurance, support, or treatment for a medical problem, how well the requested help is supplied and received, and how successful the outcome of the clinical encounter proves to be depends, mainly, on the communication and interpersonal skills of the physician involved in the interaction. Obviously, many patients visit physicians seeking diagnosis and treatment of physical disease, but there is a body of evidence indicating persons also consult physicians for psychological, social, and informational reasons.[17] Patients have two criteria for judging a clinical encounter with a physician to be good: (1) good clinical decision making by the physician, and (2) good communication between the patient and physician. Patients judge their physician to be a good communicator if he or she listens well and volunteers information and explanations to them.

Except for those who are too ill to care, most patients like to have some involvement with decisions concerning their medical problem made in the clinical encounter, and respond better to physicians who are friendly, gracious, sympathetic, and empathic than to physicians who are perceived as more dominant, directive, and controlling.[18] If a physician fails to communicate effectively with a patient during a clinical encounter or fails to develop rapport and trust with the patient, it is unlikely the involved physician will elicit all the patient information needed to supply the requested help in an efficient and skillful fashion. In addition, the patient will go away from the clinical encounter dissatisfied with the outcome of the experience. Diagnoses are only as good as the information on which they are based and good communication skills are needed to extract all the required information from patients. If physicians and patients fail to communicate effectively with each other, diagnosis and appropriate treatment may be delayed or missed altogether.[19] Dissatisfaction with a poorly conducted clinical encounter is believed to be the main reason why patients change physicians.[20] Clinical encounters are unique opportunities for physicians to build successful and loyal relationships with patients. However, to be successful in building such relationships, physicians must understand that most patients do not care *how much you know* until they know *how much you care*.[21] This can be a difficult perception for physicians to grasp because a high technology, disease-oriented medical education background does not tend to project the patient, the *person* with the medical problem, as the central figure in a medical problem solving clinical encounter.

Concern for the quality of the relationship between physicians and patients is not only a matter of respecting the feelings, needs, and perspectives of patients seeking help but also relates to the outcome of the interaction. Few criticisms directed at physicians by others have to do with their professional knowledge base, their technical expertise and clinical skills, or the actual delivery of medical care. Most criticisms of physicians and their professional behavior focus on the lack of communication and interpersonal skills exhibited by some physicians during clinical encounters. Medical care has an objective and subjective component that are perceived differently by physicians and patients. Most patients tend to assume that technical expertise will be associated with the delivery of their medical care. What patients do evaluate during a clinical encounter, however, is the human side of how that care is delivered and the compassion, warmth, empathy, courtesy, and concern for their welfare exhibited by their physician during the course of the experience. Studies link the interpersonal aspects of the physician-patient relationship with the therapeutic outcome, patient cooperation with treatment programs, and patient satisfaction with the medical experience.[22] Patient satisfaction with a clinical encounter relates more to the *content matter* of the interaction than to its *length*. Patient satisfaction with a physician relates more to his or her perception of the *quality* of time spent in the clinical encounter than to the total *length* of time the physician spends with the patient.[23] It has been shown that technical interventions by physicians, such as examinations, tests, medications, and non-drug therapy are not related strongly to patient satisfaction with the clinical encounter. On the other hand, patient education and stress counseling offered by physicians, and the opportunity to discuss their own ideas about their treatment with their physicians are related strongly to patient satisfaction with the clinical encounter.[24]

It has been suggested that clinical encounters, depending upon whether they are follow up office visits, hospital consultations, or hospital rounds, be structured around several or all of six distinct components[25]:

1. Relating to the patient.
2. Discussing reason for patient being there.
3. Conducting a verbal or physical examination or both.
4. Consideration of patient's condition.
5. Detailing treatment or further investigation with the patient.
6. Terminating the encounter.

As human beings, physicians come with varying communicating styles and personalities which have a bearing on communicating with patients. A physician's style with patients is a unique blend of behaviors determined by his or her personality, beliefs, experience, and education.[18] Because of long years of clinical education, the behavior of many physicians is disease-oriented and tends to be self-protectively authoritarian. This more traditional authoritarian approach to patient care allows a physician better control over his or her use of time and structure of the day's activities, but provides little consideration for patient wishes or convenience. An appropriate balance between physicians' needs to budget time, and patients' needs for information and medical care without long periods of waiting is difficult to achieve but must be attempted as a conscious effort by physicians. Physicians need to be aware of the effect their style and behavior has on patients, and must accept the advice that it can not be a one way street with the directional arrow always pointing in their direction.[26]

In addition to communicating styles, physicians also come with varying personalities which can influence patient communication. Some physicians are extroverted and personable by nature, while others may be more reserved and even somewhat aloof by temperament. Patients, however, are usually tolerant of the personality that comes with their physician as long as they remain convinced their physician has their best interests at heart. Satisfaction with the medical help received during a clinical encounter is influenced positively by the degree to which a physician's behavior corresponds with the patient's expectations of the physician's role in the interaction.[27] Patient dissatisfaction with a clinical encounter is greatest when the physician's actions and behavior project a cold, impersonal, and uncaring attitude toward the patient. Warmth and graciousness on the part of the physician, rather than maintenance of authority and control, associates positively with patient compliance with treatment programs and satisfaction with the clinical encounter.

THE DIAGNOSTIC INTERVIEW

Physicians should have two goals in mind when undertaking a diagnostic interview with a new patient in either an outpatient or inpatient setting. The first is to obtain sufficient information from the patient in a pleasant and efficient manner so a proper diagnosis can be approached or reached and an appropriate management plan or treatment program determined. A well conducted diagnostic interview allows the physician to elicit information about the onset, severity, and course of a patient's problems and to determine the contribution of social and psychological factors to the chronicity or prognosis of those problems.[28] His or her medical education provides the physician with the necessary tools to analyze and process the information received during the course of the interview on which he or she will take action on behalf of the patient. A successful outcome of a diagnostic interview is highly dependent upon the quality of the information received from the patient.[29] The second goal is to explain the problem and the recommended plan of action to the patient fully and clearly at the end of the interview, so the expectations both parties bring to a diagnostic interview can be achieved. Patient expectations for a diagnostic interview include: (1) their present health status needs will be made clear to them by the physician, (2) they will receive information from the physician about related health matters, (3) they may or will receive treatment for their medical problem, and (4) they will receive emotional support and reassurance from the physician.

The physician-patient relationship, so important in clinical medicine, is first established in the diagnostic interview. The most successful interviews are patient-centered, not physician-centered. Patient-centered interviews combine a careful analysis of signs and symptoms with an understanding of the patient's feelings about his or her condition and the implications of illness for daily life. This type of interview approach is most successful if combined with the interpersonal skills of listening, observing, and responding on the part of the physician. The patient-centered interview recognizes and acknowledges the patient as a person with a unique life history and a specific set of needs which occur in conjunction with a medical problem.[30] Unfortunately, some physicians fail to address these patient expectations in a satisfactory manner, thus sowing the seeds for patient resentment and animosity. Many physicians either ignore or unsuccessfully cope with their patients' worry, difficulty with activities of daily living, and social problems and physicians from predominantly procedural specialties are suspected of simply ignoring most psychosocial problems in their patients. How well the goals of physicians and patients are met in a diagnostic interview depends on the physician's interviewing and communicating skills and the satisfaction and confidence with the physician the patient takes away from this medical experience.

The diagnostic interview conducted by physicians is one of the most complex and demanding of skilled interviewing techniques.[31] It requires that physicians possess sufficient skills to be able to effectively interview and listen to patients so the maximum amount of information can be elicited from each patient.[32] An effective physician interviewer lets the patient talk at the beginning of the interview with the physician acting as a guide to the flow and direction of the conversation by asking clarifying questions. A good physician interviewer makes good use of exploratory or open-ended questions, deals with the feelings of the patient, demonstrates a willingness to listen to the patient, and accurately labels the intensity of the patient's experience.[33] From a patient's viewpoint, satisfaction with a diagnostic interview correlates positively with two outcomes: (1) patients being permitted to tell their own stories, and (2) physicians giving patients feedback about their illness and allowing them an opportunity to ask clarifying questions. Obtaining objective information from the physician about their illness and its projected treatment at the conclusion of the diagnostic interview is rated as very important by patients.[34]

Some of the skills effective physician communicators use in giving information to patients include explaining, sharing, advising, clarifying, and dealing appropriately with questions and ideas initiated by patients. It is the quality and blend of these skills that define a physician's style in conducting a diagnostic interview. Unfortunately, many physicians give a lot of advice, but little information. It has been shown that physicians frequently underestimate patients' knowledge of illness and those physicians most seriously underestimating this knowledge tend to communicate the least amount of information to patients.[35]

As is true for more general communication and interpersonal skills, medical schools also have not devoted much medical student curricular time to the teaching of interviewing skills, despite the growing importance and need for these skills. Among the deficiencies noted when interviewing skills of medical students, residents, and attending physicians have been observed and studied are interviewer insensitivity, failure to elicit all relevant patient details, developing incorrect working hypotheses from information obtained from patients, accepting informational material told to patients by others but failing to obtain primary informational material known to patient, and use of a physician-centered and controlled interviewing style.[36] Medical students in most schools are expected to learn how to conduct diagnostic interviews by repetitive practice with patients in various clinical settings, with or without direct observation by instructors. Longitudinal studies, however, indicate that medical students do not improve their interviewing skills on a uniform basis simply by repetitive practice in a clinical setting, and that on certain measures their skills actually decline from the first year of medical school to the fourth.[37] A study comparing pediatric interviewing skills of first year and fourth year medical students shows that fourth year students commonly ask leading questions, use unfamiliar medical terminology, cut off communication with patients, fail to ask questions pertaining to interpersonal aspects of the case, and rarely give reassurance or feedback to the parent.[38] Increasing recognition of the basic rights of patients to be treated as whole persons while receiving medical care, however, has fostered a growing concern that the technical competence of physicians be complemented with well developed interpersonal skills. This has led to an increase in the number of medical schools instituting programs to teach interpersonal skills, including interviewing techniques and informational gathering skills, to medical students.[39] In a review of 73 published studies of the teaching of patient interviewing skills to medical students, the authors conclude that instruction in medical interviewing techniques has generally promoted significant gains in students' interviewing skills as measured by various cognitive tests, affective instruments, and observed behavior.[37] It must be noted, however, that this type of instruction is given during the pre-clinical years in most medical schools, and little information is available to assess retention of these skills into the clinical years or, more importantly, into medical practice.

From a physician's viewpoint, the purpose of a diagnostic interview should be to achieve rapport with the patient, gather information about the presenting problem, form and validate diagnostic hypotheses, and propose a solution or resolution for the problem presented by the patient. Like most social interactions, diagnostic interviews have a content and process component, both of which can be influenced by the perceptions and beliefs the two participants bring to this interaction. Content refers to the actual verbal exchange between physician and patient that must be structured and guided in an orderly fashion so that a maximum amount of patient information can be learned for diagnostic and treatment purposes in a reasonable time frame. Process refers to what happens during the interview that clarifies the patient's and physician's emotional reactions to questioning and to the subject being discussed. Attention must be paid to the nature of patient statements and physician responses so that matters such as the logical order and flow of the interview can be observed. Process is particularly evidenced by the sensitivity and sensibility that evolve from the nuances of both verbal and nonverbal communication exchanges between physicians and patients.[40] During most social interactions, people form impressions of one another including, for patients, an impression of how good the physician seems to be at his or her job. As is true for most clinical situations, physicians involved with conducting diagnostic interviews are probably more effective as physicians if they dress and look like the public's perception of what a physician should dress and look like. Except for certain emergency situations, physicians who wear clean white coats during the clinical encounter are regarded by most patients as more effective as physicians than those who wear casual attire during the physician-patient interaction.

In structuring a diagnostic interview, physicians must allow enough time so patients are satisfied they have sufficient time to tell their story. Patients' perceptions of their physician's warmth and understanding correlates positively with their being permitted to tell their story in their own words during the diagnostic interview.[41] Providing sufficient time at this stage of the interview saves the physician time in the long run by avoiding the wastes of time caused by misunderstanding and helps build a foundation for more effective communication in the future. Physicians must avoid being perceived by patients as commanding and intimidating in their personal presence during a diagnostic interview. Physicians who conduct the interview from behind a desk, for example, are seen as trying to maintain a rigid distance between themselves and patients. It is far better to conduct the interview, if possible, in an environment that suggests equal status between physician and patient, such as sitting in facing chairs. While conducting the interview it is important for physicians to be attentive enough to pick up patient reactions and nonverbal clues. Studies of physicians videotaped while conducting diagnostic interviews show many physicians spend a good part of the time writing and reading notes, thus missing a lot of patient nonverbal information. Physicians should follow an orderly sequence when conducting diagnostic interviews so an optimal information exchange between physician and patient can occur in an efficient time frame. If no order exists within the structure of the interview, physicians find themselves constantly returning to previous bits of information in order to get all the relevant details. Following an orderly sequence in conducting the interview does not, necessarily, mean following an inflexible sequence. Good physician interviewers know that interview sequences may need to be altered on occasion depending upon the requirements of the situation, and are flexible enough to respond and adjust to these requirements.

It is believed a diagnostic interview should be constructed around five distinct steps[42]:

1. Opening the interview appropriately
2. Eliciting information
3. Sustaining the interview
4. Clarifying the problem
5. Closing the interview appropriately

A sequence that physicians can follow to elaborate on these five steps is as follows:

1. The physician establishes a relationship with the patient.
2. The physician attempts to discover or actually does discover the reasons for the patient's visit.
3. The physician conducts a verbal or a physical examination, or both.
4. The physician and, if appropriate, the patient consider the problem and its medical and social implications.
5. The physician and, if appropriate, the patient work out the details of further investigation or treatment.
6. The physician terminates the interview after giving the patient appropriate information.

Physicians can give appropriate information to patients by following a sequence such as:

1. What is wrong with you (or what I or we think is wrong with you).
2. What tests we are going to perform.
3. What I (or we) think will happen to you.
4. What treatment you will need.
5. What you must do to help yourself.

How well or how efficiently these sequences are carried out depends upon the interviewing skills of the physician. Physicians will get more information from patients during the interview by using a gently persuasive tone of voice rather than an authoritarian tone. Giving the patient a more active role in the interview process has been shown to have positive consequences in that patients are better able to express needs, articulate concerns, and make use of available resources.[43] Patients who tend to wait for physicians to take the initiative in offering explanations of their problem risk being perceived by physicians as showing disinterest or an incompetence for understanding medical matters.

Skillfull physician interviewers know to combine different types of questions to patients in order to obtain as much information as possible about the patient's problem during the diagnostic interview. The best strategy for a successful interview seems to be to give the patient more encouragement and time in which to describe the problem, rather than have the physician lead the patient along with a series of closed and short answer questions. Questions asked by physicians during the course of the interview are intended to elicit verbal information from patients and can be open-ended, clarifying, closed, personal, or impersonal in type. An open-ended question (How are you feeling today?) helps establish rapport with patients and can lead to a patient providing information about which the physician may not think to inquire. *Open-ended questions* allow some general direction to guide a patient's response but also allow a great deal of latitude for that response as open questions make people talk more. Physicians skilled in interviewing techniques can control the flow of the interview process in a courteous fashion by guiding the conversation to relevant subjects by asking *clarifying* questions, and by guiding the discussion to keep the patient to the point of the clinical encounter.

A *closed question* (Did you have the headache this morning?), by being directive, limits the patient's response to a few alternatives. Closed questions make people talk less, do not help establish rapport with patients, and limit the information received to the subject of the question. A variation of a closed question is called a *probe question* (Exactly when did the headache start this morning?). The purpose of a probe question is to build on information received from closed questions by obtaining more detailed and specific information. Each type of question serves a useful purpose in the interview process, and skilled physician interviewers know how to blend them appropriately to obtain maximum information from patients.

Physicians with poor interviewing skills frequently either fail to hear, or do not want to hear comments offered by patients. They tend to interrupt patients by imposing direct closed questions on an entirely different subject. Such an interviewing technique allows these physicians to maintain strict control over the interview, even if it means they never really hear or understand the patient's problem. It has been shown that it really does not save the physician time by disrupting the patient's opening statement, nor stopping the patient from talking. What it does most frequently is prevent the patient's real reason for coming to the interview from surfacing.[30]

At the conclusion of the diagnostic interview, or any clinical encounter with a patient, physicians must document in a written medical record their observations and beliefs about the patient and his or her medical problem. Physicians who contribute to medical records are expected to observe, diagnose. treat, and record the details of their findings and actions into a written record which documents information about a patient's health, treatment,and response to treatment, and allows its transfer to another physician or another health care facility. The written medical record must be a clear and accurate account of the pertinent information obtained from and about the patient during a clinical encounter or diagnostic interview.

CONSULTATION/REFERRAL

Physicians frequently ask other physicians to see, examine, and recommend a management program or treatment plan for a patient currently under their care, or provide some other type of medical assistance in the care of a patient. Consultations are most often requested because the consultant physician possesses special knowledge or expertise not possessed by the attending physician, or because of a request for a second opinion initiated either by the patient or the insurance carrier paying for the medical service. Both the requesting and the consulting physicians have an obligation to the patient and to themselves to ensure that the consultation process is carried out expeditiously, and that breakdowns in the consultation or patient referral process do not occur. As important and necessary as consultations are in the delivery of good medical care, poorly managed consultations can be a source of frustration and anger for patients and physicians, usually because of poor communication between the referring and consulting physicians.

For a consultation or referral to have a worthwhile outcome, communications between the physicians involved in the patient's care must be well maintained. A break in the communication process can seriously jeopardize continuity of care and, therefore, the patient's well being. In addition, communication gaps in the consultation/referral process often result in confusion, frustration, and anger on the part of the patient and his or her family. Both referring and consulting physicians should take time to ensure that all parties involved in the process are adequately informed, both initially and on an ongoing basis throughout the patient's course of treatment, so that maximum benefit will be derived from the consultation or referral.

INFORMED CONSENT

Informed consent is a physician-patient communication interaction which is required by law in order for physicians to obtain consent from patients for them to submit to physician-recommended procedures and treatments. The doctrine of informed consent obligates physicians to inform patients of the risks and harms that could possibly be associated with a procedure or treatment planned or scheduled to be performed on them as part of their physicians' diagnostic investigation or treatment of their medical problem. This explanation must include a full disclosure of the nature of the procedure or treatment to be performed, the risks involved, and the available alternatives to the proposed procedure or treatment. The purpose of this communication process is to give patients the information they need to make an informed choice as to whether to submit to a particular procedure or treatment, or to decline. Obtaining informed consent from patients by physicians is part of the therapeutic process, and should be regarded by physicians as an opportunity to improve the communication and enhance the relationship between themselves and their patients. However, the full potential of the informed consent process to improve communication and the professional relationship between themselves and patients is often not appreciated by physicians. In a study conducted in 1991 at the Mackenzie Health Center at the University of Alberta, 52 percent of surveyed residents considered obtaining consent from patients under their care as "scutwork," while only 25 percent of surveyed residents considered it an educational experience.[44]

Legally, informed consent is a consent obtained from a patient after adequate disclosure by a physician. Unfortunately, what the law regards as adequate disclosure differs from state to state, and physicians should identify the consent requirements stipulated in the state in which they practice. The law may hold physicians liable if they do not adhere to the standards for informed consent set by the legal system. These standards require a physician to obtain consent from a patient for treatment to be rendered or an operation to be performed. Patients who sue physicians for malpractice on the basis of an inadequate informed consent usually claim they were not given sufficient information by the physician about the risks associated with the procedure or treatment. Without an adequate and acceptable informed consent, the physician can also be charged with battery, and held liable for violation of the patient's rights, regardless of whether the treatment was appropriate and rendered with due care. *Battery*, which can be either a civil or criminal offense, is typically defined as unconsented physical contact.

Because of the attached legal and medical connotations, informed consent has become an uncomfortable communication process for many physicians. These attached connotations are neither competitive nor mutually exclusive, but may be given different weight by the participants in the process, thus influencing the manner in which informed consent is perceived by lawyers and physicians. The *legal connotation* of informed consent is a process designed to protect patients from invasion of their bodily integrity by physicians and other health care providers. The *medical connotation* of informed consent is a process designed to assist patients make informed decisions about whether or not to submit to procedures or treatments believed by their physicians to be for their ultimate benefit. Because of the potential for lawyers to claim lack of informed consent as part of a plaintiff's complaint in malpractice cases, many physicians have come to regard obtaining a patient's informed consent as merely a legal concept to be used by lawyers to harass them in litigation. Too many physicians have come to regard the primary purpose of obtaining a patient's signature on a consent form as protection for themselves from possible legal liability. During a time of litigious patients and defensive medicine, it is easy for physicians to forget that the real purpose of the process of informed consent is enhanced physician-patient communication, not a perfunctory exercise undertaken for the sole purpose of protecting themselves from threats of legal liability. As a consequence, the excellent potential possessed by the process of informed consent for improving physician-patient relationships tends to become obscured and unfulfilled. Physicians should regard obtaining their patients' informed consent as an opportunity for improving the bonding and communicating between themselves and their patients. It should be a dialogue not only designed to satisfy a legal requirement, but also designed to be a communication interaction between physicians and patients that explains the uncertainties in medical decision making, and helps anxious, and often frightened patients, make informed choices about their own well being and treatment.

A proper informed consent procedure has two components: (1) An oral explanation by a physician to a patient of the potential risks and harms inherent in the particular procedure or treatment being discussed and an explanation of available alternatives to the recommended procedure or treatment and (2) A printed consent form which the patient signs. This signature by the patient is intended to signify that the above discussion took place, and that the patient has read, understood, and accepts the potential risks and harms associated with the particular procedure or treatment. This signed consent form then becomes a part of the patient's medical record.

It should be understood by physicians that the consent form is not the essence of informed consent. It is merely one aspect of documenting the discussion between physician and patient which is really the essence of informed consent.

The generally accepted elements of an informed consent discussion between physician and patient are:

1. The nature of the patient's illness;
2. The recommended procedure or treatment;
3. The purpose of the procedure or treatment;
4. The likelihood of success;
5. The inherent risks and potential hazards of the procedure or treatment;
6. The available alternatives to the proposed procedure or treatment and;
7. The consequences to the patient of not performing the procedure or accepting the treatment.

In the event a patient refuses to consent to a proposed procedure or suggested treatment, the physician should carefully explain to the patient the expected consequences associated with not consenting. In addition, the physician should document clearly in the patient's medical record that, despite being fully informed and despite understanding the risks of not submitting to the procedure or treatment, the patient still chooses to refuse to submit to the proposed procedure or treatment. Such a refusal is a patient's right, and it does not diminish in any way the physician's continuing responsibility to provide the patient with the best possible medical care.

Physicians should regard obtaining a patient's informed consent as an opportunity to foster and enhance a good relationship between them, rather than regarding it as a required, but inconvenient obligation to obtain needed clearance to perform a desired procedure or treatment. A valid consent obtained after an appropriate physician-patient discussion represents an evolutionary progression from paternalistic medicine to patient-centered medicine. Being an advocate for patients means physicians must be clearer and more complete with them in their disclosures and explanations of both benefits and harms inherent in any procedure or treatment. Anxious patients seeking medical help also seek the reassurance of medical certainty, and physicians must recognize that this seeking by patients can become a communication trap for them. Unfortunately, patients seek medical certainty in a clinical environment fraught with medical uncertainty. Physicians who choose to ignore or gloss over medical uncertainties when attempting to obtain a patient's consent for a procedure or treatment do their patients a disservice, and therefore risk inviting malpractice actions by promising patients more than they or medicine can deliver. Conversely, those physicians who exaggerate or overemphasize these medical uncertainties to patients run the risk of making already anxious patients more anxious and so confused they may reject the proposed procedure or treatment simply out of fear. Physicians must be willing to admit that neither they nor their procedures and treatments are omnipotent or one hundred percent guaranteed. They must be willing to explain and discuss these medical uncertainties with patients in an honest and objective, but also a reassuring fashion. To do this properly, they must be willing to spend the time required to obtain adequate and acceptable informed consent from patients under their care.

Except for emergency or life threatening medical situations, consent must be given voluntarily by a competent patient who understands the proposed procedure or treatment with its incumbent risks and alternatives. Ideally, the physician's office is the best setting in which to hold an informed consent discussion with a patient about an invasive diagnostic procedure or an elective surgical procedure. Sufficient time for this communication opportunity, however, must be allowed in the scheduling of office patients. Advantages to the physician for obtaining informed consent from a patient in an office setting include ready availability of witnesses to the signature on the form, and a less hurried environment in which to document in the patient's medical record the facts relating to obtaining the informed consent. Also, under these circumstances, patients can not later claim they signed a consent form while under the influence of medication.

Problems with the informed consent process as it now exists have been identified. Obtaining informed consent from hospitalized patients is too often perfunctory in its performance and hurried in its presentation. Physicians other than the patient's own physician are sometimes dispatched to the bedside to explain the proposed procedure or treatment, and to obtain the patient's signature on the consent form. Anxious, frightened, and frequently intimidated patients may ask few questions, and may sign a consent form they really do not understand. It has been shown that informed consent forms for surgery are often written in confusing language, and geared to a reading level quite a bit above the reading level of the average patient.[45] This raises the distinct possibility that many patients have probably signed informed consent forms they did not read or understand. It has also been shown that, even under the best of circumstances, patients exhibit poor recall of pre-operative instructions given as part of informed consent for an operation.[46] Deficiencies perceived by patients in how the informed consent process is carried out by physicians may be an impetus for malpractice actions against them. This is particularly true if the process is carried out in a hurried and overtly disinterested manner. If physicians wish to be recognized as advocates for their patients, a start in this direction can be made by improving their approach to the informed consent process. An informed consent process that is carried out properly by a concerned and caring physician who takes sufficient time to make a full disclosure of benefits and possible risks not only improves the physician-patient relationship, but also serves to protect physicians against this particular reason for malpractice action.[47]

Physicians who are skilled in communicating with patients know that explanations offered to patients in the informed consent process afford physicians an opportunity to build supportive and trusting relationships with them. Physicians who are honest, sincere, realistic, and, at the same time, reassuring, in their explanations of risks and harms associated with specific procedures or treatments can give patients a sense that both of them will work together to get the patient through this particular medical problem. The ideal outcome of such physician-patient communication would be for the participants in the interaction to build a supportive and trusting relationship based on honesty and mutual respect in facing the uncertainties inherent in clinal practice and decision making. This ideal outcome will never be realized if physicians continue to paint pictures of unrealistic certainty for anxious and trusting patients. Seen as a dialogue in which both the cognitive and affective implications of uncertainty are acknowledged and shared, informed consent can become a powerful clinical tool.[48]

TERMINATING A PHYSICIAN-PATIENT RELATIONSHIP

A situation may arise during a physician-patient relationship when the physician wishes to terminate the relationship with the patient. This situation arises most frequently because of genuine personality conflicts which develop between the two participants in the relationship. These conflicts may linger and broaden to such an extent that the physician decides these personality conflicts interfere with his or her ability to provide optimal medical care to the patient. The physician's decision to terminate his or her responsibility to the medical care of the patient must be stated in writing to the patient with an indication of the date when this physician-patient responsibility will be terminated. In addition, the terminating physician is obliged to assist the patient in obtaining another physician and must not terminate his or her own responsibility to the patient until the new physician-patient relationshio is established. To do less is tantamount to abandoning the patient.

PHYSICIAN-GENERATED MEDICAL RECORDS

The principal reason physicians generate medical records is to document information about a patient's medical problem, treatment for the problem, and response to treatment in either an outpatient or inpatient setting, and to be able to transfer such information when requested by another physician or health care facility. Medical records are written by physicians who interview patients and their families, examine patients, review prior hospital and outpatient records, talk to referring physicians, and outline and manage a course of action for the patient's problem. Once composed, however, medical records are used to not only document the medical care received by patients, but also to serve economic and legal purposes.[49] In addition, medical records are included in computerized data bases which are used for many purposes, including treatment outcome research. It is essential, then, that physician generated medical records be factual, complete, and comprehensible because they can reach multiple audiences and will be expected to convey meaningful information to all readers. Physician generated medical records might serve different purposes, and might have differing formats, but the process a physician employs to produce clear and concisely written records is the same for all types of medical records. Physicians generating medical records should write in clear, simple prose, and show concern for the reader by avoiding ambiguity, obscure meanings, obliqueness in sentence structure, and use of medical jargon. Only abbreviations and symbols approved by the medical staff of the hospital should be used (see the Appendix). Medical records should be composed of clear and uncomplicated words, and written in a language style that flows in a continuous and sensible fashion. Before beginning to write a medical record, physicians should make a conscious and deliberate effort to think about how the record should be structured and composed, who the various audiences will be, and what the medical record should communicate to its various readers. A conscious and deliberate effort is required because it is believed that traditional medical education does not include much instruction on how to compose medical records so they can best serve the physician's purposes as well as the needs of the various audiences for the modern medical record.[50] The amount of documentation in a medical record usually increases proportionately as the patient's medical problem becomes more complex or severe. The efficient conveying of a physician's knowledge, the patient's needs, and factual data about the patient's condition to all users of a medical record requires skillful writing. The diverse nature of the modern medical community demands that physician generated medical records be written in a logical and organized fashion so they will be meaningful to their multiple audiences and for the multiple purposes for which they will be used.

The increasing availability of computer-stored medical records, and their expected use on a broad scale over the next few years, makes it essential that correct and appropriate data be entered into the medical record at all times.[51] Presently, increasing volumes of patient care data and burgeoning paperwork requirements make working with manual records difficult and time consuming.

Attending and resident physicians can spend 30 percent to 50 percent of their working time writing, searching, and copying medical records and guessing the meaning of previous medical record notations written in longhand. Deficient physician writing skills and illegible penmanship combine to obscure facts in many manually recorded medical records.[52] Because it has never been clearly determined what the minimum effective initial data base for patient care should be, the increasing availability of computerized medical record systems will allow the initial collection of patient data that is as significant and complete as possible. When this electronic technology is fully available, computer systems, instead of physicians, will do the tracking and searching for medical and patient facts with the result that medical care wll be faster and more efficient.

THE HOSPITAL MEDICAL RECORD

The *hospital medical record* is an important document because it is a written account of why a patient was hospitalized, what the diagnosis is believed to be, the evidence supporting the diagnostic conclusion, the treatment given the patient, the patient's response to treatment, and the patient's health outcome as a result of the hospital experience as noted at the time of hospital discharge. Such records include all relevant patient care data including, but not limited to, the written history and physical examination, progress notes, nurses' notes, laboratory and radiology reports, consultant reports, operative reports, and discharge summary. Patient care in hospitals is managed by numerous physicians, nurses, and other health care professionals who not only use the medical records written by physicians and nurses, but also generate medical records themselves. All persons whose responsibility it is to contribute in writing to a patient hospital medical record must be aware that the medical record is an official document that must be written with that constraint in mind. Because a large number of people can contribute to the writing of a patient's hospital medical record, and because there are multiple audiences for these records, including patients themselves, the writing of such a document takes skill and an appreciation of the multiple uses to which such records can be subjected. Not only do members of the medical care team read a patient's hospital medical record, but so do insurance evaluators, representatives of government agencies and research organizations, hospital administrators, statistical analysts, and lawyers. Courts consider the medical record to be the most reliable source of information regarding a patient's care, and of far more significance than the recollections of physicians or patients. If for no other reason, then, it is of great importance that physicians develop good record keeping habits. Good medical record documentation enhances the credibility of physicians, and may prevent malpractice actions. Lack of documentation, poor documentation, or unclear documentation in a medical record, on the other hand, helps the plaintiff in a malpractice action against a physician.

The writing of the hospital medical record has taken on increased importance in light of the effort to constrain the costs of health care and can no longer be regarded simply as an account of patient care activities and patient responses as recorded by a variety of physicians with differing views of the significance of the events being recorded. Medicare and third party payer documentation requirements now exist and hospital reimbursement for the care of many patients depends, in large part, on the accuracy and adequacy of the information recorded in the patient hospital medical record. These medical records are regarded as integral components of hospital quality assessment and quality assurance programs and physicians must be certain all information essential to the requirements of these programs is recorded. The medical care provided to patients must be documented factually and specifically and in sufficient detail in the hospital medical record to permit continuity of care and peer evaluation of the care provided. Physicians can strengthen the professional and clinical aspects of a hospital medical record by adding carefully written notes that explain their findings and reasoning used to arrive at their professional judgments in regard to their actions on behalf of the patient. Also useful in strengthening the professional validity of a patient's medical record is the practice of supporting clinical decisions with written relevant literature citations when appropriate.

Because hospital medical records have multiple audiences, medical record room personnel have had to become more demanding of physicians in regard to kinds of data that must be in the medical record. PRO (Peer Review Organization) regulations stipulate, for example, that if a patient is admitted to a hospital the record must state the physician's reason for deciding to hospitalize the patient as opposed to outpatient observation or home care, including geographic and psychosocial factors, if relevant. The record must include a discussion of how outpatient treatment failed and reasons why the medical problems were not resolved during previous recent admissions for the same diagnosis, if applicable. The medical record must contain a description, written in general terms, of the physician's plan for the patient during this particular admission, including reasons for any limited treatment plan, if appropriate. The recorded physical examination of the patient must include vital signs, an assessment of patient distress, an assessment of the acuteness and severity of illness, and a description of the patient's frailty, dependence, or dementia, if any. Aside from the observation that good medical practice dictates the timely completion of a patient's hospital medical record, federal regulations and laws in some states require that certain entries be made in the record within specified time periods following a patient's hospital discharge. In addition, hospital bylaws or regulations usually define a stated time period during which patient hospital medical records are to be completed following patient discharge. In most hospitals, failure to comply usually carries some penalty for the offending physician, most often a monetary fine or a temporary loss of admitting privileges.

Readers of a hospital medical record should be able to obtain an understanding of what the patient and the physician perceived the medical problem to be, the diagnosis or differential diagnoses under consideration, and the proposed plan of study and treatment. Laboratory and radiolologic reports, comments about their relevance to the patient's condition, and the patient's progress during the hospital period should be evaluated in frequent and dated progress notes written legibly by the physician to show that the physician did follow up on the plan of action determined for the care of the patient. Appropriate consultations and suggestions for additional studies or tests are entered into the record, dated, and their significance to the care of the patient commented upon in appropriate progress notes written legibly by a physician. Notes prepared by nurses, physical therapists, social service workers, and other health care personnel should be entered into the record, dated, signed or initialed by the one making the entry, and their significance to the patient's progress and recovery commented upon in notes written by the attending or principal physician. If surgery or other invasive procedure is recommended as part of the treatment plan, the hospital medical record must reflect that a truly informed consent to the surgery or invasive procedure was obtained from the patient or from someone legally allowed to speak for the patient. If surgery is performed, a dated and signed operative report must be part of the hospital medical record. Information in the hospital medical record should facilitate communication among physicians and other health care professionals treating the patient and allow easy evaluation of therapy and patient progress. If arranged in proper chronologic order, information contained in the various segments of a hospital medical record should flow like a well constructed novel with the plot unfolding in a logical and orderly fashion toward the conclusion of the patient's hospital experience. Although physicians may spend countless hours keeping current by reading and attending continuing medical education courses, there may be little, if any, direct benefit transferred to patients and patient care if physicians are unable to orchestrate appropriate patient management by the proper use of a complete hospital medical record.

Because these records are maintained, retrieved, and studied by many people, they must be written in a clear and orderly fashion. The writing rule for these records is the same as that governing all medical writing. The text of the record should be composed of lucid, easily understood, and uncomplicated words structured into sentences that progress in a continuous and sensible flow. Comments added to the hospital medical record must be written clearly and legibly and pertain to the medical condition or medical problem under consideration. All entries made in a patient's hospital medical record must be signed or initialed by the person making the entry. Unless an obvious error has occurred in recording data in a patient's medical record, no change or deletion should be made in the medical record once the note or data has been made. Pages of a patient's medical record should never be removed, torn out, or cut. If it should become necessary to correct a previously written entry in a patient's hospital medical record, the legally appropriate method of correcting an entry requires single line deletion, correction, and initialing by the person making the correction. However, a physician, or anyone else, should never alter a medical record after being notified of a lawsuit. To do so may lead to serious consequences and legal ramifications for the person altering the medical record.

It must be appreciated by all who add handwritten notes to patient charts that such notes have to be written in a legible manner. Courts in many jurisdictions have held that an illegible medical record documents a failure on the part of physicians and hospitals to maintain a proper record. An illegible record, in addition, may well impair the ability of the hospital staff to provide proper patient care. Physicians, notorious for possessing poor penmanship skills, must keep constantly aware of the absolute necessity for making legible entries in a patient's medical record. Without a legible record, it may not be possible to defend a malpractice action because, in some situations, illegible records may be considered worse than no record at all. In addition, the use of medical jargon and an excessive amount of abbreviations in physicians' notes should be avoided, because hospital medical records have become increasingly important as legal documents essential to both the proper defense and prosecution of professional liability actions against physicians and hospitals. A carelessly written or poorly documented patient hospital medical record is of little help to a physician's defense in a malpractice action and can be a source of acute embarrassment to the physician if read aloud in a courtroom. Although medical records are the property of the hospital and are maintained for the benefit of the patient, the physician, and the hospital, patients do have a right of access to the information contained in their own medical record. Physicians who are involved in the writing of patient medical records should bear in mind that patients in this country have a legal right to see their medical records if they wish. This legal right, however, does not extend, carte blanche, to medical records of psychiatric patients or patients undergoing treatment for drug or alcohol abuse. These particular records are subject to access by appropriate persons only by means of a court order.

Traditional patient hospital medical records, as written by physicians, have tended to focus on the biomedical aspects of the patient's presenting medical problem, with few entries exploring and recording in depth what patients think and feel about their illness.[53] Such medical records lack information that should be recorded about what patients understand and feel about their medical problem, how they are coping with the effects of acute or chronic disease or disability, the treatment they are receiving and, in some instances, their impending death. In traditional medical records, patient symptoms tend to be presented as depersonalized abstractions by physician writers, and little or nothing is included about the ideas, thinking, and feelings of the patient who should be the central figure in a hospital medical record.[54] It seems apparent a consensus exists in this country that our medical care system must become more socially conscious and responsive to the needs of its patients. Thus, modern medical care requires that physicians, in addition to describing the biomedical features of a disease process, develop the ability to recognize and elicit psychosocial data that are germane to the total care of the patient, and document in the patient's hospital medical record the impact of the illness on the patient's life and its meaning for the patient.[41]

HISTORY AND PHYSICAL EXAMINATION

The history is the patient's spoken story and, as such, is the most general source of information about the patient and focuses the rest of the medical evaluation. The history taking format establishes a mode for the orderly documentation of historical data in the clinical care of patients, regardless of whether the clinical care is delivered in an inpatient or outpatient setting. Information gathered from the patient in the diagnostic interview and documented in the medical record by the physician forms the basis for hypothesis generation and initial clinical problem solving by the physician.[55] The history is a fundamental aspect of clinical practice and it is essential that physicians possess the skills needed to establish effective relationships with patients and to elicit patient information that is both accurate and relevant to an understanding of the patient's problem. The patient's history at its best is a narrative which can and should have form and beauty in its written form. Physicians must appreciate that patients have the central role in the interaction of history giving and history taking and must learn to collaborate with patients in writing patients' histories. Two additional skills physicians should possess to assist in achieving a successful diagnostic interview are the skill of listening and observing, and the skill of performing an effective physical examination. The physical examination as performed by the physician can be simply a way of seeking some clinical information about the patient's physical status or it can be expanded into an impressive and powerful ritual which can have therapeutic implications for the patient. Some patients are disappointed by the physical examination performed on them because their physicians tend to perform it in a stylized and casual manner. A good and thorough physical examination, in addition to adding important clues to the decision making process, can have a therapeutic effect on the patient by impressing him or her with the physician's ability and thoroughness.[56] Despite the agreed upon importance for physicians to possess good interviewing skills, and the ability to record in the medical record in a clear fashion patient findings pertinent to the clinical problem under observation, medical records have long been known to be marred by errors introduced by physicians deficient in eliciting adequate patient histories or by physicians performing inadequate physical examinations.[57]

Medical students are instructed in patient interviewing and medical record keeping skills by means of introductory courses in clinical skills during medical school. They need help, however, in making the transition from an excessively detailed written medical record and one that communicates succinctly what is needed to care for the patient.[58] It has been noted frequently that a history and physical examination written by a third year medical student on a new patient averages seven to ten pages, but later, when the same student has entered clinical practice, this document seldom exceeds two pages. This marked decrease in the amount of detailed patient information provided in the written medical record is not based on any formula taught in medical school but is, apparently, based on guessing how much documentation is necessary and balancing that estimated amount against the time constraints imposed by clinical practice. In that context, it is instructive to note that students graduating from medical schools have reported that rarely were they observed taking a medical history and doing a physical examination during clinical training.[59]

The formats used most frequently by physicians to record patient information elicited during a diagnostic interview in which a medical history is obtained and a physical examination is performed are the traditional outline format, and the problem oriented medical record.

Traditional Outline Format

Prefaced by the chief complaint as expressed by the patient, the *traditional outline format* uses the history of present illness to begin the documentation of the information obtained from the patient during history taking and physical examination. As presented in the traditional medical record, the history of present illness is a limited narrative account, presented usually in the physician's words, of what recently happened in the patient's life and why he or she has sought or has been referred for medical opinion or hospitalization. This format follows the following outline:

- Chief complaint;
- History of present illness;
- Past medical history;
- Family history;
- Personal history, habits, occupation, and environmental factors;
- Review of systems;
- Summary and working diagnosis;
- Signature of physician writing the medical record.

A perceived need for shifting the focus of medical records produced by the traditional format from limited narrative accounts written from the viewpoint of the physician to a more patient oriented document has led to the suggestion of transforming such chronicles into stories focused more specifically on the beliefs and fears of the patient regarding his or her illness.[60] Traditionally, the account of a patient's present illness as recorded in most hospital medical records has been mostly a second hand account written by a physician. Constructing medical narratives as stories rather than chronicles is believed to add the voice of the patient to the medical record, thus identifying and preserving information that is believed necessary for optimal patient care. Recording the subjective information of what the patient knows and feels about his or her illness or disability gives a balance previously missing from hospital medical records. The effort to produce such a balanced medical record can prove beneficial to both principals in the medical interaction by promoting better physician-patient rapport and communication, and improving the level of patient satisfaction with the medical care that is being delivered. When recorded in clear and simple terms by the physician, this patient-centered informational document stands as a testimony to the physician's interest in the patient as a fellow human being.

A variation of the traditional outline format, which allows the patient more input into the process, is suggested for recording the results of the diagnostic interview.[61] In this suggested format, the patient's presenting problem is approached gradually and not before the physician has a "feel" for the patient's personality, well being, past health, and relevant psychosocial factors. The suggested outline sequence for this variation is as follows:

- Introduction (tell me about yourself);
- Patient's lifestyle, occupation, hobbies, interests;
- Family history;
- Past health: Include a list of current or frequently used medications and a chronologic listing of surgical procedures;
- Present illness;
- Other problems identified by the patient;
- Review of systems;
- Summary of problems identified by physician and patient;
- Patient encouraged to volunteer any neglected information or worries.

THE PROBLEM-ORIENTED MEDICAL RECORD

The *problem-oriented medical record* is a format based on the concept of organizing all relevant patient data around each identified medical problem.[62,63] The problem-oriented medical record contains a complete list of the patient's problems, including both clearly established diagnoses and all other unexplained findings that are not yet clear manifestations of a specifc diagnosis, such as abnormal physical findings or symptoms. The objective of a problem-oriented medical record is to present evidence of concise, organized, and disciplined thinking in eliciting a history, selection of diagnostic procedures and treatment, interpretation of findings, as well as information about plans for the patient's total needs. The technique for constructing problem-oriented medical records takes learning and practice to master which has limited its general acceptance to some degree. Parts of this technique can be combined with the more traditional outline format to give the final result a more problem based orientation. An advantage of the problem-oriented medical record is its adaptability to computer storage and retrieval.

Regardless of which format is selected to record patient information in the hospital medical record, physicians must remain aware of societal changes that can influence the practice environment and the types of information that should be included in patient medical records. Clinical research aimed at evaluating treatment outcomes in terms of achieved patient benefits will tend to focus interest on health status assessment and estimates of health related quality of life for patients. This means the medical record will have to speak to health outcomes people feel and care about such as length and quality of life, functional ability or disability, appearance, pain, anxiety, and peace of mind. The medical record will need to reflect the patient's evaluation of his or her sense of well being, the patient's preference among available treatment options, and the patient's personal evaluation of the physical, mental, and social burden of his or her medical problem.[64]

For most of this century, the older segment of the population in this country has increased far more rapidly than any other age group and this age group is itself getting older, with the percentage of persons over 85 years growing rapidly. Population statistics suggest this trend will continue. The Census Bureau projects that the number of persons over age 65 years living in this country by the year 2000 will be about 35 million and should reach 52 million by the year 2020. In addition, it is projected that the average life expectancy by the year 2020 will be 82.0 years for women and 79.2 years for men. As the number of elderly people increases, so will the incidence of chronic diseases and the spectrum of medical problems encountered by physicians will more and more reflect the characteristics of this age group.[65] People do not age in a uniform way, and older people differ from each other more than those in any other age group. Older people are the heaviest users of medical care in this country, and medical care for elderly patients rarely encompasses a single complaint. Management of multiple active problems in this segment of the population is the rule. It is important to determine which problems are most pressing and to establish a set of priorities, so that problems deemed important by the patient be identified and effectively managed.[66] Understanding an elderly patient's subjective interpretation of his or her degree of disability can be helpful to physicians in setting these priorities. Flexibility on the part of the physician interviewer in determining the multiple chief complaints of elderly patients is a necessary skill for effectively managing the medical care of elderly patients.

By the time of medical school graduation, physicians are presumed to have learned patient interviewing skills, and to have mastered the ability to assemble and write a patient medical record based on a patient's history of the medical problem and the physician's physical examination, but evidence exists to cast that presumption in some doubt.[67,68] These studies suggest many students lack the skill to elicit patient information efficiently and completely, others make many errors in conducting a physical examination, and still others lack the skills necessary to translate acquired patient information into clear and useful written medical records. Details relevant to the important communication process of conducting an appropriate diagnostic interview would appear to be neglected in the formal education of many medical students. In most medical school curricula, little time is devoted to formal education in patient inteviewing skills or the skills required to assemble and write a competent patient medical record. A lot of teaching that does occur seems to focus on what questions students should ask to elicit details of physical illness with little attention paid to the psychological and social aspects of the patient and his or her medical problem. Teaching of these clinical skills in medical schools should concentrate more on helping medical students to develop a more holistic and patient-centered approach to patient care, and to the creation of more meaningful physician generated medical records.

PROGRESS NOTES

The purpose of *progress notes* in a patient's hospital medical record is to record the progress, or lack of progress, of the physician-generated treatment plan in solving or ameliorating the medical problems for which the patient was admitted to the hospital. Progress notes need to be pertinent, relevant, and material, recorded in a narrative writing style using clear and understandable language so all readers of the medical record can follow the progress of the patient without the assistance of translators or cryptographers, and signed or initialed by the progress note writer. Entries should be made in a timely fashion and in chronological order, with both date and time of entry recorded. Usually written daily, progress notes should record any change in the patient's complaints or physical findings, and should evaluate reported radiologic and laboratory studies as these reported results relate to the patient's diagnosis, treatment, or response to treatment. Physicians must comment in progress notes on findings recorded by consultants, on any unexpected laboratory or radiologic results, any untoward clinical events sustained by the patient, and respond to any contradictory observations recorded in the medical record by nurses or other health care professionals. Any change in the physician's thinking in regard to diagnostic impression, diagnostic efforts, or patient management should be explained in a progress note.

OPERATIVE REPORT

Dictated *operative reports* must contain the following factual information:

1. Patient's name, medical record number, date of hospital admission, and date of operation.
2. Names of surgeon and assistants.
3. Name of surgical procedure performed.

4. Type of anesthetic agent used.
5. Name of anesthetist.
6. Pre-operative diagnoses.
7. Post-operative diagnoses.
8. Indication for surgery.
9. Position and preparation of patient.
10. Type of incision used.
11. Findings at operation.
12. Surgical procedure performed.
13. Technical points of operation, such as sutures, drains, etc.
14. Type of wound closure used.
15. Description of tissue removed and its disposition.
16. Volume of fluids lost by patient.
17. Amount of fluids or units of blood administered to patient.
18. Condition of patient upon conclusion of operation.

Physicians dictating operative reports should take great care to include a description of all technical steps that occurred during the performance of the surgical procedure, even to the extent of including information that might seem obvious to any surgeon. When dictating the operative report for a seemingly routine appendectomy, for example, specifically state and document that the appendiceal artery was ligated during the procedure. If the patient should have bleeding complications postoperatively, the presence of three words, "appendiceal artery ligated," can be extremely helpful to the surgeon should a subsequent malpractice action arise.

The language used in the operative report should be crisp and understandable so as to provide a medically sophisticated reader with a clear picture of what took place during the operation. Physicians who dictate operative reports should possess a sense for words and sentences. Consider, for example, this sentence which can be found as the concluding statement in thousands of dictated operative reports, "The patient left the operating room in good condition." An editorial purist would be inclined to ask the physician dictating such a sentence whether the patient used a mop or a broom to put the operating room in good condition. It is the patient, not the operating room, who has to be documented as being in good condition at the conclusion of the surgical procedure. The appropriate meaning of the sentence becomes clear when it is rewritten to state, "The patient was in good condition on leaving the operating room."

Discharge/Narrative Summary

The *discharge* or *narrative summary* is an account of the patient's medical experiences while hospitalized and should be written in the past tense, using a narrative writing style. The discharge summary should specify the patient's principal diagnosis that necessitated hospital admission, in addition to other diagnoses that required diagnostic or therapeutic action. Included in a discharge summary should be a discussion of any abnormal laboratory, radiologic. or nursing observations in addition to commenting upon tests whose results had not yet been reported to the attending physician at the time of patient discharge. The discharge summary should indicate the patient's response to treatment if treatment was a part of the hospital experience.

The final section of a discharge summary should discuss the disposition and follow up plans for the patient. These notations should indicate the level of the patient's ability to function, the support and caregiver arrangements that have been provided for the patient, details of diet and medications, activities allowed, and patient education data provided to the patient. The recording of instructions given to the patient in the hospital setting is required by the Joint Commission on Accreditation of Healthcare Organizations and should include any instructions given to the patient, including restrictions of activity, diet, warning symptoms that may require the patient to call sooner, office appointments, and plans for the future. If the patient posed special problems to the medical or nursing staffs while hospitalized, such as being uncooperative, unstable, or leaving the hospital against medical advice, these particular problems should be noted in the discharge summary. A statement detailing the follow up visit plan for the patient is the usual way to close a discharge summary. In some hospitals, a copy of a letter written by the attending physician to the referring physician may be used in place of a discharge or narrative summary. The attending physician must sign the discharge or narrative summary.

OFFICE MEDICAL RECORDS

Although *office medical records* are often regarded by physicians as more informal and relaxed as compared to patient hospital medical records, it is well to remember that particular view of these patient records is not shared by the legal profession. In truth, office medical records are considered to be official medical documents, and the same constraints apply to them as apply to patient hospital medical records because these medical records constitute a part of a patient's total medical record. Patients have the right to obtain access to the information contained in office medical records, and office medical records can be subpoenaed. It can be anticipated that at some time in the near future office medical records, just like patient hospital medical records, will be subject to review for quality of care purposes. Information gathered by the physician about the patient in the history taking and physical examination part of the diagnostic interview in the office should be recorded in a style and format with which the physician is comfortable. Once the physician has adopted a comfortable and satisfactory writing style and format for office medical records, he or she should stick to it so that other readers of the office record can follow a patient's course with a minimum of difficulty. What needs to be documented in office medical records is what truly and realistically occurs in the office between patient and physician or other office personnel. Patient related telephone calls, dispensing of medications, specific instructions for postoperative care or rehabilitation plans, informed consent, referrals to other physicians for consultation, or unusual office incidents involving the patient, or refusal of recommended tests or treatment by the patient, should be documented in the patient's office medical record. Too many patient office medical records appear to be written for a single reader who possesses the same private knowledge as the physician who writes the record.

The rule governing the writing of office medical records is the same rule that applies to all medical writing. Notes made in office medical records must be written in clear, easily understood, and uncomplicated words made into sentences that flow in a continuous and sensible fashion. Notes made in office medical records, including progress notes, are usually short, concise, and tend to emphasize only critical and important points about a patient's diagnosis, treatment, and progress toward recovery. Office medical records should specify what tests, radiologic examinations, or consultations have been ordered, the reasons for ordering them, and the results when this information becomes available. If handwritten, office medical record notes must be legible, and all office record notes, whether handwritten or dictated, must be free of medical jargon and excessive use of abbreviations. Personal or belittling remarks about patients have no place in a hospital or office patient medical record. If ever tempted to put such remarks in a patient medical record, physicians would do well to remember that, in this country, patients have a legal right to see their own medical records, and to bear in mind their written medical record might be read aloud in a courtroom at some future date.

References

1. American Board of Internal Medicine. *A Guide to the Awareness and Evaluation of Humanistic Qualities in the Internist*. Portland, Ore: American Board of Internal Medicine; 1985.
2. Schroeder SA. Clinical intensity versus cost containment: Conflicting pressures on hospital care. *Trans & Studies of the College of Physicians of Philadelphia*. 1990; Series 5, 12(2): 175-205.
3. Osmond H. God and the doctor. *N Engl J Med*. 1980; 302(10): 555-558.
4. Parsons T. *The Social System*. New York: Free Press; 1964.
5. Siegler M, Osmond H. *Models of Madness, Models of Medicine*. New York, NY: Macmillan; 1974.
6. Gartland J.J. Guidelines for tomorrow. *J Bone Joint Surg*. 1979; 61-A: 467-471.
7. Annas GJ, Glantz LH, Mariner WK. The right of privacy protects the doctor-patient relationship. *JAMA*. 1990; 263(6): 858-661.
8. Scott N, Weiner MF. Patientspeak: An exercise in communication. *J Med Educ*. 1984; 59: 890-893.
9. Connell CM, Crawford CO. How people obtain their health information. A

survey of two Pennsylvania counties. *Public Health Rep.* 1988; 103 (2): 189-195.

10. Wiener JM, ed. *Behavioral Science* New York, New York: John Wiley & Sons; 1987.

11. Cohen DL, McCullough LB, Kessel RW, Apostolides AY, Alden ER, Heiderich KJ. Informed consent policies governing medical students' interactions with patients. *J Med Educ.* 1987; 62(10): 789-798.

12. Lazere A. Shame and humiliation in the medical encounter. *Arch Intern Med.* 1987; 147: 1653-1658.

13. Crown S. Failures of communication. *Lancet.* 1971. 1: 1021-1022.

14. White EB. Department of Retrospection. A study of the clinical "we." *Trans. & Stud. of the College of Physicians of Philadelphia.* 1985. Series 5, 7(4): 295-296.

15. Tumulty PA. The art of healing. *Johns Hopkins Med J.* 1978; 143: 140-143.

16. Billings JA, Stoeckle JD. *The Clinical Encounter. A Guide to the Medical Interview and Case Presentation.* Chicago: Year Book Medical Publishers, Inc; 1989.

17. Barsky AJ. Hidden reasons some patients visit doctors. *Ann Intern Med.* 1981; 94(1): 492-498.

18. Tase P. Doctors' Style. In: Pendleton D, Hasler J, ed. *Doctor-Patient Communication.* London, England: Academic Press; 1983: 75-85.

19. Hendren RL. Communication and Interviewing. In: *Behavioral Science.* JM Wiener, ed. 197-204. New York, New York: John Wiley & Sons; 1987.

20. Schwartz H. Through the eyes of patients. *PennaMed.* 1986; 89(10): 42-46.

21. Jackson P. Building relationships with patients. *Amer Acad Orthop Surg Bull.* 1988; 36(4): 4-5.

22. Comstock LM, Hooper EM, Goodwin JM, Goodwin JS. Physician behaviors that correlate with patient satisfaction. *J Med Educ.* 1982; 57: 105-112.

23. Ware JE, Snyder MK. Dimensions of patient attitudes regarding doctors and medical care services. *Med Care.* 1975; 13(8): 669-682.

24. Brody DS, Miller, SM, Lerman CE, Smith DG, Lazaro CG, Blum MJ. The relationship between patients' satisfaction with their physicians and perceptions about interventions they received. *Med Care.* 1989; 27(11): 1027-1035.

25. Byrne P, Long BEL. *Doctors Talking to Patients.* London. H.M.S.O.; 1976.

26. Goitein M. Waiting patiently. *N Engl J Med.* 1990; 323(9): 604-608.

27. Larsen DE, Rootman L. Physician role performance and patient satisfaction. *Soc Sci Med.* 1976; 10: 29-32.

28. Guckian JC, ed. *The Clinical Interview and Physical Examination.* Philadelphia: J. B. Lippincott, Co, 1987.

29. Kahn GS, Cohen B, Jason H. The teaching of interpersonal skills in U.S. medical schools. *JMedEduc.* 1979; 54: 29-35.

30. Weihs K, Chapados JT. Interviewing skills training- a study. *Soc Sci Med.* 1986; 23(1): 31-34.

31. Tapia F. Teaching medical interviewing; A practical technique. *Br J Med Educ.* 1972; 6: 133-136.

32. Stewart MA. What is a successful doctor-patient interview? A study of interactions and outcomes. *Soc Sci Med.* 1984; 19: 167-175.
33. Werner A, Schneider JM. Teaching medical students interactional skills. A research-based course in the doctor-patient relationship. *N Engl J Med.* 1974: 290(22): 1232-1237.
34. Stiles WB, Putnam SM, Wolf MH, James SA. Interaction exchange structure and patient satisfaction with medical interviews. *Med Care.* 1979; 17(6): 667-679.
35. Waitzkin H, Stoeckle JD. The communication of information about illness. *Adv Psychom Med.* 1972; 8: 180-215.
36. Platt FW, McMath JC. Clinical hypocompetence: The interview. *Ann Intern Med.* 1979; 91: 898-902.
37. Carroll JG, Monroe J. Teaching medical interviewing: A critique of educational research and practice. *J Med Educ.* 1979; 54: 498-500.
38. Helfer RE. An objective comparison of the pediatric interviewing skills of freshman and senior medical students. *Pediatrics.* 1970; 45(4): 623-627.
39. Preven DW, Kacher EK, Kupfer RB, Waters JA. Interviewing skills of first year medical students. *J Med Educ.* 1986; 61: 842-844.
40. Thompson TL. *Communication for Health Professionals. A Relational Perspective.* New York, Harper & Row; 1986.
41. Enelow AJ, Swisher SN. *Interviewing and Patient Care.* 3rd ed., New York, NY: Oxford University Press, Inc; 1986.
42. Monahan DJ, Grover PL, Kavey REW, Greenwald JL, Jacobsen EC, Weinberger HL. Evaluation of a communication skills course for second-year medical students. *J Med Educ.* 1988; 63: 372-377.
43. Tyson PA, Leonard RC. Giving the patient an active role. In: Skinner JH, Leonard RC, ed. *Social Interaction and Patient Care* Philadelphia, Pa: J.B.Lippincott Co; 1965: 120-127.
44. Hayward RSA, Rockwood K, Sheehan GJ, Bass EB. A phenomenology of scut. *Ann Intern Med.* 1991; 115(5): 372-376.
45. Grundner TM. On the readability of surgical consent forms. *N Engl J Med.* 1980; 302(16): 900-902.
46. Hutson MMcD, Blaha JD. Patients' recall of preoperative instruction for informed consent for an operation. *J Bone Joint Surg.* 1991; 73-A: 160-162.
47. Koop CE. Exasperation on both sides of the stethoscope. *Amer Coll of Surg Bull.* 1991; 76(2): 8-17.
48. Gutheil TG, Bursztajn H, Brodsky A. Malpractice prevention through the sharing of uncertainty. *N Engl J Med.* 1984; 311(1): 49-51.
49. Nisonson I. The medical record. *Amer Coll Surg Bull.* 1991; 76(9):25-26.
50. Pagano MP, Mair, D. Writing medical records. *J Tech Writ and Commun.* 1986; 16(4): 331-341.
51. McDonald CJ, Tierney WM. Computer-stored medical records. Their future role in medical practice. *JAMA* 1988; 259(23): 3433-3440.
52. Mamlin JJ, Baker DH. Combined time-motion and work sampling study in

a general medical clinic. *Med Care*. 1973; 11: 449-456.

53. Maguire GP, Rutter DR. History-taking for medical students.1. Deficiencies in performance. *Lancet*. 1976; 2: 556-558.

54. Engel GL. The deficiencies of the case presentation as a method of clinical teaching. Another approach. *N Engl J Med*. 1971; 284(1): 20-24.

55. Woolliscroft JO, Calhoun JG, Beauchamp C, Wolf FM, Maxim BR. Evaluating the medical history: Observation versus write-up review. *J Med Educ*. 1984; 59: 19-23.

56. Bates B. *A Guide to Physical Examination*. 4th. ed. Philadelphia: J.B.Lippincott Co; 1987.

57. Burnum JF. The misinformation era: The fall of the medical record. *Ann Intern Med*. 1989; 110(6): 482-484.

58. Physicians for the Twenty-First Century. *Subgroup Report on Clinical Skills*. *J Med Educ*. 1984; 59(2): 139-147.

59. Stillman PL. Use of standardized patients to evaluate clinical skills. In: Singer I, ed. *Proceedings of the Conference on Physician Competence: Whose responsibility?* Chicago, Ill: American Medical Association; 1988: 71-77.

60. Donnelly J. Righting the medical record. Transforming chronicle into story. *JAMA*. 1988; 260(6): 823-825.

61. Sullivan SN. Clinical hypocompetence: The interview. *Ann Intern Med*. 1980; 93: 573.

62. Weed LL. Medical records that guide and teach. *N Engl J Med*. 1968; 278(11): 593-600.

63. Weed LL. Medical records that guide and teach (concluded). *N Engl J Med*. 1968; 278(12): 652-657.

64. Berwick DB. Health services research and quality of care: Assignments for the 1990s. *Med Care*. 1989; 27: 763-771.

65. Kerzner LJ, Greb L, Steel K. History-taking forms and the care of geriatric patients. *J Med Educ*. 1982; 57: 376-379.

66. Omenn GS. Prevention and the elderly: Appropriate policies. *Health Affairs*. 1990; 9(2): 80-93.

67. Aloia JF, Jonas E. Skills in history-taking and physical examination. *J Med Educ*. 1976; 51: 410-415.

68. Wiener S, Nathanson M. Physical examination. Frequently observed errors. *JAMA* 1976; 236(7): 852-855.

11

Computers in Medical Communicating

Marvin E. Gozum, M.D.

The fundamental characteristic of medicine is the growth in knowledge that rapidly translates into increased information to be assessed and used by physicians in patient care. If not organized and controlled in some fashion, this growing amount of information would overwhelm students, teachers, and practitioners. Information-handling technologies and telecommunications are basic tools of modern society, and their ability to organize and control this growing information base has been of inestimable value to the practice of medicine. Because physicians are essentially information processors, how they process, record, retrieve, use, and communicate information dominates the practice of medicine. This task, once onerous and time consuming, has been eased to a remarkable degree by computer technology. The enabling technology that has allowed the development of convenient systems to collect, store, organize, retrieve, and disseminate enormous amounts of information is the computer and related information-managing technology.

WHY A COMPUTER?

In the last 12 years there has been phenomenal growth in the number of personal computers used in medicine, business, and homes. Computers can be found in laboratories, factories, photocopiers, bank machines, and even microwave ovens. There are many reasons for the rapid growth of computers, but if a single characteristic could be selected, it would be versatility. A computer system, also called *hardware*, can simultaneously serve its "user" as a typewriter,

---

Marvin E. Gozum, M.D., is Clinical Assistant Professor of Medicine; Chief, Section of Medical Informatics Division of Internal Medicine, Department of Medicine; and Chief, Section of Medical Consultation, Wills Eye Hospital, Philadelphia.

checkbook, ledger, phone book, or video game simply by changing its program, or *software*. Computer capabilities continue to increase monthly so that expensive, high-powered machines, once affordable only by a few scientists in scattered laboratories, are now found in most offices at a fraction of the original cost. Tasks once possible only with specialized equipment can now be performed by computers with appropriate software, and writing and communicating is no exception. For example, computers can now permit persons to literally create publications from their own desks.

COMPUTERS AS A WRITERS' TOOL: THE WORD PROCESSOR

One of the most popular programs for any computer is a word-processing program or word processor. A *word processor* is either a computer program or a dedicated computer that allows writers to type and edit manuscripts, like a typewriter, without the need for paper copy until documents are ready for printing. At the present time, word processors have replaced typewriters as the chief tool for producing documents. Although a typical word processor provides basic typing and editing functions, most modern programs include built-in dictionaries and thesauri. Modern word processors can print in various type styles and sizes, include graphs and charts, merge pictures, and produce typeset-quality documents.

The evolution of word-processor capabilities has also added some functions that are difficult to use. In order to market programs, software companies have added more functions to gain an edge over competitors and also to justify increased program costs. Many of these functions may never be used by physician writers (such as built-in calculators). Thus, three points need to be remembered when purchasing word processors. First, a program should be easy to use. Most of a writer's computer time should be spent writing, not deciphering how to operate the program. Thus, ease of use is considered a program feature, and this will be marked on the package or emphasized by the salesperson. Second, a physician should buy a program for current use, not for future needs. Basic word processors now offer similar capabilities, and market forces have made the cost of basic word processors almost identical. It is difficult to determine future electronic writing needs, but it has been shown that most additional word-processor capabilities that add to the cost and complexity of a program are never used by most writers. It is usually the added functions that differentiate most word processors today. Lastly, a physician should estimate the maximum writing volume required and insure that the program is capable of editing that size of text. Cheap word processors typically limit editing to increments of 17 to 20 pages of single-spaced text, while more expensive programs are limited only by the computer's "system memory." More expensive word-processing programs for IBM-PC clones and Apple Macintosh computers allow editing increments of over several hundred pages of single-spaced text.

Many academic, corporate, and business users find word-processor file-formats important. The *file-format* of a word processor is the method used by programs to store documents on a computer. It may be necessary to share these "computer documents" among users in an institution but, unfortunately, the file formats of different word processors are, generally, incompatible. Programs may be purchased, or are included with some word processors as features, that convert between different formats. Converting formats may be an important feature if file-format documents need to be shared with other users such as publishers. IBM-compatible word processors support a limited universal format, called ASCII text, a simple text format that can be shared between programs. ASCII text was designed in the 1960s as a file-format for text, but now has only limited capabilities. ASCII text stores only text and margination data, but cannot save modern word-processor formats such as type styles, superscripts, subscripts, or mathematical symbols.

There are computers dedicated to word processing that are computers designed to run a specific word-processing program built into the computer. These devices are half the cost of a typically non-dedicated computer system and are often portable, but their word-processing programs cannot be changed to accommodate software innovations. Dedicated word processors usually come with draft-quality printers, non-standard file-formats, and inadequate word-processing capabilities by today's standards. If portability and cost are an issue, the rapid developments in portable computers, which can run word processing software, have made such portable computers a better choice in price, performance, flexibility, and software upgrades than dedicated word-processing computers.

COMPUTER AS EDITOR: THE GRAMMAR CHECKERS

Computer programs called *grammar checkers* are available that have limited proofreading and editorial capabilities. These programs are capable of checking grammar, usage, style, and spelling to produce more concise texts. For example, a statement such as:

> It is commonly known that undesirable elements may resort to felonious methodologies to achieve their ends.

may be simplified to:

> Undesirables may perform crimes.

It is important to consider accuracy, ease of use, and compatibility with word-processing software when purchasing proofreading programs. These factors are the principle characteristics of grammar checkers and will be emphasized by both salesmen and product literature. Many computer magazines provide valuable assessments of grammar-checking programs. Grammar checkers are an excellent substitute for human proofreading.

COMPUTER AS TYPESETTER: THE DESKTOP PUBLISHER

Desktop publishers are programs that allow computers to typeset documents and arrange graphics in preparation for publication. Unlike word processors, desktop publishing produces documents similar to professional journal pages, textbook pages, or newspaper columns, but desktop publishers lack the breadth of editing capabilities found in word processors. Laser printers and modern desktop publishers produce typeset-quality pages that rival a professional equivalent, the Linotype. Desktop publishers allow users to produce high-quality publications that rival professionally created periodicals. Desktop publishers, however, are of limited use for physician writers because medical journals usually request material with limited formatting. Because of their popularity, however, many modern word processors incorporate some features of desktop publishers as special capabilities. Physicians should be careful not to purchase expensive word-processor-desktop publishers that do more than they actually need.

GRAPHICS

Graphics is a generic term for the free-hand drawings, photographs, or charts that are used in documents. Prior to computers, graphics had to be drawn or created professionally to be suitable for publication. Now, special computer programs have replaced humans in the production of graphics. Many complex programs require computer skills but, overall, they simplify the work of professional graphic artists.

Computer as an Art Tool: Drawing Programs

The simplest programs for graphics replace paints, brushes, pens, charcoal, and inks in the production of graphics and are called *drawing* or *painting programs*. Using a "light pen" or "mouse" (computer devices for moving a pointer on the computer screen), an artist can draw images free-hand and add embellishments much as a graphic artist would on paper. Good paint programs have four characteristics: control of drawing tools as its non-computer equivalent, ease of use, large selection of tools, and a wide range of colors. Paint programs rely on the artist to provide quality graphics, so a judgment of the appropriateness of a program rests with the user. Generally, a minimal graphics program must use a mouse or light-pen, will support at least 256 colors, and will "pre-draw" circles, polygons, straight lines, rectangles, and squares of various sizes and colors. A basic drawing program must support the following tools: flood-fill, air-brush, variable shape and size paint brushes, text-entry with variable fonts, and cut-and-paste editing. Features beyond these basic functions will determine the overall cost of the program. Historically, graphic features were set as a "standard" by the Xerox PARC project, popularized by the Macintosh computer.

Computers as Slide Makers: Presentation-Graphics Programs

Speaking engagements and presentations often require the use of graphics. Most speakers use slides, transparencies, and paper charts as visual aides. Although drawing programs produce art, it is often necessary to lay out graphics in preparation for shooting film, transparencies, or chart production. Lettering in slides must often be a certain size and type to be effective. Text, images, and charts should be properly centered on slides. Recognizing this need, software manufacturers have created programs to automate the production of visual aids in terms of format, style, and layout. Audiovisual services used to take about an hour to manually produce a single slide. With *presentation-graphics programs*, the production time for a good slide is less than one minute, and it can be created by the occasional computer user. Design uses up most of the time spent creating slides on computers, but then the slide must be printed. For an occasional user, it is cost effective to deliver computer disks with finished images to a production facility for printing. The cost of color printers and slide-making equipment, although decreasing with time, remains high and is not a worthwhile investment for an occasional user. Attempts to print images by photographing the computer screen produce inadequate images.

When shopping for presentation-graphic programs, remember that special features and custom capacities increase program cost and operational difficulty. Graphic formats from these programs should be compatible with the production facility used to make the finished visual aids. If slides require embedded graphics or variable shades of color for slide backgrounds, then a presentation-graphic program is ideal. Otherwise, for less demanding requirements (such as standard white-on-blue slides or white-on-black slides containing only text), simple word-processor files with text centered on the page, printed in a Courier font at 14-to-18-point sized type will be sufficient for most production facilities. Most production facilities support many graphic formats, including slide production from standard word-processor formats, so it is wise to consult with the production facility to discover which programs they support. Software companies that produce presentation-graphic programs usually offer a 24-hour express-mail service to create slides from their programs, so the absence of a graphics service nearby is not a limiting factor.

Computer as Photographer: Image-Processing Programs

With so many steps involved in producing photographs, such as lighting, position, film characteristics, and printing, multiple photographs are usually taken of subjects until one or a few images meet the requirement of the author or publisher. Professional photographers often "touch-up" photographs to minimize blemishes or highlight important areas. A similar touch-up process can be performed with computers by an expert user. Two tools are needed in addition to a computer: a desktop or hand image scanner and *image-processing software*. Despite the ease of use of personal computers, image processing still requires users to understand the effects of complicated image-processing methods on photographs. Image-processing programs require fast computers with high-resolution screens and a large computer RAM memory. Criteria for selecting programs, then, depend heavily on the users' knowledge of image-processing methods. Expensive programs have greater image-processing capabilities, giving the user more resources with which to manipulate images.

Imaging methods offer great ability to manipulate the contents of photographs. A photographed subject can be removed, altered, enhanced, clarified, or discolored to obscure original features or distort reality. The complexity of computer methods for image analysis almost limits image processing to professionals, but many basic features can be performed by casual users. Most users may simply need to label, add pointers, highlight, crop, or frame photographs. A hand scanner and a drawing program will perform these tasks admirably.

COMMUNICATIONS BY COMPUTER

As a communications tool, writing has distinct advantages over radio's spoken words or television's images. Facts can be presented clearly and unambiguously, and documented for later reference. Documents can be copied and distributed cheaply to many individuals. Documents can be read at leisure by readers. However, the time it takes to typeset and print a document limits the speed with which documents can be distributed. For specific audiences, *computer networks* have the advantage of communicating and distributing documents with the speed of cable television.

Computer networks refer to computers that are connected, through specialized connectors and cables, to a cable system that links other computers together. These networks are not limited to personal computers but have, traditionally, connected many mainframe computers across the country. Network subscribers often have specialized needs, and have tended to be in the military, in industry, and at universities. To increase their outreach, network administrators have joined their networks to other networks, allowing communications throughout the world. Within these networks, subscribers can send computer-generated documents or scanned images to specific recipients, or to all subscribers. Thus, the advantage of a large distribution for documents can be realized without printing or distribution delays. However, these advantages require the addressee or audience be within the network.

Such a broad country-wide network is often referred to as a Wide Area Network, or WAN, contrasted to an office or a building network, often called a Local Area Network, or LAN. In many institutions, LANs serve as the media by which office personnel communicate with each other, replacing the established inter-office memo method.

Network communications are still limited to large institutions, but it is possible for individuals with an interest in the network's area of specialization to subscribe. Using a large, ubiquitous "network"--telephone lines and a modem (a device connecting computers to phone lines)--individuals may subscribe to fee-based services that offer connections to networks. Over the last 15 years, the most popular of these services has been CompuServe. CompuServe houses large computers that offer thousands of gateways to networks. CompuServe also provides hundreds of additional services such as access to databases for news, medicine, law, and consumer goods.

For computer users with narrower interests, many institutions run computer bulletin board services, or BBSs. These are similar to CompuServe, but are usually free, and are limited to the users registered with the owner of the BBS. States have local computer clubs that maintain lists of phone numbers for access to these BBSs.

SPECIAL WRITING CONSIDERATIONS USING COMPUTERS

Word processors have, for the most part, replaced typewriters as writing tools. Of the many functions available in these computer programs, six basic concepts remain the cornerstone of word-processor-based writing.

Choose a word processor that presents your text as it will appear when it is printed on paper. This function, called *wysiwyg* (pronounced weeseewhig), stands for "what you see is what you get." Since formatting and appearance are essential to finished text, this feature will save printing errors and your time.

Because words, sentences, and paragraphs can be moved around in a word processor, it is easier to write outlines directly with word processors than it is to draft outlines on paper. Ideas unrelated to the outline can be written down immediately and organized later.

Not all characters that appear on a computer screen in a word processor can be printed. These special non-printing characters are called *control* characters. These special characters that have no alphabet equivalent are used for control functions, such as setting typestyle, character size, ends of lines, paragraphs, or tabs. Other control characters may stand for characters in other languages, such as those in German, French, or Spanish, or symbols in mathematics. All word processors have different methods to type control characters; knowledge of this "invisible" character set will allow the proper printing of non-English words. Most computer manufacturers follow the ASCII standard, which defines control and alphabet characters for 256 codes. Some manufacturers, such as IBM, have extended the character set for their own needs. Word-processor manuals provide guidance for access to these codes.

Search-and-replace functions in word processors can be used for special purposes. Search-and-replace will search for a particular word and place the cursor (a point on the computer screen that indicates where newly typed characters will appear) on that word, or, if "replace" was invoked, replace the searched word with the selected new word. Search-and-replace is almost always case sensitive, and will recognize the difference between capital and lower-case letters. Search-and-replace functions always search for characters within words. Most word-processor programs, regardless of price, have these capabilities:

1. Case-sensitive sentence or fragment searches can be done by adding a single space before and after the search sentence;
2. Bookmarks can be left anywhere on documents by leaving a stream of characters unlikely to be duplicated elsewhere, for example, a line of *x's:* xxxxxxxxxxxxx;
3. Unfamiliar words, such as Latin phrases, may be written as a pseudonym left for substitution until a proper word is found;
4. Word processors can be used to search through databases saved from services such as CompuServe.

Most word processors are capable of *file-merge*. When a document is loaded into a word processor, it is called the *current document*. Another document can then be merged or joined with the current document to effectively merge the contents of the two documents. The point of merging is marked by the cursor's last location. A practical use for file-merge is to take versions of other documents that have been saved and incorporate these versions into the current document. Previously saved versions may be sections of literature searches, quotes from other documents, or quotations from other writers. File-merge becomes very useful in "boilerplating," as described below.

Physicians in clinical practice frequently have to write letters in which a great deal of patient detail must be repeated. Previously composed letters may be used repeatedly for different purposes, not unlike form letters. "Form letters" may be individually addressed by word processors, giving them the advantage of a personal touch. Whole documents, paragraphs, and sentences can be reused in new documents. These reusable sections are known as *boilerplate*, and, while more expensive word processors support this feature, file-merge can perform a similar feature. Using file-merge, the writer simply merges a document containing boilerplate sections with the current document, then adds whatever additional statements are needed. Boilerplate sections can be written for insurance company purposes, patient addresses, closing statements, opening statements, abnormal laboratory studies, parts of physical examinations, or even entire normal physical examinations. Boilerplating can add detail and legibility, correct spelling, and ensure proper grammar to that part of physician correspondence where its use is appropriate.

In moderately priced word processors that support boilerplating directly, physicians will find a *mail-merge* function. Once set and turned on, mail-merge links a document--usually a file of addresses or opening sentences--to another document, and can print individually addressed documents as a batch without further user intervention.

WHAT COMPUTERS ARE BEST FOR YOU?

A computer system consists of the components, called *peripherals*, that are needed to perform the functions for which the computer was purchased. A basic computer system consists of a system unit (the "box" containing the computer power supply and hard-drive memory), video monitor, printer, and *operating system software*. Operating system software are programs like MSDOS that coordinate the peripherals to work together and provide a common milieu for application programs. *Application software programs* are programs designed for specific work, such as a word-processor or graphics programs. An up-to-date computer must also come with a minimum of 100 megabyte of hard-disk space, 4 megabyte of RAM memory, and a 3.5-inch floppy disk drive. Recognizing the need for such systems, some manufacturers bundle all necessary peripherals and software as a fixed package, such as the word-processors previously described.

Most users today must decide between three computer systems that, in decreasing order of popularity are: IBM-PC clones, Apple's Macintosh, and Unix Workstation machines.

IBM-PC CLONES

Originally produced by International Business Machines (IBM) as the IBM PC (personal computer), these machines have been successfully copied, enhanced, and sold under various manufacturer's names, and are universally referred to as *PC clones*. The PC clones of today are much more powerful than the original IBM PC of 1982. Because they have the largest installed base of personal computers, the PC-clone market offers the largest selection of computer programs, lowest prices in software, lowest prices per hardware system, and the largest range of software and hardware options. Unfortunately, PC clones and peripherals lack a standard and, consequently, subtle differences exist among different PC clones and peripherals. These differences often can cause problems with programs or peripherals that require a high level of computer literacy to solve. IBM has released a family of computers called the PS/2 (Personal System Two), whose hardware is incompatible with PC clones, but which maintains software compatibility. The PS/2 line is well designed and more costly, but has not proven to be too successful. PC-clone manufacturers have enhanced the original design of IBM, and have developed highly cost-effective machines that have proven to be more popular than the PS/2 line.

Historically, system prices have ranged from $300 (for the original PC) to about $5500 for top-of-the line PC-clone computer systems. PS/2 prices are about 50 percent higher than clone system prices. System processors determine the capacity and speed of computers, with the most current being the 80386 and 80486 processor families. A recommended basic system for a new user consists of a 386DX, running 33 MHz or faster; 4 megabytes of memory; a 100-megabyte hard disk; a 3.5 inch floppy drive; a SuperVGA card and SuperVGA color monitor of .28mm dot pitch or less; an MS DOS 5.0 (or greater) operating system, and Microsoft Windows software. As of this writing, such a computer system costs about $1300 or less.

APPLE MACINTOSH

Apple introduced the Macintosh computer in 1984 and revolutionized the computer industry with a computer that offered ease of use rivalled only by typical household appliances. Prior to the introduction of the Macintosh (and still typical of today's PC clones), computer systems lacked standard programs and peripherals. The Macintosh system offered simplicity and a standard, making the need for basic computer literacy unnecessary and producing a dedicated following of Macintosh users. Ahead of its time, the Macintosh was designed for graphics applications and remains highly popular among graphic artists. Macintosh software is slightly less varied, less prolific, and is generally priced slightly higher than PC clones. Macintosh software, however, is consistently of the highest quality and is the system of choice for graphics work. As the machines age and new improvements come out, Macintosh hardware upgrades have been costly and require sending the computer back to Apple or to one of its distributors. Among PC-clone users, upgrades can often be done by users at home and at lower cost. As the sole manufacturer of entire computer systems, Apple is in the position to dictate its prices. Although Macintosh system costs have decreased tremendously, an equivalent PC-clone system costs 50 percent less. Most users tend to buy complete systems from Apple. A recommended basic Macintosh system consists of the monochrome Macintosh Classic II or equivalent; an 80-megabyte hard drive; 4 megabytes of RAM memory; and a 7.0 operating system at a cost of about $1200. To add a color monitor, a new Macintosh system requires a separate video monitor, making the total cost about $2,000 for the Macintosh LC, or $3000 for the II series.

UNIX WORKSTATIONS AND OTHER COMPUTERS

The Unix operating system requires a large computing capacity, and was designed in the 1970s to allow several people to use a computer simultaneously. Unix systems are dominated by the SPARC Station manufacturer, Sun Microsystems. Unix has traditionally been the operating system of choice for minicomputers in academia, but their power is now almost matched by the PC clones and new Macintoshes. Unix-capable machines can be purchased from vendors (usually in industry or academia), and are used primarily to run software of high capacity, such as in automotive design. In specific disciplines, some faculty members may spend their entire working hours on powerful Unix machines, thus the name "Unix Workstations." Although Unix machines can run PC-clone and some Macintosh software, their cost is higher than other systems. Taking all into consideration, Unix systems are not cost effective for individual users.

Commodore, a survivor of the home-computer wars of the 1970s, still manufactures the Commodore Amiga computer system. Formerly the cheapest reliable system available, it cannot compete against the breadth of the PC clones or the Macintosh today.

When choosing a computer system for professional or personal use, physicians need to consider families of software, peripherals, and costs incurred over the life of the computer. For performance and cost effectiveness, PC clones like Compaq and Dell are a good investment, provided the user is aware that basic computer literacy will be required for efficient operation of the machine. If you consider acquiring basic computer literacy a high price to pay for meeting your computing needs, the Macintosh family is an excellent choice, even though these systems are more expensive than PC clones.

PRINTERS

Four types of printers are available. Choice of an appropriate printer should be based, mostly, on a consideration of the use for which it is needed. A very high-quality printer would not be needed, for example, if its intended use is only to print pages of data. Physicians can make the best judgment about the speed, quality, and convenience of any printer by a demonstration of its capabilities. Such a test is available on every printer through a built in self-test, which can be run independently of a computer in a sales showroom.

The quality of *dot-matrix printers* may be viewed as that of a typewriter. The quality of dot-matrix printing today meets or supersedes that of the daisy-wheel printer (now obsolete). Inexpensive printers, costing about $120, are capable of producing highly legible print that appears to be the product of a high-quality typewriter, called "near-letter-quality output." Dot-matrix printers can also produce carbon copies. Dot-matrix printers are mechanically reliable, but are noisy in operation. Printers by Epson, Panasonic, and Okidata have dominated the dot-matrix market. The more features a printer has, the better a value it is for its price. Compare dot-matrix printers on their print speed and their quality of print. The speed of printing is measured in characters per minute or *cp/m*. Dot-matrix printers produce two levels of print quality: (1) *draft mode*, which is fast and produces letters of more primitive shape and lighter density; and (2) *near-letter quality* (NLQ) mode, which is slower and produces a high-resolution type that is difficult to distinguish from the product of a high-quality typewriter. Printers that feature high cp/m are best; the minimum should be 120 cp/m in draft mode and 12 cp/m in NLQ mode. Another feature to look for is the number of *pins* that strike an inked ribbon and form each character. Inexpensive printers use 9 pins, while more expensive printers use 24 pins. Generally, more pins produce better NLQ printing at higher speeds, but a good 9-pin printer can produce the same quality NLQ at a lower cp/m rate. A third feature to look for is the capacity to control the feed of two types of paper on demand: *tractor paper* (continuous sheets with holes on the left and right margin), and *single sheets*. Tractor paper is ideal for reviewing drafts, while single-sheet paper allows convenient printing on stationery. A fourth feature to consider when evaluating printers is its quietness in operation. Also, consider cost: a replacement ribbon for a dot-matrix printer costs about $6, and lasts for over 1000 single-spaced pages. Finally, graphics printing is not a strong feature of dot-matrix printers. At best, graphics printing by dot matrix resembles the kind of monochrome graphics typically found in newspapers.

Ink-jet printers print by spraying tiny droplets of ink on to paper. Most ink jets accept only single sheets. Because the droplets in an ink jet are minuscule and numerous, they provide quieter operation and superior print quality than dot-matrix printers. Ink-jet printers that print in color are available. The most reliable ink-jet printers are made by Hewlett Packard, and cost about $300 for a standard printer and $600 for a color printer. Ink-jet printers cannot print in draft mode, cannot use tractor paper, cannot make carbons, and have higher operating costs. On the other hand, ink jets reproduce graphics well. A replacement ink-jet cartridge costs about $20 and lasts for about 500 single-spaced pages.

Laser printers work on the same principles as photocopying machines. Laser printers contain built-in computers and operate quietly. Their computers control a laser that burns characters on paper and produces shades of grey, and the size of the computer's memory determines the capabilities of the printer. More expensive than other printers, laser printers produce type of superior quality; of near-typeset quality compared to other printing devices. They are ideal for physician correspondence and manuscripts. However, the complex design of laser printers increases the breakdown rate and the need for more frequent maintenance. The design of the laser's computer and its internal software determine the laser printer's chief characteristics, print quality, and speed. Laser printers were popularized by Hewlett Packard, who leads the market with reliable printers. Laser printers have the same disadvantages of ink-jet printers, and should be judged on print quality, which must be seen and compared to typeset pages, and the number of full-text pages produced per minute (*ppm*). Current standards are set by Hewlett Packard's Laserjet III series, at 6 ppm. Laser printers cost from $600 up. A toner cartridge for a laser printer costs about $75 and lasts for about 1000 single-spaced pages. Some companies offer to refill cartridges for half the cost, a frequent practice that is discouraged by manufacturers of toner cartridges. Color laser printers are available, starting at $2500. Monochrome graphics printed by laser printers are of excellent quality.

Thermal-transfer printers work like dot-matrix printers, except they use heater wires that burn a special heat-sensitive paper. Small, lightweight, slow, and capable of running on batteries, thermal-transfer printers produce only type in draft mode or poor NLQ mode and are often used in portable computers. Available usually as 9-pin printers, they have all the disadvantages of ink-jet printers, and use special roll paper. However, thermal printers are mechanically simple, robust, reliable, and quiet. Thermal printers are used for their portability, and cost from $250 to $500, with Kodak printers dominating the market. Thermal paper costs about $10 per roll. Thermal paper printouts, however, must be photocopied to be saved, as they fade with age.

Historically, software vendors for PC clones developed many applications that maximized the use of dot-matrix printers for business correspondence; thus, a dot-matrix printer for about $120 does well with PC-clone systems. Macintosh systems are graphics oriented, and acceptable printouts are created only by ink jet and laser printers. The Apple Stylewriter (an ink-jet printer), and the Apple LaserPrinter are excellent choices for about $300 and $1300 respectively. When graphics printing is important, a laser printer is ideal. For color printing, the Hewlett Packard Color Inkjet Printer produces acceptable business graphics. Color laser printers are very expensive, and at present do not produce images of photographic quality.

PROGRAMS TO CONSIDER

The most useful programs are listed under six categories and divided by computer system. This list is *not* meant to be comprehensive.

Program Type	PC Clone	Macintosh
Word Processors		
General	Microsoft Write*	MacWrite
Full function	WordPerfect	Microsoft Word
(thesaurus and	Microsoft Word	WordPerfect
dictionary included)	AmiPro	
Grammar checkers	Grammatik	Correct Grammar
		Grammatik Mac
Drawing	Microsoft Paint*	MacDraw
Desktop Publishing	Ventura Publisher	Aldus Pagemaker
	Aldus PageMaker	Adobe Systems
	Adobe Systems	Ready, Set Go!
Presentation Graphics	Microsoft Powerpoint	Aldus Persuasion
	Harvard Graphics	Microsoft PowerPoint
Communications	Microsoft Terminal*	Smartcom II
	Procomm	MicroPhone II

*These are free programs that come with Microsoft Windows software.

Resource Bibliography

Greenes RA, Shortliffe, EH. Medical informatics. An emerging academic discipline and institutional priority. *JAMA*. 1990; 263: 1114-1120.

Haynes RB, McKibbon A, Walker CJ, Ryan N, Fitzgerald D, Ramsden MF. Online access to MEDLINE in clinical settings. A study of use and usefulness. *Ann Intern Med.* 1990; 122: 78-84.

McDonald CJ, Tierney WM. Computer-stored medical records. Their future role in medical practice. *JAMA*. 1988; 259: 3433-3440.

12

Improving Medical Writing and Communication Skills

WRITING AND SPEAKING SKILLS

Writing and speaking are powerful and persuasive forms of medical communicating and physicians should be strongly encouraged to continually broaden and improve their skills in the techniques of both forms. It is also important for physicians to understand that each form of communicating has different characteristics because the written word is more formal than the spoken word. There is a need, therefore, for physicians to not only be aware of the structural and stylistic differences between written and spoken language, but also to understand and appreciate how each form of medical communicating can be used most effectively.

Writing Skills

Developing acceptable writing skills should be a major aim for physicians because the nature of the medical profession is such that physicians can not escape the need to write, be it a patient's medical record, a letter to a referring physician, or an article for submission to a medical journal. However, the abilities of physicians to use writing as an effective communication skill has been harshly criticized by a variety of experts over the years. Physician writing has been described as filled with confused thought and ambiguity, ungrammatical and pretentious constructions, subspecialty jargon and neologisms, and reflecting a general ineptitude with the English language. Consider this sentence from a program abstract appearing in the printed program for the annual meeting of a national medical organization: "To this date, however, there have been no published studies correlating gross intra-articular anatomy and the compartments of the ankle that can be instrumented under arthroscopic visualization." The fact that there is no such verb as "instrumented" in the English language did not deter this physician author from coining a neologism. Learning about the topic and about the writing itself comes in refining diction, rethinking structure, and questioning meanings. The ability to write well to support effective critical analysis, logical arguments and meaningful interpretations, comes for most physician writers only after constant practice in writing and rewriting, in addition to thinking hard about writing as a learned skill.

Because writing is an important form of medical communicating, clarity in writing has to be considered a vital element of effective medical communicating. Clear thinking and clear writing should exist as a single linked activity. Unfortunately, the expressed criticisms of physicians' writing abilities speak to a lack of clarity in much of the material written by physicians. The purpose of medical writing of any type is to communicate information to readers, and transmission of information by the written word is part of the service and teaching obligations of the medical profession. Physicians who write for any professional purpose must have their expressed ideas understood exactly so that no possibility for misinterpretation or misunderstanding can creep into the written material. This goal can be achieved only by stating each expressed idea as clearly and simply as possible in words and sentences that are carefully crafted in a methodical fashion. It is almost impossible to misinterpret or misunderstand information that is presented in uncomplicated direct sentences written in simple and clear language. Misinterpretation and misunderstanding of written information usually accompanies writing that is convoluted, confusing, and ambiguous.

Regardless of whether a physician is writing a history and physical examination on a new patient, a progress note on an old patient, or a medical article for submission to a peer reviewed journal, the goal set for the writing effort should be the same. This goal is the transfer of precise and accurate information from physician to reader by the use of language that is grammatically correct and clearly understandable. In this context, writing is the intellectual act of expressing meaning through language. The more physicians know about the resources of the English language, the more likely it becomes that what physicians write will not only be written in proper form but also will be more understandable to readers. Medical writing is a form of technical writing and differs in style from the style used in literary writing. A good medical writing style is characterized by objectivity, brevity, and crispness in the written material and is achieved by way of plainness, simplicity, and orderliness in the writing effort. When asked to describe the appearance of the sky, for example, a literary author might write: "A sparkling clear azure blanket floats lazily overhead." By contrast, a medical writer would say: "The sky is blue and cloudless."

The ability to write clearly and in logical sequences is generally regarded as an important and desirable skill for physicians to possess but, judging from the way many physicians write, seems to be a professional skill more honored in the breach than in the attainment. Physicians should have a sense of pride in the writing they produce and in the written material to which they sign their names. Writing that is grammatically incorrect, badly structured, or conveys a confusing message should be rejected, revised, and rewritten until correct. Medical writing of any type can always be improved by proper word choice, shortening sentences, correcting grammatical errors, simplifying the vocabulary, and cutting out verbiage. Being able to transmit a clear and unambiguous message by what is written is a key characteristic of a good physician communicator.

Good medical writing reflects the writer's ability to think logically, and physicians who possess good writing skills combine clarity of thought with common language so readers understand clearly what has been written. Effective writing requires that physicians also possess certain technical skills such as a facility for the language, along with a sense of grammar, syntax, and writing structure that allows them to turn vague thoughts into words, sentences, and paragraphs on a sheet of paper or on a computer screen. Good physician writers know to not use more words than are necessary to express the intended meaning clearly, know to not use superfluous adjectives and adverbs, and know to not use complicated phrases in places where single words would serve just as well. Because physicians bear a heavy responsibility to convey clear and accurate information in their written material, they can fulfill this responsibility best by using precise rather than vague words, concrete rather than abstract terms, and familiar rather than unfamiliar words and phrases. To write effectively, physicians should also possess a good vocabulary, a feel for good sentence structure, an ability to string words together in sentences that are pleasing to read, a sense for appropriate word choice, and the good judgment to write to the language level of the projected readership. Medical writing, for whatever purpose, should be grammatically correct, simple in its construction, clear in its meaning, and pleasing to read.

Faults most commonly encountered in material written by physicians are careless writing, confusing writing, and verbose writing. The sheer awkwardness of expression exhibited by some competent physicians when they try to write and the ineptitude with ordinary English revealed by other physicians is only too commonplace. In many instances the cause of careless physician writing appears to be thoughtlessness, because physicians who habitually write in a careless and imprecise manner should know better by virtue of their educational background. Consider this carelessly composed sentence written by a physician in the hospital medical record of a patient admitted for a bone graft operation to repair a fracture nonunion of the tibia:

> There was some attempt at healing while being casted with some fracture callus but the patient still has gross motion at the fracture site and no increase in the amount of healing on x-ray over the past couple of months.

All the significant information is contained in this sentence but it hardly reads as a sentence constructed by a person as well educated as a physician. Physicians are trained to think in logical sequences when determining diagnostic possibilities and treatment plans for patients. Notes that physicians write on hospital charts documenting these diagnostic and therapeutic decisions should reflect this same logical sequencing, so as to avoid sentence structures that only confuse readers. If the physician who wrote the note quoted above followed that advice, the note could have led the reader along a clear logical line of thought in less words and would have read as follows:

> Although there was some attempt at fracture healing while the patient was casted, persisting nonunion of the fracture developed. Now there is gross motion at the fracture site and repeated x-rays have demonstrated no increase in fracture healing.

The real danger with careless and imprecise medical writing, however, is that it could convey careless and imprecise information about a patient's medical condition which could be detrimental to a patient's health outcome.

A sentence can be structurally correct, yet not be concise in its meaning so that it conveys information to readers in an improper or confusing fashion, or in a pedantic or equivocal manner. Such sentences often have to be read and reread before readers can gain insight into the physician writer's intended meaning. Consider this sentence written by a physician in a patient's hospital medical record:

> Admitted with symptoms suggestive of congestive heart failure, she requested a private room so she could be alone and undisturbed and her family was contacted about details of her past medical history.

Physicians who write sentences such as the one quoted above have neither learned nor appreciated that words are the tools of thought and, consequently, lack the ability to write logically or convey meaning clearly. The bad writing that such physicians produce is, more often than not, the outward and visible form of an inward confusion of thought.

Other physicians seem to fall in love with their own words and, as a consequence, produce writing that is verbose and overwritten. Such physician writers have failed to develop the emotional distance from their own words that good writers must have in order to edit their own material and craft their words and sentences into a style that is crisp and lean. Overwritten material always contains redundancies in words and ideas that annoy readers and waste their time. As far as medical articles written by physicians are concerned, the text should contain the essence of the study being reported, not all peripheral information in endless detail. Other physician writers have a fondness for new words or neologisms, current buzzwords, and technical jargon. Use of unnecessary and undesirable technical jargon has become a bad habit of many physician writers and needs to be recognized by them as a bad habit and corrected.

Combining a good vocabulary with a feel for crisp and correct sentence structure and an ability to link well selected words together in sequences that are easy and pleasing to read is the formula for an effective writing style that can produce good medical writing. In turn, good medical writing conveys its message to readers with clarity and simplicity, flows together easily, and does not seem awkward when read. The fact that good medical writing is crisp, lean, and objective in its composition should not preclude it being composed with grace and style and a sense for pleasing word selection and fit. Graceful medical prose helps convey clear messages to readers and carries them along a continuing line of thought in which paragraphs are linked so that readers do not start a new paragraph wondering how it relates to the one just finished. The ideas and information contained in the written material should be presented to readers in sequences that follow logical patterns that are immediately apparent to readers. The best advice for physicians who wish to improve their writing skills is to learn to write in such a manner that the information they wish to bring to readers will be clearly understandable to them on the first reading, and will be phrased so that the conveyed information is incapable of being misinterpreted or misunderstood by readers.

Speaking Skills

Physicians who wish to be more effective in commanding the attention of listeners in order to move them toward the position advocated by their spoken message can accomplish this by learning and using the techniques developed for this powerful form of medical communicating. In contrast to medical writing, medical speaking allows a greater freedom of personal expression in how the material is presented because content, organization, and delivery, the major elements of this form of medical communicating, are less restrictive than the elements associated with medical writing. The ability to speak effectively, and deliver a message that is both useful to and remembered by listeners, rests on the principles of good organization and preparation, and knowing something of the type and interests of the audience and their familiarity with the subject matter of the presentation. Proper organization and preparation are largely dependent upon having adequate time to research and plan what has to be said, followed by organization and production of the material that will make up the content of the talk. In preparing material for vocal presentation to an audience, physicians must be alert to possible differing levels of knowledge and familiarity with the subject matter of the talk among members of the audience, and take special care in preparing their remarks so that all members of the audience can understand and follow the development of the points being made by the speaker.

Regardless of the size of the audience, the location of the setting, or the prominence of the meeting at which a physician is scheduled to speak, success in the endeavor rests upon having good material to present, good organization and preparation of the material to be presented, and a pleasing style of delivery of the material when the talk is presented. A pleasing delivery style is enhanced by good vocal tone and use of voice modulation where appropriate. Presentations at important meetings should be delivered from a prepared text, practiced for delivery and timing until perfect, and illustrated with carefully selected slides that are professionally produced and shown in correct order at the proper time. Few things are more annoying to a medical audience than a disorganized and ill prepared speaker who, in all likelihood, will deliver a disjointed and wandering message Physician speakers should cover the material and points they wish to make in a clear, organized, and succinct manner and in their allotted time period. Successful accomplishment of this goal by physician speakers requires good organization of the material to be presented and practice in the technique of oral presentation. The best advice for physician speakers is to come to the lectern fully prepared with a well organized and well rehearsed talk. Instructions regarding speaking style and delivery and the showing of slides will assist in adding to the professionalism of the presentation but will, in no way, substitute for good material, good organization of the material to be presented, and good preparation and practice for the actual presentation.

COMMUNICATION AND INTERPERSONAL SKILLS

During the nineteenth century the writer, Robert Louis Stevenson, described physicians as the flower of civilization, and it is instructive to speculate why physicians of that century might have deserved such an accolade. During Stevenson's time medical science was minimal, medical technology was primitive, and diseases were rampant and frequently fatal. Yet, despite these almost overwhelming handicaps, physicians cared for patients with the limited resources of the time, but their most potent weapon was their ability to inspire their patients' trust and confidence. This element of charismatic authority, wielded in a positive sense by physicians of that era, encouraged patients to help and heal themselves. For this, more than for their medical skills, physicians were regarded as humanitarians and, as humanitarians, were accorded Stevenson's floral tribute. But, from the time physicians received this floral tribute to the present, Stevenson's flower seems to have wilted. Society now tends to believe the medical profession has lost sight of its idealism and professionalism, and has become a profession whose primary goal seems to be professional self-interest and greed rather than the welfare of their patients. Lack of a warm and caring attitude by physicians, coupled with their perceived overemphasis on the technological aspects of patient care are the reasons most frequently given by society to justify their present assessment of physicians.

Justified or not, physicians, once revered as humanitarians, are now widely perceived as possessing little actual regard for the individual patient. Many of the interpersonal problems now arising out of the physician-patient interaction are thought to be caused by modern physicians' believed lack of balance between emphasis on curing and emphasis on caring. This perceived lack of balance is fueling some developments in medical care that point up the need for physicians to look more closely at their own communication and interpersonal skills. Some managed care organizations are beginning to ask their patients to rate physicians' communications skills and availability as well as the technical aspects of the care received. These organizations believe that the potential for patient satisfaction with the clinical encounter to encourage increased revenue through high quality adds weight to the value of incorporating these patient measurement techniques into their total quality assurance programs. Patients appreciate and acknowledge modern medicine's scientific advances and the technical expertise and professional skills displayed by modern physicians, but decry what they believe are physicians' detached and uncaring attitudes and behaviors toward them as patients. Dissatisfaction with the interpersonal and communication skills exhibited by many present day physicians has contributed to the perceived wilting of Stevenson's flower, and to the recorded decline of medicine's professional image in the eyes of society. Improvement in the communication and interpersonal skills of physicians will help convert these expressed dissatisfactions by some patients into a realization that physicians do indeed represent a caring profession whose primary goal is not professional self-interest but, rather, a sincere concern for the welfare of their patients.

The physician-patient relationship is an important aspect of patient care because it pledges the physician to the moral code of the profession, which requires a physician to act for the welfare of the patient. Successful patient care, then, is highly dependent on effective communication between physician and patient. Skillful communication, in reference to interactions between physicians and patients, relates to physician and patient behaviors which are of particular importance to the flow of information between them. Physicians must master the ability to communicate effectively with patients so their intentions and meanings relative to these interactions can be conveyed to patients in a clear and understandable manner. In clinical interactions with patients, physicians not only have an obligation to diagnose and treat appropriately, but also to inform and advise the patient about his or her illness and its treatment, and to perform these functions with the courtesy expected of a professional person. However, continued expressed patient dissatisfactions with communication and interpersonal skills of physicians remains a strong reminder that improvement in these vital physician skills is needed.

In a privately circulated document entitled "Personal Remembrances of a Heart Patient," an anatomy professor at an East Coast medical school had this to say about his own remembered medical experiences eighteen years after coronary artery bypass surgery:

> As I look back at what I have been through, not only the experience of the operation but the other hospital stays, I am struck by one major problem which stands out far above all others. Physicians are well trained to address the health problems of the patient regarding identification and treatment of a disease state. They are usually poorly trained in dealing with the patient as a person and providing the kind of emotional support which the patient often desperately needs. Training is similarly weak in understanding the

fears and concerns of the family. Not all physicians lack these skills, of course. I was fortunate to have some very caring and supportive doctors. But in our fast-paced world where the time spent with each patient is minimized to maximize profit, skills which may have been addressed often are not used. Our medical schools are faced with an information explosion and the temptation, too often realized, has been to emphasize the technology rather than the patient. Young people, therefore, often do not acquire these interpersonal skills and the lay public progressively sees doctors as highly competent professionals providing excellent technical support, but with a coldness and lack of basic understanding or concern for their needs other than to provide an answer to a specific medical problem. Our medical schools must not let physicians be trained to be just another technician, doing a task, collecting a salary, and going home. Medicine is the art of healing humanely--it's about people helping people! Anything less should be unacceptable.

Criticisms of physicians by patients focus mostly on a lack of communication and interpersonal skills and lack of a caring attitude exhibited by physicians during clinical interactions with them. While impressed with medicine's scientific achievements, these expressed criticisms speak to the disenchantment of patients with what they perceive to be as careless, callous, thoughtless, or nonexistent psychosocial attitudes exhibited by some physicians. At its best, the physician-patient relationship brings science, kindness, and the moral power of medicine to the care of a single human being in need of medical help. At its worst, it spawns patient resentment and anger, and an increase in malpractice actions. For patients, no other human experience duplicates the intimacy, candor, physical access, and vulnerability of seeing a physician for a health problem. Unfortunately, for too many patients, the high technology and narrow specialization of modern medical practice tend to dehumanize the clinical encounter with some physicians. Fault for this situation lies partly with the medical education process which emphasizes science while providing little opportunity for instruction in communication and interpersonal skills. It is also important to note that erosion of social and humanistic concerns, and the lack of interest in these components of medical care displayed by some physicians, have been identified as being correlated with advanced medical training and the production of physicians whose behavior toward patients emphasizes curing over caring. Because of long years of clinical education, the behavior of many physicians toward patients is not patient centered but, rather, is disease oriented and tends to be self-protectively authoritarian. Such physicians have forgotten, or never learned, that technology can never completely replace touch in dealing with sick people, and that technology applied with compassion has a greater chance of healing than technology applied without compassion.

Physicians, once revered as humanitarians, are now often depicted as money oriented entrepreneurs, armed with mechanical gadgets, self-referral facilities, and high technology tests for diagnosis, but possessing little actual regard for individual patients. These criticisms will continue, and possibly worsen, until physicians and medical educators come to understand that patients are asking that physicians become more humanistic in their interactions with them. It seems clear that patients want physicians who interact with them as people, and consider their psychological and social features as well as the physical in their assessments and treatments. They want physicians who are compassionate and ethically sensitive, and who communicate empathy and sensitive concern to them in a warm and effective manner. Improvement in the communication and interpersonal skills of physicians can begin to occur only when physicians are willing to acknowledge, and accept as valid, the general sense of the criticisms directed toward their displayed psychosocial attitudes as perceived by patients.

To become effective communicators, physicians must learn to become effective listeners. Good physician communicators know the importance of listening more and talking less in clinical encounters with patients. It remains an interesting paradox that many patients hold their own physicians in high regard yet, at the same time, agree with these publicly expressed criticisms of the medical profession as a whole. The difference between the public's opinion of their own personal physicians and physicians as a professional group is known as the "image gap." Reversing this public perception of physicians' communication and interpersonal skills should be an important objective for the medical profession, because failure to do so risks opening the door to profound changes in the health care system, which could adversely affect the delivery of optimal patient care.

Interactions with Patients

Physicians need to appreciate that illness can create an abnormally sensitive emotional state in many patients, and reacting with appropriate sensitivity to such patients can be a difficult challenge for many physicians. Even if the physician brings superb clinical skills and an extensive scientific knowledge base to the clinical encounter, an effective patient response may not result unless these technical skills are tempered with understanding, compassion, and courtesy toward the patient as a person in need of medical help. Physician interactions with patients, in addition to providing professional assistance for specific health problems, should be associated with a subjective process that is sensitive and emotionally supportive, and includes an understanding of the patient, his or her personality, and his or her distress. To be effective, physician communications with patients must convey concern and compassion, and provide patient information because the object of the communication activity is an anxious patient, a fellow human being, apprehensive about his or her own state of health. Physicians who are able to communicate well with patients have the ability to combine patient information with courtesy and common sense. Other characteristics that are important to good personal communicating between both participants are empathy, trust, honesty, caring, and respecting each other's right to communicate. A crucial part of the bond between physician and patient is complete trust in the physician's honesty and sincerity toward the patient. Two additional characteristics of importance to physician communication abilities are listening to patients and the use of gentle humor to neutralize or alleviate stress. Patients seem to be more agreeable to physician recommendations about treatment when the patient believes he or she is not treated as just another medical problem, but, rather, is treated respectfully as a distinct individual by a physician who understands the requirements of a good physician-patient interaction, and who shows interest, attentiveness, and empathy toward the patient.

The core of the physician-patient relationship is the ability of the two participants in the clinical interaction to talk freely and openly with each other. Patients have become more demanding and more articulate in their expectations of effective communication with physicians, and judge their own physician to be a good communicator if he or she listens well and volunteers information and explanations to them. Physicians know, but need to be reminded from time to time, that medicine is still an area in which one physician, by bringing together the qualities of a knowledgeable and skillful clinician and a warm, caring, and supportive humanist, can make a vital difference, not only to a sick patient, but to the surrounding social environment as well. Giving attention to patients by paying heed to their concerns is a most important, yet often underemphasized, aspect of a physician's responsibility to patients. This is not only a self evident need for good patient care, but also a necessary element in the structuring of a successful physician-patient relationship. The truly competent physician knows that knowledge, clinical skills, interpersonal skills, and the ability to communicate well with patients are all important components of modern medical practice. Skillful physician communicators know that the manner and style of how they communicate with patients is as important to good patient care as any other aspect of the physician-patient relationship.

Patients consider a sense of confidence a desirable trait for their physicians to possess, and want to believe their own physicians are omnipotent in medical matters. However, physicians who foster or encourage a false sense of confidence in patients do these patients a cruel disservice. Wise physicians recognize that the realities of modern medicine with its attendant uncertainties make confidence tempered by honesty and sincerity a better course for them to follow. The truth of the matter is that many gaps exist in the knowledge base of medicine and many clinical decisions made on behalf of patients rest on an uncertain knowledge base because of these gaps. It is this uncertain knowledge base underlying modern medicine that often makes it impossible for physicians to know with certainty which among several courses of action, or inaction, will produce the best, or even an acceptable, outcome for patients.[1] Physicians, acting responsibly in clinical interactions with patients, should neither disregard these uncertainties in a false sense of confidence, nor be paralyzed into inaction by them. Medical uncertainties affecting clinical decision making exist, and this fact needs to be acknowledged by physicians and accepted by patients. In areas of clinical uncertainty, the wise physician uses his or her best clinical judgment to guide the patient in an honest and sincere manner. This allows the selection of a course of action for the patient based on forthright input from the physician, and an expression of preference by the patient. In addition to identified gaps in the medical knowledge base which make the outcomes of physicians' clinical decisions uncertain at best, the continuing effort to constrain health care costs can be expected to generate initiatives which will force physicians to give patients a larger voice in decision making relative to their own health needs.

It seems apparent a consensus is developing in this country that our medical care system must become more socially conscious and responsive to the needs of its patients. Many advocates for change in the way physicians practice medicine argue for a new model of medical practice, a model in which responsibility for decision making about patient care is shared between physician and patient. This developing consensus has induced a gradual shift from a paternalistic "doctor knows best" type of medical practice to a more egalitarian model characterized by the consent process and shared decision making. This is not to deny that doctors may very well know what is best for patients. Knowing what is best for patients is an acceptable reason for acting on their behalf, provided patients are fully informed of the reasons for the actions and are offered the opportunity to be part of the decision making process if they so desire. Counter arguments that clinical practice is best managed by the old style "doctor knows best" attitude, and that communication skills have little impact on patient care outcomes seem to be losing credibility in light of social science research findings over the past two decades that indicate that just the opposite is probably closer to the truth. Increasing recognition of the basic rights of patients to be treated as whole persons while receiving medical care has fostered a growing concern that the clinical competence of physicians be complemented with well developed communication and interpersonal skills. It seems quite likely that physicians of tomorrow, to be considered competent, will need to possess not only good clinical skills, but also will need to be skilled in ethical decision making as well as possess good communication and interpersonal skills.

Physician Behaviors and Attitudes

The physician-patient relationship, so crucial to effective patient care, is established at the time of the first clinical interaction between them. How well or how badly this newly established relationship develops will be influenced mostly by the behaviors and attitudes each participant brings to the encounter, and how each participant judges the outcome of the visit. This encounter is a test for physicians' interpersonal skills as these skills relate to physician behaviors and attitudes which are of particular importance to physician acceptance by patients. Dramatic technical advances in medical science are not as well understood or appreciated by patients as the warm, personal care offered to them by physicians in an unhurried way. Just as important as medical expertise and the proper use of new technologies is the ability of the physician to show legitimate concern, to be there during the bad times, and to provide hope even to the incurable.[2] Those physicians who have a sincere concern as to how they relate to patients are usually those who also understand the patient benefits generally associated with those affective components of good patient care known as the art of medicine and bedside manner. A patient's assessment of the clinical encounter generally reflects the professional attitudes of the physician, as those attitudes relate to these affective components of patient care. Patients are most satisfied with their interactions with physicians when competent medical care is provided to them in a compassionate, warm, and concerned manner, and are less satisfied with the interaction if the physician projects as impersonal, hurried, or more businesslike. Relationships between physicians and patients are often impaired because of careless communication between them, which can spill over into tangled relationships and even malpractice suits. Fault for a poor relationship can lie with either party to the interaction. Physicians may be abrupt, impersonal, and in a great rush to move on to the next patient. Patients may be demanding, overly dependent, distrustful, hostile, or uncooperative with medical suggestions and recommendations.

Both physicians and patients are subject to multiple forces which influence their behaviors in clinical situations. When sick, patients lose control of their familiar day to day routines, and must replace this lost sense of control with a sense of trust in those who are caring for them. It is when those who are caring for patients fail to appreciate this sense of trust instinctively afforded them by sick patients, and respond to these patients in autocratic, impersonal, or indifferent ways that the seeds for a poor physician-patient relationship may be sown. Physicians, by virtue of their educational background and clinical training, tend to take charge of clinical encounters with patients and often appear to be directive and controlling in their actions and behaviors toward these patients. This may be appropriate physician behavior in emergency medical care situations, but may not be as appropriate in more elective medical care situations. Authority exercised properly by physicians in medical care situations can be therapeutic and associated with positive patient responses. Patients will accept some domination from those physicians they have invested with authoritative experience and competence. This type of authority, characterized by benign paternalism and domination, can be an ingredient of beneficial medical care, particularly for worried, anxious, or dependent patients. On the other hand, authority exercised by physicians in a thoughtless, insensitive, or autocratic fashion, is resented by patients, and can have a negative and distressing effect on a physician-patient relationship. If a physician's sense of authority is accentuated by behavior that is insolent, vain, or arbitrary, or shows a clear lack of empathy for the patient, the outcome can be poorly received and ineffective medical care. As far as it is humanly possible under the conditions and constraints of the clinical environment, physicians should strive to treat patients as they, themselves, would wish to be treated if their roles in the clinical interaction were reversed. Most patients like to have some involvement with the decisions made concerning their own medical problems and respond better to physicians who are friendly, cordial, gracious, and sympathetic than to physicians who are perceived as more dominant, directive, and controlling. Patient dissatisfaction with the outcome of a clinical encounter with a physician is greatest when the physician's actions and behaviors during the encounter project a cold, impersonal, and uncaring attitude toward them as patients.

Too many physicians regard the scheduling of patient office visits as nothing more than a method of ordering their own convenience. The amount of time a patient must wait to see a physician is closely related to a patient's assessment of the value of the visit. Patient waiting time is influenced by a variety of factors, some of which are beyond the control of the physician, but an effectively structured scheduling system with smooth patient flow through the office can increase patient satisfaction with the care and attention they receive. If the schedule flow is disrupted by demands of emergency patient care or other unforeseen events, waiting patients should be kept informed of the delay and its cause, and offered an opportunity to reschedule the visit if desired. The use of medical jargon, appearing hurried or giving patients the sense of begrudging them adequate time to be heard, or conveying the perception of a pretentious, condescending, or paternalistic attitude on the part of the physician are the most frequently encountered barriers to effective communication between physicians and patients in face to face clinical interactions. Such physician behavior is antithetical to the qualities of humanism, caring, ethical behavior, and patient advocacy, which are the core elements of medicine's professionalism. All of these frequently encountered barriers to effective physician-patient communication can be easily remedied if physicians just decide to make the effort to correct these less than optimal behaviors.

Warmth, graciousness, and information giving on the part of a physician, rather than maintenance of authority and control, associate positively with patient satisfaction with clinical interactions with physicians. Patient satisfaction with a physician also relates more to their perception of the *quality* of the time spent in the interaction than to the total *length* of time physicians spend with them. Few patients are sufficiently knowledgeable to correctly assess the quality of the technical component of care they receive during a clinical encounter with a physician, but patients can, and do, evaluate the human side of how their medical care is delivered, and the compassion, warmth, empathy, courtesy, and concern for their welfare shown by their physician during the medical experience. How well physicians rate in this patient evaluation depends on how well physicians understand and make use of the skills of what is regarded as the "art" of medicine, and the requirements of acceptable social behavior between fellow human beings. There are some qualities beyond pure medical competence that patients need and look for in their physicians during periods of sickness. They want reassurance, and want to be looked after and not just looked over. They want to be listened to, they want to believe they are in their physician's thoughts, and they want to believe it makes a very big difference to their physician whether they live or die.

In most non-emergency medical care situations, physicians reactions to patients' medical needs will include one or more of the following responses: (1) they do something to, or for, the patient, (2) they tell the patient what to do, (3) they help the patient help himself or herself, or (4) they combine all three responses. The strongest physician-patient relationships are built by combining all three responses. Physicians need to realize that believing just the first or second response is sufficient identifies a physician with a rigid professional attitude. Physicians with good communication and interpersonal skills are flexible enough to combine these three responses to ensure satisfying clinical interactions with patients.

In the moment to moment challenges of an intensive care unit, or an operating room, a physician's technical skills and emergency decision-making capabilities are more important to patients than communication skills. In most non-emergency medical care settings, however, patients need physicians who treat them with humaneness and caring and provide them with empathy, communication, and patient education information. Wise physicians employ all their skills to potentiate and motivate patients and try to inspire confidence in them. Patients who seem to be getting the most out of their treatments are the ones who admit being inspired by their physicians. A knowledgeable and skillful clinician who is able to use benign charismatic authority to inspire confidence in patients is every person's perception of the ideal physician. It is the persona of the physician just as much, and frequently more, than what the physician does that creates an environment for healing. Sick, worried, and dependent patients are reassured and buoyed by caring and friendly physicians who look like physicians are generally expected to look. As superficial as it may appear, the physician's white coat seems to symbolize for many patients the magic of medicine, and these patients tend to associate the physician's white coat with medical science, compassion, and hope.

Physicians who are skilled at establishing rapport and trust with patients are more likely to be characterized as open-minded and flexible, and to exhibit positive attitudes toward people. Insightful and sensitive physicians have learned to interpret and respond to the nuances of both verbal and nonverbal communication exchanges between patients and themselves. The ability to establish rapport and trust with patients must also include the physician's ability to deal with intimately emotional material associated with patients and, on occasion, patients' families. Unfortunately, some physicians tend to avoid dealing with such material because of personal discomfort with it. Sensitive and caring physicians approach emotion-laden clinical encounters with patients with the knowledge that empathy is the clinician's essential tool in understanding the patient and his or her problem, and recognize the differing effects on patients of pity, sympathy, and empathy. Pity rarely helps distressed patients, sympathy commonly helps them, but empathy always helps patients. As applied to the physician-patient interaction, *empathy* is the feeling relationship that develops when the physician understands the patient's problem as if he or she was the patient and sees the medical situation through the eyes of the patient. An empathic physician can identify with a patient yet, at the same time, maintain sufficient professional distance so as to be able to make appropriate clinical decisions on behalf of the patient. Physicians who do not, or can not, develop empathic relationships with patients tend to maintain a more rigid distance from their patients in the mistaken belief that this attitude strengthens their image as authority figures, and increases their power to reassure patients. Neither a physician's depth of knowledge nor interviewing skills will be sufficient to provide effective and compassionate patient care unless the physician's behavior and attitude during the clinical interaction convey to the patient the sense that, for the physician, addressing the patient's needs ranks above all other considerations.

Patient care is improved if all members of the medical care team communicate and work well together in an environment of mutual trust. Unfortunately, the insensitive, arrogant, and outmoded behaviors of some physicians alienate members of their medical care teams, making an environment of mutual respect virtually impossible to achieve. Nurses and allied health personnel view themselves as professionals who should be expected to make more independent judgments within the framework of the medical care team, but many physicians have a difficult time adjusting to this concept. As a consequence, some physicians respond by showing little respect for the opinions of nurses and allied health professionals, rarely listening or accepting their views, resorting to outmoded male-female stereotyping, and, on occasion, even verbally abusing team members in public. These arrogant and unacceptable behaviors by some physicians toward other members of the medical care team have stimulated many hospitals to start what is called collaborative practice. This is a system of patient care management in which physicians, nurses, and other members of the medical care team approach patient care problem solving as a group, rather than individually as was formerly the case.

Interviewing Patients

It is in the interview process with new patients that physicians are expected to obtain the patient related information needed for them to take the appropriate actions necessary to diagnose and treat the problem for which the patient seeks help. A primary goal for physicians when undertaking new patient interviews is to obtain sufficient information from patients, and patients' families if appropriate, in a pleasant and efficient manner so a proper diagnosis can be approached or reached, and an appropriate management program or treatment plan determined. Interviews with new patients can be more complicated than many physicians realize if all the needed information is to be obtained in a reasonable time frame. Those knowledgeable about interviewing techniques believe the diagnostic interview with a new patient is one of the most complex and demanding of skilled interviewing techniques. Physicians' behaviors and attitudes, as well as their communication and interpersonal skills, influence and shape their interviewing skills, so it should be no surprise to notice that some physicians are instinctively better patient interviewers than others. What is surprising, however, is the information that, despite its obvious importance to good patient care, relatively little time is afforded in traditional medical school curricula for the teaching of physician interviewing skills. This is particularly unfortunate in light of the knowledge that successful interviewing techniques have been taught and used in other occupations for years.

For patient interviews to be successful, physicians need to possess sufficient skills to be able to question patients carefully and listen to their responses attentively, so the maximum amount of relevant information can be elicited. Physicians will get more information from patients during these interviews if they project as genuine in their concern for the patient and his or her problem, and if they ask their questions in a gently persuasive tone of voice rather than an authoritative tone. The outcomes of interviews will be improved if physicians give patients more time and encouragement in which to describe their medical problem, rather than, as so frequently happens, leading patients along with short answer questions and frequent interruptions of their stories. In structuring new patient interviews, physicians must schedule enough time so patients are satisfied they had sufficient time to tell their stories to physicians. Giving patients a more active role in the interview process has been shown to have positive consequences in that patients are better able to express needs, articulate concerns, and cooperate with diagnostic and treatment suggestions. Patients' perception of their physicians' warmth and understanding correlates positively with their being permitted to tell their stories in their own words to their physicians during the interview process. Obtaining objective information about their illness, proposed treatment, and prognosis from physicians at the end of the interview is also rated as very important by patients.

The most successful patient interviews from a patient care standpoint are those that are patient-centered as contrasted to physician-centered interviews. Good patient-centered interviews combine a careful analysis of the patient's symptoms and signs with an understanding of the patient's feelings about his or her condition and the implications the illness might have for his or her daily life.[3] This type of interview approach is most successful if combined with the interpersonal skills of listening, observing, and responding on the part of the physician. A patient-centered interview recognizes and acknowledges the patient as a person with a unique life history and a specific set of needs which occur in conjunction with a medical problem for which the patient seeks help. Physicians who are skilled at conducting patient-centered interviews are usually able to obtain more patient information that is germane to the medical problem at hand than are those physicians who are not so skilled.

An effective physician interviewer lets the patient talk at the beginning of the interview with the physician acting as a guide to the flow and direction of the conversation. Physicians skilled in interviewing techniques can control the flow of the interview process in a courteous manner by guiding the conversation to relevant subjects, and guiding the discussion to keep the patient to the point of the interview. Good physician interviewers make effective use of exploratory or open-ended questions, deal with the feelings of patients, demonstrate a willingness to listen to patients, and are able to appreciate the intensity of the experience for patients. Skilled physician interviewers know how to combine different types of questions to patients so as to obtain as much information as possible about the patients' problems. Each type of question serves a somewhat different purpose in the interview process, and skilled physician interviewers know how to blend them to obtain maximum information from patients in a reasonable time frame. Good physician interviewers understand that interview sequences may need to be altered on occasion, depending upon the requirements of the situation, and are flexible enough to respond and adjust accordingly. The best strategy for a successful physician interview with a new patient is to give the patient more time and encouragement in which to describe his or her problem, rather than leading the patient along with a series of closed and short answer questions, interspersed with frequent interruptions of the patient, in a physician-centered attempt to expedite the patient interview process.

Giving Information to Patients

The complaint from patients that they get little useful information about their own health needs from physicians is a frequently heard criticism of the medical care system. Most patients want to have their health status needs made clear to them by physicians, and are unhappy with those physicians who do not or will not explain to them in a full and clear fashion their medical problem and the recommended plan of treatment. Some of the skills effective physician communicators use in giving information to patients include explaining, sharing, advising, clarifying, and dealing appropriately with questions and ideas generated by patients. It is the quality and blend of these skills that defines a physician's style in conducting a clinical encounter with a patient and influences how successful the outcome of the encounter will be judged to be by the participants. Unfortunately, many physicians give a lot of advice, but little information to patients. If physicians fail to give patients the information they want to receive, and fail to address their expectations in a manner satisfactory to them, they risk being the object of patient resentment and animosity. How well the goals of physicians and patients are met in clinical interactions depend, greatly, on the physicians' interviewing and communication skills, and the satisfaction and confidence with the physicians patients take away from this medical experience.

Physicians need to possess good communication and interpersonal skills to be able to extract all necessary information from patients, and must be willing to share with them information about diagnosis, treatment, and prognosis of their medical condition. If physicians and patients fail to communicate effectively with each other, the objectives of the clinical interaction may not be met, and diagnosis and appropriate treatment may be delayed or missed altogether. Many present day patients are surprisingly well informed about medical matters and resent physicians who do not give them clear and logical information about their medical problems, and who do not provide them with sufficient time to discuss details of their own health status. Good physician communicators understand that the fruits of well considered conversations with patients and patients' families are understanding and motivation, peace of mind, and increased confidence in the physician. While giving information to patients and patients' families, the words physicians select to use in these conversations should be carefully chosen to give hope, when possible, to the concerned patient, and his or her family. On occasion, these can be very emotional conversations and physicians must be sensitive enough to the situation to ensure their chosen words do not give offense. Physicians must be alert to the profound positive or negative effect the words they use in conversations with patients can have on them and on their well being.

Patients often want more information about their own health situation than most physicians believe they do. Consequently, physicians tend to underestimate patients' desires for information about their own medical problems, and tend to misperceive the process of information giving. It has been shown that most physicians actually spend very little time giving information to patients, with a little more than one minute in encounters lasting about twenty minutes believed to be an accurate average estimate. In addition, physicians think they spend much more time informing patients about their medical conditions than they actually do. It is believed physicians, on average, overestimate the time they spend giving information to patients by about a factor of nine. Patients, and their families, often become resentful when they are given little diagnostic, therapeutic, or prognostic information by physicians, or when their physician provides little effort or time to answer questions and communicate information to them in a meaningful way. Patient resentment against a physician's inability, neglect, or refusal to communicate details of patient management to them or their families in a manner that stimulates an effective communication exchange has been the generating stimulus for many malpractice actions against physicians.

How effectively or ineffectively physicians give information to patients and their families can be influenced by the same factors that influence the process and outcome of the clinical encounter itself. Vocal transmission of information to patients by physicians is related to characteristics of: (1) patients (sex, age, education, social class, and prognosis); (2) physicians (social class, background, income, and perception of patients' desire for information); and (3) the clinical environment (private office, clinic, number of patients to be seen, etc.) Too often, physicians maintain a style of high control which includes little feedback to patients, but does include many physician initiated questions, frequent interruptions of the patient's story, and neglect of the social and physical environment in which the patient lives and functions. Information given to patients can also be positively or negatively influenced by accompanying nonverbal clues expressed, knowingly or unknowingly, by physicians. It must be admitted that giving patients adequate and appropriate information about their condition, treatment, and prognosis, does add to the time physicians spend in each clinical encounter. What may be gained by this time expenditure, however, could be immeasurable. The time physicians spend giving useful information to patients increases the patients' respect and regard for the physician, and is interpreted by patients as a display of concern and support by the physician which acts to ease their fears and worries, and may even contribute to a faster recovery by such patients.

Physician Medical Records

The principal reasons physicians write medical records are to document information, and to transfer information about a patient's medical problem, treatment for the problem, and response to treatment in either an outpatient or inpatient setting. Once composed, however, medical records can be used to not only document the medical care received by patients, but also to serve peer review, economic, and legal purposes. Medical records are included in computerized data bases which have many uses, including quality assurance and quality assessment efforts, and treatment effectiveness outcomes research. It is essential, then, that physician generated medical records be factual, complete, and fully understandable because they may reach multiple audiences and will be expected to convey meaningful information to, potentially, multiple readers. Physicians who write medical records are expected to observe and record details of their findings and actions on behalf of patients into a written record which not only documents these observations and actions, but which also should allow the transfer of meaningful patient information to other physicians or to other patient care facilities. In order to fulfill their principal purpose appropriately, written medical records must be accurate, clearly documented, easily understandable, and sufficiently detailed accounts of the pertinent information obtained by physicians, nurses, and other health professionals from and about patients during a clinical encounter, diagnostic interview, or hospital experience.[4]

Too many physician generated medical records read as if they were written for the single reader who, alone, possesses the same private knowledge as the physician who composed the record. In addition, poor physician writing skills and illegible penmanship combine to obscure patient details and treatment facts in many manually recorded medical records. Physicians who generate medical records need to begin the process with an understanding of the importance of writing them in a clear and direct fashion so they are easily understandable to all future readers. The production of good patient medical records takes a conscious and deliberate effort on the part of physicians because it is believed that traditional medical school education does not include much instruction on how to compose medical records so they can best serve physicians' purposes, as well as the needs of the various audiences who now read and review the modern medical record. This conscious and deliberate effort in writing a medical record includes avoiding ambiguities, obscure meanings, obliqueness in sentence structures, and use of medical jargon in the construction of text. Only approved abbreviations and symbols should be used in the written text (see the Appendix). Physician generated medical records, in order to fulfill their principal purposes in a manner that improves the overall efficiency of the recorded patient care, should be composed of clear, direct, and uncomplicated words and sentences, and written in a language style that flows in a continuous and logical fashion.

The hospital medical record is a particularly important document because it represents the written account of why a patient is hospitalized, what the diagnosis is believed to be, the evidence supporting the diagnostic conclusion, the treatment given the patient, the patient's response to treatment, and the patient's health outcome as a result of the hospital experience as noted at the time of hospital discharge. Courts of law consider the medical record to be the most reliable source of information regarding a patient's medical care and far more significant than the recollections of physicians and patients themselves. Because a large number of people contribute to the compiling of a patient's hospital medical record, and because there are multiple audiences for these records, including patients themselves, the writing of such a document takes skill and careful thought, and an appreciation of the multiple uses to which such records can be subjected. Physicians can strengthen the professional and clinical aspects of a hospital medical record by adding carefully written notes explaining their findings and reasoning used to arrive at their professional judgments in regard to actions taken on behalf of the patient. Also useful in strengthening the professional validity of a patient's medical record is the practice of supporting clinical decisions made on behalf of patients with written relevant literature citations when appropriate.

The writing of a hospital medical record has taken on increased importance in light of the national effort to constrain the costs of health care. These records can no longer be regarded simply as accounts of patient care activities and patient responses to treatment as recorded by a variety of physicians and other health professionals with differing views of the significance of the events being recorded. Medical care provided to patients must be documented factually and specifically and in sufficient detail in the hospital medical record to permit continuity of care and peer evaluation of the care provided. Medicare and third party payer documentation requirements now exist, and hospital reimbursement for the care of many patients depends, largely, on the accuracy and completeness of the information recorded in the patients' hospital medical records. Medical records are regarded as integral components of hospital quality assurance and quality assessment programs, and physicians must be certain all information essential to the needs of these programs is included in medical records for which they are responsible. Readers of a patient's hospital medical record should be able to obtain a clear and complete understanding of what the patient and physician perceived the medical problem to be, the diagnosis or differential diagnoses under consideration, the proposed plan of study and treatment, and the patient's response to the medical care received. If a reader of a hospital medical record is unable to learn or understand the details of a patient's illness and hospital experience because the medical record is poorly constructed, poorly written, or inadequate in its documentation of essential patient care details, such a hospital medical record can be said to have failed to fulfill its principal purpose.

TEACHING MEDICAL WRITING AND COMMUNICATION SKILLS IN MEDICAL SCHOOLS

Medical Writing

It seems clear from the amount of criticism heaped on physicians' writing skills that marked improvement in this skill is needed. While some writing experts believe writing ability can not be taught, others believe writing can be learned as a skill, and it is to the further development of this skill that more attention needs to be paid in medical schools. Medical educators have generally failed to appreciate that writing is a poorly developed skill in the majority of medical school applicants and most medical schools have yet to provide formal instruction in writing skills in their curricula. It is apparently assumed by medical educators that entering medical students bring writing skills with them in a state of sufficient development to make further attention unnecessary, but available evidence and the continuing criticism voiced about physician writing skills cast considerable doubt on this assumption. It appears accurate to state that a large number of students enter medical schools with poorly developed writing skills. In 1991, a method to evaluate writing skills of students was added to the MCAT examination and the scores achieved in writing were the lowest of the four areas assessed in the examination. The best way to address this deficiency would be for prospective medical students to learn writing skills during the high school and college educational process, but acceptance and implementation of this possible solution is highly unlikely. The next best way to improve physician writing skills is to teach them while physicians are medical students. Formal instruction in writing as a medical communicating skill needs to be included in medical school curricula if the present deplorable state of physician writing is to be improved.

Writing courses developed for medical students can be simple in design and limited in scope and emphasis if medical educators accept the view that medical writing is a form of technical writing and, as such, differs markedly in purpose and style from literary and creative writing. This is neither a new nor a novel view, but is the concept by which medical writing is now being taught in some colleges, graduate schools, and medical schools.[5] Medical writing can be taught as a form of technical writing in medical schools, with the major teaching effort focused on learning to express oneself with clarity in the crisp and lean style of good medical writing. Medical school writing courses, in addition to reviewing with students the fundamentals of grammar, syntax, and sentence structure, and trying to develop in them a facility for the use of the English language, should concentrate on teaching future physicians how to achieve clarity, accuracy, precision, logic, and discipline in their writing. Physicians use logical sequencing in arriving at diagnostic conclusions and treatment plans, and their written material should reflect appropriate use of the English language presented to readers in similarly derived logically written sequences.

The communication tasks requiring writing skills which physicians carry out most frequently in their professional lives include writing office medical records, letters to referring physicians, patient histories and physical examinations, progress notes, discharge summaries, peer reviewed medical articles, and grant proposals. Although these represent important, complex, and different writing tasks which physicians carry out with varying degrees of frequency or infrequency, it appears most medical schools do not offer medical students formal instruction on how to perform these writing tasks. Courses developed to teach writing skills to medical students should be designed with the primary intent of teaching medical students how to express themselves clearly and correctly in written form, and should focus their teaching emphasis on these seven writing tasks which physicians carry out most frequently in their professional lives. In addition, opportunities for medical students to practice and sharpen their writing skills should be woven into the fabric of the entire medical education process.

Communication Skills

If future physicians are to be regarded as more sensitive and empathic toward patients as fellow human beings, and are to be regarded as more attentive to their medical care needs, medical schools will have to give greater emphasis to the nurturing of appropriate physician attitudes and behaviors toward patients and to the development of better physician communication and interpersonal skills.[6] Strongly positive educational efforts should begin early in the course of medical school education and extend throughout the entire curricula in order to teach and enhance the humanistic interpersonal and communicating skills of future physicians. Certain personal values, usually associated with medical school curricula overly oriented toward technology, may be antithetical to inculcating in medical students a proper understanding of the need for and value of warm and empathic relationships with patients. If these latter qualities are to be valued and emphasized in medical practitioners, they must be taught, nourished, and kept in proper balance throughout the entire course of medical school education. In addition to gaining medical knowledge and learning clinical skills in medical schools, future physicians must learn a set of appropriate behaviors and attitudes which will serve to connect physicians' professional, scholarly, and personal preparations for medical careers with the patients and society they are preparing to serve.[7] The practice of modern medicine is a complicated mixture of demands because it is both a highly technical healing science, and a more amorphous healing art which should be practiced with compassion, concern, and an appropriate respect for those fellow human beings who become ill or injured. In order for future physicians to be most effective in this more socially aware practice environment, medical educators must include in their curricula instruction in these affective components of patient care. These are extra demands to place on medical students, but they need to understand how important this aspect of medical practice will be to them if they aspire to satisfying professional careers. Medical school curricula should be modified to provide medical students with the understanding and tools to address these important patient needs while, at the same time, maintaining their own professional effectiveness.[8]

Although a crucial element of physician communication and interpersonal skills, and despite the evident importance and need for these skills in practice, most medical schools at the present time do not devote much curricular time to the teaching of interviewing skills to medical students.[9,10] The important communication aspects of conducting effective diagnostic interviews with patients, and instruction in the skills required to assemble the information and write competent patient medical records would appear to be neglected parts of the formal education of many medical students. Among the deficiencies noted when the interviewing skills of medical students and residents have been observed and evaluated are interviewer insensitivity toward patients, failures to elicit all relevant patient details, developing incorrect working hypotheses from information obtained from patients, and use of physician-centered and controlling interviewing styles. In most medical schools it appears that medical students learn how to conduct patient interviews by repetitive practice with patients in various clinical settings, with or without direct observation by instructors. Evaluation of this interviewing technique, however, indicates that medical students do not uniformly improve their interviewing skills simply by repetitive practice in a clinical setting, particularly if their role models are residents or junior instructors who may have poor interviewing skills themselves. The teaching of interviewing skills to medical students that does occur tends to focus on what questions students should ask to elicit details of physical illness, with little attention paid to the psychosocial aspects of the patient and his or her medical problem.

Interviewing skills can be taught to students as has been demonstrated repeatedly in other occupations. Many interviewing techniques exist and appropriate ones can be selected for use in teaching interviewing skills to medical students.[11-16] Any interviewing technique selected for use in medical student teaching should have the following features:

1. The essential elements of interrelationship skills should be isolated, defined, and taught to medical students in a systematic fashion.
2. Students should practice these skills in either simulated or actual interpersonal situations.
3. Immediate feedback on their performance should be given to students.
4. Training in these skills should take place in relatively small groups so instruction can be individualized.
5. The dynamics of group process should be used in order to promote both support and stimulation for learning.

More time and effort must be devoted in medical schools to teaching medical students the clinical skills of patient interviewing and writing patient medical records. Such expanded efforts should concentrate more on helping medical students develop a more holistic and patient-centered approach to patient care and on the creation of more meaningful physician generated medical records.[17]

It must be made clear to all medical students during the course of their medical education that, while medical knowledge and clinical skills remain the cornerstones of good patient care, the catalysts for transforming good patient care into effective patient care are the communication and interpersonal skills of individual physicians. Among the needed interpersonal skills that physicians should possess are a sensitivity to each patient's needs, an awareness of the effect of illness on the patient's life, role in life, and function in society, and an appreciation for the effects of illness on the patient's family. It has been noted that effective communication skills are not routinely acquired by medical students in existing medical school education programs, but educating medical students in communication skills during medical school has been shown to be both feasible and effective.[16] Appropriate instruction in developing and broadening these skills, therefore, should become an integral part of the medical education process.

A program designed to teach communication skills to medical students should have several objectives, including introducing students to the language of communication and the principles of dynamic information exchange, teaching students the format and process of the medical interview, and offering students a variety of opportunities to practice communication skills during their medical student years. Specific skills which should be included in a communication skills course for medical students include:

1. How to interview patients so the interviewer can obtain all relevant health information from them.
2. How to give information to patients and patients' families in an appropriate manner.
3. Instruction in the value and use of physician inter-personal styles which enhance patient satisfaction with the clinical interaction, and compliance with recommended diagnostic and treatment programs.

4. Instruction in basic counseling skills to enable physicians to become better equipped to assist patients withstand the impact of potentially distressing diagnoses and medical or surgical procedures.

Courses designed to teach communication and interpersonal skills to medical students are now given in a few medical schools and these courses can be used as models to assist other medical schools initiate similar courses.[18-20] Some medical schools may wish to design their own programs based on the adequacies or limitations of the resources available to them for these additional educational programs. The process in these schools could begin by appointing a faculty task force charged with reviewing, evaluating, and selecting relevant published studies on teaching communication, interpersonal, interviewing, and writing skills to medical students. Based on this selected source of information, this task force would then recommend the design of a course which, to achieve optimal results, should be taught on a continuing basis through the four years of the medical education process. Being knowledgeable about the adequacy or limitations of their own institution's resources for this additional educational effort, it can be expected that the task force would select realistic teaching methods and techniques from the total available knowledge base. This would afford the task force an opportunity to design their own medical communicating skills course to recommend to the dean and to the curriculum committee. A faculty task force used to design such an educational program would need enlightened leadership and probably should be chaired by a representative of the Dean's office or a faculty person selected specifically because of special interest or expertise in the body of knowledge underlying the teaching of communication skills to medical students. In medical schools where no such educational programs exist, a useful next step could be the appointment of a faculty Committee on Medical Communicating Skills to monitor, evaluate, revise, and improve the program until such time as the medical communicating skills program is running smoothly and productively. At that point, oversight of the performance and effectiveness of the medical communicating skills program could be turned over to the medical school's curriculum committee or whatever mechanism the particular medical school uses for oversight responsibility in its teaching programs.

Physicians, medical educators, and medical students do need to have an interest in and a concern for their own abilities, and the abilities of other physicians, to communicate with patients and others. The abilities of physicians to communicate well with patients and others is assuming increasing importance in the delivery of effective patient care, and every indication suggests that the presence, or absence, of these abilities will take on added significance as time passes. Organized medicine is beginning to realize that, to be most successful, it must represent patients' interests before the economic interests of physicians. If today's physicians take the time and make the effort to listen to patients, they will hear these patients tell them that improvement in the communicating and interpersonal skills of physicians is needed.

The physician-patient relationship is a primary bond that frequently acts as another form of social support to influence the health of patients. Recognizing the particular importance of this relationship, and recognizing how critical good communication is to this relationship, is especially important at present when threatened or real changes in health care delivery methods, quality assurance efforts, and health care financing, could place this relationship at some risk. A good relationship between physicians and the public they serve is not a new requirement for practitioners but, rather, one that has been recognized as a critical alliance for a long time. The physician uncle of René Laennec, the French physician credited with inventing the stethoscope, reputedly advised his nephew as Laennec began his eighteenth century medical practice that, even though doctors might think it silly, doctors hold their credit solely from the public and it would be foolish for young doctors not to respect this role of the public.

References

1. Eddy DM. Medicine, money, and mathematics. *Bull Amer Coll Surg.* 1992; 77(6): 36-49.
2. Zollinger RM. Let's improve our image. *Bull Amer Coll Surg.* 1992: 77(4): 7-13.
3. Weihs K, Chapados JT. Interviewing skills training--a study. *Soc Sci Med.* 1986; 23(1): 31-34.
4. Pagano MP. *Communicating Effectively in Medical Records: A Guide for Physicians.* Newbury Park, Calif: Sage Publications; 1992.
5. Haneline D, Turpin ER. Results of the AMWA higher education survey demonstrate increasing link with academia. *J Amer Med Writers Assoc.* 1991; 6(3): 10-16.
6. Bickel J. Human values teaching programs in the clinical education of medical students. *J Med Educ.* 1987; 62: 369-378.
7. Federman DD. The education of medical students: sounds, alarums, and excursions. *Acad Med.* 1990; 65(4):221-226.
8. Maheux B, Delorme P, Beland F, Beaudry J. Humanism in medical education: A study of educational needs perceived by trainees of three Canadian schools. *Acad Med.* 1990; 65: 41-45.
9. Carroll JG, Monroe J. Teaching medical interviewing: A critique of educational research and practice. *J Med Educ.* 1979; 54: 498-506.
10. Preven DW, Kachur EK, Kupfer RB, Waters JA. Interviewing skills of first-year medical students. *J Med Educ.* 1986; 61: 842-844.
11. Cassata DM, Harris IB, Bland CJ, Ronning GF. A systematic approach to curriculum design in a medical school interview course. *J Med Educ.* 1976; 51: 939-942.
12. Dobbs HI, Carek DJ. The conceptualization and teaching of medical interviewing. *J Med Educ.* 1972; 47: 272-276.
13. Kahn GS, Cohen B, Jason H. The teaching of interpersonal skills in U.S.

medical schools. *J Med Educ*. 1979; 54: 29-35.

14. Kauss DR, Robbins AS, Abrass I, Bakaitis RF, Anderson LA. The long-term effectiveness of interpersonal skills training in medical schools. *J Med Educ*. 1980; 55: 595-601.

15. Pacoe LV, Naar R, Guyett IPR, Wells R. Training medical students in interpersonal relationship skills. *J Med Educ*. 1976; 51: 743-750.

16. Sanson-Fisher R, Maguire P. Should skills in communicating with patients be taught in medical schools? *Lancet*. 1980; 2: 523-526.

17. Reiser SJ. The clinical record in medicine Part 2: Reforming content and purpose. *Ann Intern Med*. 1991; 114(11): 980-985.

18. Branch WT, Arky RA, Woo B, Stoeckle JD, Levy DB, Taylor WC. Teaching medicine as a human experience: A patient-doctor relationship course for faculty and first-year medical students. *Ann Intern Med*. 1991; 114(6): 482-489.

19. Friedman CP, deBliek R, Greer DS, Mennin SP, Norman GR, Sheps CG, Swanson DB, Woodward CA. Charting the winds of change: evaluating innovative medical curricula. *Acad Med*. 1990; 65(1): 8-14.

20. Monahan DJ, Grover PL, Kavey REW, Greenwald JA, Jacobsen EC, Weinberger HL. Evaluation of a communication skills course for second year medical students. *J Med Educ*. 1988; 63: 372-378.

21. Sanson-Fisher R, Fairbairns S, Maguire P. Teaching skills in communication to medical students--a critical review of the methodology. *Med Educ*. 1981; 15: 33-37.

Appendix

THOMAS JEFFERSON UNIVERSITY HOSPITAL
APPROVED ABBREVIATIONS LIST
1992

A

a	above
Aa DO$_2$	areolar arterial oxygen gradient
A2	aortic second sound
a	before
aa	equal parts of each
AAA	Abdominal Aortic Aneurysm
AAROM	Active assistive range of motion
ARROM	Active resistive range of motion
Ab.	abortion
abd.	abdominal
ABG	arterial blood gases
AC	Acromioclavicular
A.C.	anterior chamber
a.c.	before meals (Latin--*Ante Cibum*)
ACB	aorto coronary bypass
ACTH	adrenocorticotrophic hormone
AD	right ear
ad. lib.	as desired
ADH	antidiuretic hormone
A.D.L.	activities of daily living
Adm.	Admission
ADR	adverse drug reaction
ADU	acute dialysis unit
AEA	above elbow amputation
AFB	acid fast bacilli
AFP	alpha 1-fetoprotein
A/G	albumin globulin ratio
Ag	antigen
AGA	Appropriate Gestational Age
Aggl	agglutination

AGL	acute granulocytic leukemia
AGN	acute glomerulonephritis
AHF	Antihemophilic Factor
AI	Aortic insufficiency
AIDS	acquired immunodeficiency syndrome
A.J.	ankle jerk
AKA	above knee amputation
A line	Arterial Line
alb.	albumin
Alk.	alkaline
ALG	antilymphocyte globulin
ALS	amyotrophic lateral sclerosis
ALT	alanine aminotransferase
a.m.	morning
A.M.A.	against medical advice
amb.	ambulate, ambulatory
ANA	antinuclear antibody
Ant. Tib.	anterior tibialis
Ao	aorta
AP	anteroposterior
A+P	ausculation and percussion
APAP	acetaminophen
APB	Abductor Pollicis Brevis
APTT	activated partial thromboplastin time
aq	water, aqueous
AR	aortic regurgitation
ARF	Acute renal failure
A.R.O.M.	artificial rupture of membranes
AROM	active range of motion
art.	arterial
AS	left ear
ASA	aspirin
AST	antistreptolysis-O
ASCVD	Arteriosclerotic Cardiovascular
ASD	atrial septal defect
ASHD	Arteriosclerotic Heart Disease
A-Fib	atrial fibrillation
AT	Achilles Tendon
atr	atracurium
ATN	acute tubular necrosis
AU	each ear (both ears)
A-V	arteriovenous
AVM	arteriovenous malformation
ax	axillary

B

b	below
B	Block
BAEP	brainstem auditory evoked potential
BE	barium enema
BEA	below elbow amputation
b.i.d.	twice a day (Latin--*bis indie*)
bili.	bilirubin
BILI T/D	bilirubin total and direct
bl. cult.	blood culture
BKA	below knee amputation
BLE	both lower extremities
BM	bowel movement
BMR	basal metabolic rate
BOA	born on arrival
B.P.	blood pressure
BPH	benign prostatic hypertrophy
BR	Brachioradialis
B.R.P.	bathroom privileges
BS	blood sugar
b.s.	bowel sounds
BSA	body surface area
BSO	bilateral salpingo-oophorectomy
BSP	bromsulphalein
BUE	both upper extremities
BUN	blood urea nitrogen
Bx.	biopsy

C

Cl-C9	complement components
c	with (Latin--*cum*)
C	centigrade
CA	cancer or carcinoma
Ca.	Calcium
CABG	coronary artery bypass
CAD	coronary artery disease
CAH	chronic active hepatitis
Cal.	calories
cap. or caps.	capsules
cath.	catheter
CAVH	continuous arteriovenous Hemofiltration
CAVHD	chronic arteriovenous hemodialysis
CBC	complete blood count
CBI	continuous bladder irrigation

CC	chief complaint
cc	cubic centimeter
CCK-PZ	cholecystokinin-pancreozymin
CCU	Coronary Care Unit
CEA	carcinoembryonic antigen
CF	complement fixation
CGN	chronic glomerulonephritis
CHD	coronary heart disease
CHF	congestive heart failure
CID	Cervical Immobilization Device
CLL	chronic lymphocytic leukemia
chol.	cholesterol
CL	chloride
cm.	centimeters
C.M.J.	carpometacarpal joint
CML	chronic myelocytic leukemia
C.N.S.	central nervous system
CO	cardiac output
CO_2	carbon dioxide
COAGS	coagulation studies
compd.	compound
cont.	continued
COPD	chronic obstructive pulmonary disease
CPK	creatine phosphokinase
CPK 2 MB	creatinephosphokinase c isoenzymes
CPR	cardiopulmonary resuscitation
CPT	chest physiotherapy
CR	cast room
Cr	creatine
CRF	chronic renal failure
CRNA	certified registered nurse anesthetist
C&S	culture & sensitivity
CSF	cerebrospinal fluid
CSR	central supply room
CT. scan	computerized tomographic scan
CV	cardiovascular
CVA	cerebrovascular accident
C.V.P.	central venous pressure
Cx	cervix
CXR	chest x-ray
Cysto	cystoscopy

D

D-stik	dextrostix
D&C	dilatation and curettage

APPENDIX

D/C	discontinue
D&E	dilatation and evacuation
Diag. or dx	diagnosis
Derm.	dermatology
DG	decibels
D.I.	diabetes insipidus
DIC	disseminated intravascular coagulapathy
diff.	differential test
decr. or	decreased
dig.	digit
D.I.P.	distal interphalangeal joint
disch.	discharge
Disp.	dispense
DL	direct laryngoscopy
DM	diabetes mellitus
DNA	deoxyribonucleic acid
DOA	dead on arrival
dobut	dobutamine
DOE	dyspnea on exertion
DP	dorsalis pedis (pulse)
D.P. flap	delto-pectoral flap
DPT	diphtheria, tetanus toxoid, and pertussis
Dr.	doctor
D.R.	delivery room
DSD	dry sterile dressing
DT's	delirium tremens
dTC-d	tubocurare
DTR	deep tendon reflexes
DUB	dysfunctional uterine bleeding
DVT	deep venous thrombosis
D/W	dextrose in water

E

EB	Epstein-Barr
EBL	estimated blood loss
ECG (EKG)	electrocardiogram
ECT	electroshock treatment
ECRB	Extensor Carpi Radialis Brevis
ECRL	Extensor Carpi Radialis Longus
ECU	Extensor Carpi Ulnaris
EDB	Extensor Digitorum Brevis
EDC	estimated date of confinement
EDI	Extensor Digiti Indicis
EDL	Extensor Digitorum Longus
EDQ	Extensor Digiti Quinti

EEG	electroencephalogram
EGD	esphagogastroduodenoscopy
e.g.	for example
EHL	Extensor Hallucis Longus
ELC	electrolytes
ELF	elective low forceps
ELISA	enzyme-linked immunosorbent assay
elix.	elixer
EMD	Electric Mechanical disassociation
EMG	electromyogram
EMT	Emergency Medical Technician
EMT-P	Emergency Medical Technician--Paramedic
enf	enflurane
ENT	ears, nose and throat
EOM	extraocular movement
epi	epinephrine
epid	epidural
EPB	Extensor Pollicis Brevis
EPL	Extensor Pollicis Longus
ER	emergency room
ERcP	endoscopic retrograde
ESR	erythrocyte sedimentation rate
ESRD	end stage renal disease
ESWL	extracorporeal shock wave lithotripsy
etc.	and so forth
$ETCO_2$	end tidal carbon dioxide
ETOH	ethyl alcohol
ETT	endotracheal tube
EUA	examination under anesthesia
Ext.	external

F

5 FC	5-fluorocytosine
5 FU	5-fluorouracil
F.	Fahrenheit
FAM. M.D.	family doctor
F.B.	foreign body
F.B.S.	fasting blood sugar
FCR	Flexor Carpi Radialis
FCU	Flexor Carpi Ulnaris
FDL	Flexor Digitorim Longus
FDP	Flexor Digiti Profundus
FDS	Flexor Digiti Sublimus
fem-pop	femoral popliteal bypass

APPENDIX

F.H.	family history
FHL	Flexor Hallucis Longus
fib	fibula
FI02	fraction of inspired 02
fl.	fluid
fl. ext.	fluid extract
FPB	Flexor Pollicis Brevis
FPL	Flexor Pollicis Longus
ft	feet
F.T.S.G.	full thickness skin graft
FU	follow-up
FVC	Forced Vital Capacity
FUO	fever of unknown origin
Fx.	fracture
Fetal Position & Presentation:	
	LOA left occiput anterior
	LOT left occiput transverse
	LOP left occiput posterior
	ROA right occiput anterior
	ROT right occiput transverse
	ROP right occiput posterior
	LSA (RSA) left (right) sacrum anterior
	LSP (RSP) left (right) sacrum posterior
	LFA (RFA) left (right) frontoanterior
	LFP (RFP) left (right) frontoposterior
	LMA (RMA) left (right) mentoanterior
	LMT (RMT) left (right) mentotransverse
	LMP (RMP) left (right) mentoposterior
FSH	follicle-stimulating hormone
FTA-ABS	fluorescent treponemal antibody

G

g.	gram
GA	general anesthesia
Ga	Gauge
Gastroc.	gastrocnemius
GCS	Glasgow Coma Scale
GE	gastroesophageal
G6PD	glucose-6-phosphate dehydrogenase
GPA	gravida para abortus (indicates the number of pregnancies, births, and abortions; i.e. G1 P1 A0 is a woman who has had 1 pregnancy, 1 child, and no abortions)
GGTP	gama glutamyl transpeptidase

GI	gastro-intestinal
G/dl	grams per deciliter
GPS	General Protective Screening
gr.	grain
Grav. I	primigravida
Grav. II, etc.	indicating a woman of so many pregnancies
GS	Gastrocnemius-soleus
gt.	drop
gtt.	drops
GTT	glucose tolerance test
GU	genito-urinary
Gyn	gynecology

H

HAA	hepatitis antigen
HAL	hyperalimentation
halo	halothane
HbCO	% Carboxyhemoglobin saturation
HbMet	% Methemoglobin saturation
HBV	hepatitis B surface antigen
HCO$_2$	Bicarbonate
HCTZ	hydroclorothiazide
HBV	hepatitis B virus
HBsAG	hepatitis B surface antigen
Hgb	Hemoglobin
HBP	high blood pressure
HC	head circumference
HCO$_3$	bicarbonate ion
Hct	hematocrit
HCVD	hypertensive cardiovascular disease
HDL	high density lipoprotein
Hemi (L) (R)	hemiplegia--(left) (right)
HIV	Human Immunodeficiency Virus
H/H	hemoglobin/hematocrit
HMD	hyaline membrane disease
H.O.	House Officer
H/O	history of
H&P	history and physical
hpf	per high powdered field (used only in describing urine sedimentation)
H.P.I.	history of present illness
hr.	hour
H.S.	hour of sleep
HTN	hypertension

APPENDIX

ht.	height
Hx.	history
$H_2 0$	water

I

I-131 or I-125	radioactive iodine
IC	individual counseling
ICP	intracranial pressure
ICU	intensive care unit
ID	Infectious Disease Service
IDDM	insulin dependent diabetes mellitus
I&D	incision and drainage
IDV	Intermediate Dialysis Unit
Ig.	immunoglobulin
IgG	immuno globulin G
IgA	immuno globulin A
IgM	immuno globulin M
IgD	immuno globulin D
IgE	immuno globulin E
IHSS	idiopathic hypertrophic sub-aortic stenosis
I.M.	intramuscular
IMB	intermenstrual bleeding
IMP	impression
IMV	intermittent mandatory ventilation
inc or	increase
in	inches
INH	isoniazid hydrochloride
I&O	intake and output
IPPB	intermittent positive pressure breathing
ISDN	isosorbide dinitrate
isof	isoflurane
I.Q.	intelligence quotient
Irrig.	irrigate
IU	international unit
I.U.D.	interuterine device
I.U.P.	intrauterine pregnancy
I.U.P.D.	intrauterine pregnancy delivered
IV	intravenous
IVP	intravenous pyelogram

J

JSC	Jefferson Surgical Center

K

K	potassium
KCL	potassium chloride
Kg.	kilogram
KJ	knee jerk
KUB	kidney, ureter bladder (x-ray plane film of abdomen)
Kc	Kilo calories
KVO	keep vein open

L

L or Lt.	left
LA	left arm
lab.	laboratory
LAO	left anterior oblique
LAD	left anterior descending
LAT	left anterior thigh
lat.	lateral
lb.	pound
LBBB	left bundle branch block
LDH	lactase dehydrogenase
LFT	Liver Function Test
LG	left gluteus
LGA	large for gestational age
LH	luteinizing hormone
LHRH	luteinizing-hormone-releasing hormone
lido	lidocaine
LIH	left inguinal hernia
liq.	liquid
LLD	left lateral decubitus
LLE	left lower extremity
LLL	left lower lobe lung
LLT	left lateral thigh
LMD	local medical doctor
L.O.C.	Level of Consciousness
LP	lumbar puncture
lpf	low-power field
LT	long term
LTL	laparoscopic tubal ligation
LUA	left upper arm
LUE	left upper extremity
LUL	left upper lobe--lung
	RLL right lower lobe--lung
	RML right middle lobe--lung
	RUL right upper lobe--lung

APPENDIX 241

LLQ	left lower quadrant--abdomen
LUQ	left upper quadrant--abdomen
RLQ	right lower quadrant--abdomen
RUQ	right upper quadrant--abdomen
LMP	last menstrual period
LNMP	last normal menstrual period
LOC	Loss of consciousness
LPN	licensed practical nurse
LV	left ventricle
LVH	left ventricular hypertrophy
L&W	living and well
Lymphs	lymphocytes

M

m	murmur
M	male
M 1	mitral first heart sound
MA	mentum anterior
MAC	monitored anesthesia care
MAE	moving all extremities
Mag. Cit.	magnesium citrate
max	maximum
MBD	minimal brain dysfunction
MBR	micro bilirubin
MCA-STA	middle cerebral artery--superficial temporal artery
MCCU	medical coronary care unit
mcg	microgram
MCH	mean corpuscular line
MCL	mid-clavicular joint
M.C.P.	metacarpo-phalangeal joint
MCT	medium chain triglycerides
MCV	mean corpuscular volume
M.D.	physician
Med.	Medicine
Meds.	medicine
mEq	milliequivalent
mEq/L	milliequivalent per liter
mg	milligram
Mg	magnesium
mg %	milligrams per hundred milliliters of fluid
MH	menstrual history
Mi	myocardial infarction
mic	minimum inhibitory concentration
MIC	maternal infant care

MICU	Medical Intensive Care Unit
min.	minute
mM	millimole
MMT	manual muscle test
ml	milliliter
mmHg	millimeters of mercury
MO	mineral oil
MOM	milk of magnesia
mono	monocyte
Mos.	months
MP	mentum posterior
MPAP	mean pulmonary artery pressure
MR	mitral regurgitation
MRI	magnetic resonance imaging
MS	multiple sclerosis
Msec	Milliseconds
M/sec	meters per second
MS04	morphine sulfate
MTP	Metatarsal Phalangeal Joint
MTX	methotrexate
MU	million units
MUGA	multigated angiogram
MVI	multivitamin
MVA	mitral valve area

N

N	normal
N_2O	Nitrous Oxide
NA	not applicable
na	sodium
NaCl	sodium chloride
NB	newborn
NCV	nerve conduction velocity
NEC	necrotizing enterocolitis
neg.	negative
Neuro	neurological, neurology
NG	nasogastric
NIDDM	noninsulin dependent diabetes mellitus
NICU	Neurosurgical Intensive Care Unit
NKA	no known allergies
NKDA	no known drug allergies
noct.	nocturnal
NPH	neutral protamine hagedorn E

NPO	nothing by mouth
N.R.	no repeat
NS	neurosurgery
N/S	normal saline
NSR	normal sinus rhythm
NSS	normal saline solution
NTG	nitroglycerin
N&V	nausea and vomiting

O

O_2	oxygen
OA	occiput anterior
OB	obstetrics or obstetrical
OBS	organic brain syndrome
OCC	occasionally
O_2-cap	oxygen capacity
O.D.	right eye (Latin--*oculus dexter*)
oint.	ointment
O/N	Oral/Nasal
OOB	out of bed
OP	Opponens Pollicis
op.	operation
OPD	outpatient department
OPG	ocularpneumoplethysmography
OR	operating room
ORIF	open reduction internal fixation
Orth.	orthopedics
O.S.	left eye (Latin--*oculus sinister*)
osc.	oscillatory
O_2 sat.	oxygen saturation
O.T.	occupational therapy
OT	old tuberculin
Oto.	otolaryngology
O.U.	each eye (Latin--*oculus uterque*)
oz.	ounce

P

P	pulse
p	after
P2	pulmonic heart sound
P (A-a) O_2	alveolar-arterial oxygen pressure difference in mmHg.
P (a/A) O_2	Alveolar/arterial oxygen pressure ratio
PA	pulmonary artery

PA	pulmonary artery
P-A	posterioranterior
PAC	premature atrial contraction
PACU	post anesthesia care unit
PAP	pulmonary artery pressure
pan	pancuronium
para	paraplegia
PAS	periodic acid-shift
PAT	paroxysmal atrial tachycardia
pat.	pattern
PBI	protein bound iodine
p.c.	after meals
PCA	patient controlled analgesia
PCO_2	oxygen pressure
Pcn.	penicillin
PCWP	pulmonary capillary wedge pressure
PD	peritoneal dialysis
P.D.R.	Physicians' Desk Reference
PE	Physical Exam
Ped.	pediatric
PEEP	positive end expiratory pressure
PEG	pneumoencephalogram
per	by
PERLA	pupils equal and react to light and accommodation
pH	hydrogen ion concentration
P.H.	past history
Pi	phosphorus
PICA	posterior inferior cerebral artery
PICU	pediatric intensive care unit
PID	pelvic inflammatory disease
P.I.P.	proximal interphalangeal joint
PIP	peak inspiratory pressure
P.I.Q.	performance intelligence quotient
PKU	phenylketonuria
PL	Palmaris Longus
pl	pleural
ptts.	platelets
PMB	post menopausal bleeding
p.m.	afternoon
pmh	past medical history
P.M. & R.	physical medicine and rehabilitation
PNS	peripheral nerve stimulator
p.o.	by mouth

POC	products of conception
PO$_2$	oxygen partial pressure (tension)
PLT count	Platelet count
polys	polymorphonuclear leukocytes
post op	postoperative
pp	post prandial
P.P.	post partum
PPD	purified protein derivative
p.r.	per rectum
PRE	progressive resistive exercise
pre-op	preoperative
prep.	prepare for
p.r.n.	as often as necessary
P.R.O.M.	premature rupture of membranes
PROM	passive range of motion
Pro-Time	prothrombin time
P.S.	pulmonic stenosis
pss	physiologic saline solution
Psychol.	psychology
pt.	patient
P.T.	physical therapy
PTA	prior to admission
PTC	percutaneous transhepatic cholangiogram
PTH	parathyroid hormone
PTR	prothrombin ratio
PTT	partial thromboplastin time
Pulse Ox	pulse oximeter
PVC	premature ventricular contraction
PVD	peripheral vascular disease
PWB	patient weight bearing
PWP	pulmonary wedge pressure

Pelvic Measurements:

DC	diagonal conjugate
Oc	obstetrical conjugate
bisp.	bispinour or interspinour diameter
IT	intertuberous
Ant. (or) Post Sag. D.	anterior (or) posterior sagittal diameter

Q

q	every
q 4 hr	every four hours, etc.
qh	every hour

qhs	at bedtime
q.i.d.	four times a day
qns	quantity not sufficient
quad	quadriplegia
quant.	quantity
qs ad	insufficient quantity to make

R

R or rt.	right
R. or Resp	respirations
RA	right arm
R.A.	rheumatoid arthritis
RAO	right anterior oblique
RAT	right anterior thigh
RBBB	right bundle branch block
rbc	red blood cells
RBC	red blood count
RF	renal failure
Receiv.	receiving
Ref.	Referring
reg.	regular
RG	right gluteus
Rh	rhesus blood factor
RIA	radioimmunoassay
RICU	respiratory intensive care unit
RIH	right inguinal hernia
RLE	right lower extremity
RLL	right lower lobe--lung
RLQ	right lower quadrant--abdomen
RLT	right lateral thigh
RML	right middle lobe--lung
RN	registered nurse
R.N.D.	radical neck dissection
R/O	rule out
ROM	range of motion
ROS	review of systems
RPR	rapid plasma reagin
RR	recovery room
RRE	round, regular, equal
RRR	regular rate and rhythm
RT	Rate
RTC	return to clinic
RUA	right upper arm
RUE	right upper extremity
RUL	right upper lobe--lung

RUQ	right upper quadrant--abdomen
RV	right ventricle
Rx	prescription, therapy, or treatment

S

s	without
SA	sacrum anterior
SAB	subarachnoid block
SaO_2	arterial oxygen saturation
sc	subcutaneous
SCCU	surgical coronary care unit
SCI	spinal cord injury
SD	standard deviation
SDA	Same day admission
SEP	systolic ejection period
SGA	small for gestational age
S.H.	social history
sibs.	siblings
SIADH	syndrome of inappropriate antidiuretic hormone
SICU	surgical intensive care unit
Sig.	label as
SLA	sacrum L anterior
SLE	systemic lupus erythematosus
SLP	sacrum L posterior
SLT	sacrum L transverse
SMA 12, 6 & 7	automated laboratory testing
SMR	submucous resection of nasal septum
SNP	sodium nitroprusside
SOB	short of breath
sol	solution
S.O.S.	may be repeated once if urgently required
S/P	status post
SP	sacrum posterior
spec.	specimen
sp.gr.	specific gravity
SPO_2	Oxygen saturation by pulse oximetry
SPROM	spontaneous premature rupture of membranes
SPU	short procedure unit
SRA	sacrum right anterior
SROM	spontaneous rupture of membranes
SRP	sacrum right posterior
SRT	sacrum right transverse
ss	a half
SSE	soap sudsenema
SSD	social security disability

ST	short term
staph	staphylococcus
stat	immediately and once only
strep	streptococcus
STS	serologic test for syphillis
STSG	split thickness skin graft
subj.	subjective
subling. or SL	under the tongue or sublingual
supp.	suppository
Surg.	surgery or surgical
Sx	signs
SUX	succinylcholine
SV	spontaneous ventilation
SVG	saphenous vein graft
SVR	systemic vascular resistance
syr.	syrup
S-O-A-P	Subjective-Objective-Assessment-Plan
Sz.	Size

T

T	transfer
T1	tricuspid first sound
T3	triodothyronine
T4	Thyroxin
TA	Tibialis Anterior
T & A	tonsillectomy and adenoidectomy
Tab.	tablet
TAB	therapeutic abortion
T.A.H.	total abdominal hysterectomy
TB	tuberculosis
Tbsp.	tablespoon
temp	temperature
THR	total hip replacement
T.I.	tricuspid insufficiency
TIA	transient ischemic attack
TIBC	total iron binding capacity
t.i.d.	three times a day
TJUH	Thomas Jefferson University Hospital
TL	tubal ligation
TM	tympanic membrane
TMJ	temporomandibular joint
TMT	Tarsal Metatarsal Joint
TOF	Tetralogy of Fallot
tol.	tolerated

APPENDIX

TP	Tibialis Posterior
TPL	thiopental
TPN	total parenteral nutrition
TPR	temperature, pulse, respiration
Tr.	tincture
TRH	thyrotropin-releasing hormone
trach	tracheostomy
T/S	Champion Trauma Score
T.S.	tricuspid stenosis
TSH	thyroid stimulation hormone
tsp.	teaspoon
TU	trauma unit
TURB	transurethral resection of bladder
TURP	transurethral resection of prostate
TV	tidal volume
tx.	traction

U

U	unit
UA	urinalysis
UDS	Urine Drug Screen
UE	upper extremity
UGI	upper gastro-intestinal
ung. or oint.	ointment
UPJ	uretero pelvic junction
URI	upper respiratory infection
Urol.	urology
UPS	U.S. Pharmacopoeia
UTI	urinary tract infection
UVJ	uretero vesical junction

V

vag	vagina	
VC	vital capacity	
VCT	venous clotting time	
VD	venereal disease	
VDRL	venereal disease research laboratory	
Ve	minute ventilation	
vec	vecuronium	
Vertebrae:		
	C1 C8	Cervical vertebrae
	T1 T12	Thoracic vertebrae
	L1 L5	Lumbar vertebrae
	S1 S5	Sacral vertebrae

Vit.	vitamin when followed by a specific letter, i.e. Vit. A
VO	verbal order
VP	Ventriculoperitoneal
VS	vital signs
Vtx	vertex

W

W	white
Wass.	Wasserman
WBC	white blood cells
W/C	wheel chair
WD	well-developed
WN	well-nourished
WNL	within normal limits
W.P.	whirl pool
Wt.	weight

X

x	times
xmatch	cross match

Y

Yrs.	years
YY/MM/DD	year/month/day